BRIGHT TRIUMPHS FROM DARK HOURS

Also by **DAVID HEENAN**

Flight Capital

Double Lives

Co-Leaders
WITH WARREN BENNIS

The New Corporate Frontier

The Re-United States of America

Multinational Organization Development
WITH HOWARD PERLMUTTER

TURNING **BRIGHT**
ADVERSITY **TRIUMPHS**
INTO **FROM DARK**
SUCCESS **HOURS**

DAVID HEENAN

Foreword by Warren Bennis

A Latitude 20 Book

UNIVERSITY OF HAWAI'I PRESS
HONOLULU

To Alex and Malia

© 2010 UNIVERSITY OF HAWAI'I PRESS
All rights reserved
Printed in the United States of America
15 14 13 12 11 10   6 5 4 3 2 1

University of Hawai'i Press books are printed
on acid-free paper and meet the guidelines for
permanence and durability of the Council on
Library Resources.

Designed by Julie Matsuo-Chun
Printed by The Maple-Vail Book Manufacturing Group

LIBRARY OF CONGRESS CATALOGING-IN-
PUBLICATION DATA

Heenan, David A.
  Bright triumphs from dark hours : turning
adversity into success / David Heenan ; foreword
by Warren Bennis.
      p. cm.
  "A Latitude 20 Book."
  Includes bibliographical references and index.
  ISBN 978-0-8248-3430-2 (hardcover : alk. paper)
  1. Success—Case studies. I. Title.
  BF637.S8H394 2010
  155.2'4—dc22
                                        2009029817

No problem of human destiny
is beyond human beings.

—JOHN F. KENNEDY

Contents

FOREWORD

THE STORY SEEMS AS OLD AS METHUSELAH. Following a string of losses, the directors of a company launch an intensive search for a corporate messiah. Eventually, they find one, a miracle worker, who, it seems at the time, can restore customer confidence, employee morale, and, most important, operating income. But, just months after the appointment, disillusionment sets in and the would-be savior is terminated unceremoniously.

Sound far-fetched? In the teeth of the recent financial crisis, the American landscape is littered with such dark clouds. The corner office has become a revolving door, as boards and shareholders become ever more demanding. Increasingly, heading an important organization is like being one of the kings in ancient Crete who had extraordinary power and access to every perk and pleasure—but only for a time. After his year of absolute power, the king was put to death. For contemporary leaders, the emperor's throne isn't nearly as comfortable as it used to be. As the top job becomes more and more tenuous, tackling the near-impossible becomes critical.

Nor are these gargantuan challenges confined to corporate titans or to the private sector. Take sports, for instance. From my perch at the University of Southern California, I'm an unabashed Trojans fan. So I was shocked when our charismatic assistant football coach, Lane Kiffin, left USC for the black hole of professional coaching, the top slot at the Oakland Raiders. Less than two years later, the team's aging autocrat, Al Davis, abruptly pink-slipped the thirty-one-year-old Kiffin—his fifth head coach in seven years. Fortunately, Kiffin landed on his feet, snaring the top coaching job at the University of Tennessee.

Today, we are seeing more and more dark hours—nightmarish situations where talented men and women, quite often for reasons beyond their control, seem destined to walk the plank. No doubt, we've all—at one time or another—encountered times of gloom and despair. I used to think I wanted to be a university president. And for seven long years, I did just that. The problem was I wanted to *be* a university president, but I didn't want to *do* a university president—a role often described as notoriously hellish. Less than three years into my tenure, I had a moment of truth. At four o'clock in the morning—weary of bone and tired of soul, I found myself muttering, "Either I can't manage this place, or it's unmanageable." Consequently, I shucked the brass ring for opportunities that allowed me to achieve my brightest triumphs: to write, teach, and lecture on a wide variety of topics.

I have to add now—I hope not too defensively—that peering back through the shining ether of thirty years of time, I feel more capable of writing about servant leadership with more authority than I would have had as a full-time scholar. To this extent, I believe David Heenan's thinking and writing have marinated over time, depositing a more profound conceptual heft and gravitas than had he remained a distinguished Wharton scholar.

In this well-timed book, Heenan examines why some of us are able to sidestep life's most serious setbacks and go on to greatness. He knows this subject. A well-respected corporate executive, business school dean, and former Marine, he has encountered his own share of the best and worst of times, as Dickens put it. It is this authenticity that allows him to lay out an intellectual road map—a set of directions any of us can follow to confront some of life's most daunting challenges. While *Bright Triumphs From Dark Hours* offers no major formula, no quick fix, it does provide hard-hitting strategies for turning gloom into prosperity.

Read this groundbreaking book and you'll discover some simple truths about overcoming adversity. Part mediation, part how-to manual, *Bright Triumphs* illustrates through the prism of ten extraordinary individuals that confronting a hellhole is not the end of the world. According to Heenan, it could even be a required speed bump on the road to success—to, in his words, a *Bright Triumph*.

WARREN BENNIS
Santa Monica, California
August 2009

ACKNOWLEDGMENTS

MANY FRIENDS AND COLLEAGUES contributed to this book. Earlier versions of the manuscript were critiqued by Warren Bennis, Jerry Porras, Kent Keith, Dan and Peter Boylan, Vance Roley, Dave Bess, and Reg Worthley. Brett Uprichard gave my ideas flight and elegance. I also owe special thanks to Jim Bouton, Warren Keegan, Dick Tomey, Marty Jaskot, Sampson Parker, Tadanobu Kashiwa, Hiroshi Yasuda, Robert Witt, Nanci Kincaid, Warren and Carolyn Luke, Dick Gushman, Zap Zlatoper, Clint Churchill, and Marc, Eric, and Jennifer Heenan.

Many thanks, too, to those who allowed or encouraged me to tell their stories: Joel Klein, Shirley Ann Jackson, Pattie Dunn, Bill Snyder, Joanne Boyle, Scott Waddle, Gary Guller, and Steve Case. Others who gave me insight into their lives include Bill Ouchi, Julia Levy, Laban Coblentz, Theresa Bourgeois, David Haviland, Alan Cramb, Bill Jahnke, Debbie Lammers, Mary Bitterman, Jon Wefald, Sean Snyder, Jim Epps, Bob Krause, Bob Shoop, James Coffman, Mark Janssen, Joan Friederich, Sandy Barbour, Lindsay Gottlieb, Tom Fargo, Al Konetzni Jr., Jay Fidell, Dave Cole, John Agee, Miles Gilburne, and Dan, Carol, and Jean Case.

At the University of Hawai'i Press, I had the pleasure of working with a talented team of wonderful professionals, especially its CEO, Bill Hamilton, who edited my first two books at Addison-Wesley. *Bright Triumphs From Dark Hours* benefited tremendously from his wisdom and vigor. In addition, I want to thank Kent Keith of Greenleaf Center for Servant Leadership. His friendship, advice, and encouragement led to writing this book. Despite the pressures of creating his own most recent writing success, *Peaks and Valleys*, Spencer Johnson also greatly inspired me to hone my finished manuscript.

Roger Jellinek of the Jellinek & Murray Literary Agency saw the project through—guiding and inspiring me every step of the way. Joyce Libby and Ann Ludeman polished my writing. Once again, Martha Miller's competence, diligence, and unfailing good cheer contributed greatly to the book's completion. Finally, my wife and co-leader, Nery, has been at my side throughout this project. As with my earlier books, she organized my interviews, read and commented on successive versions of the manuscript, and helped shape its principal arguments. To this loving and most constructive critic goes a very special *Mahalo*.

DAVID HEENAN
Honolulu
August 2009

ABOUT THE AUTHOR

DAVID HEENAN is a trustee of the Estate of James Campbell, one of the nation's largest landowners, as well as a visiting professor at Georgetown University. Formerly, he served as chairman and CEO of Theo. H. Davies & Co, the North American holding company for the Hong Kong–based multinational Jardine Matheson. He has been vice president for academic affairs at the University of Hawai'i and, before that, dean of its business school.

Educated at the College of William and Mary, Columbia University, and the University of Pennsylvania, Heenan has served on the faculties of the Wharton School, the Columbia Graduate School of Business, and the University of Hawai'i. His articles have appeared in such leading publications as the *Harvard Business Review*, the *Sloan Management Review*, the *Wall Street Journal*, the *New York Times*, and the *Christian Science Monitor*. He is author or coauthor of six other books, including *Flight Capital* and *Double Lives*.

Heenan lives in Honolulu, Hawai'i. He can be reached at davehee@aol.com.

INTRODUCTION

Hope begins in the dark, the stubborn hope
that if you just show up and try to do the
right thing, the dawn will come. You wait and
watch and work: you don't give up.

—ANNE LAMOTT

BY EVERY CONVENTIONAL MEASURE, J. K. Rowling was mired in her darkest hour. Her exceptionally short-lived marriage had imploded. She had been sacked and was as poor as it was possible to be in modern Britain without being homeless. "By every usual standard," she admits, "I was the biggest failure I knew."

Against all odds, the spunky single mother poured her energies into finishing the only work that mattered to her—a book about a boy wizard. However, the publishing world hadn't caught up with her genius. Twelve publishers rejected her manuscript before a small London house picked up *Harry Potter and the Philosopher's Stone.* And the rest is history.

How did Rowling defy life's calamities and go on to greatness, while others pack it in? The billionaire author credits tenacity as the reason she weathered the storm. "Rock bottom became the solid foundation on which I rebuilt my life," she told a recent Harvard University graduating class at commencement.

Like Rowling, we are all confronted with our own dark hours: equally traumatic, life-altering events. Some of us are unshakable in our belief that anything is possible if we find the courage to forge ahead. Others, however, can't seem to escape the jaws of defeat.

Hero or zero? Both courses are available to you. As industrialist Henry Ford, who had more than his share of dark clouds, once put it: "Think you can, think you can't; either way, you'll be right."

Bright Triumphs From Dark Hours affirms the conviction that *you can.* We challenge those who choose to cling to the dark side, and celebrate others like megaseller Rowling, who are able to face adversity—and transform near-defeat into a bright triumph.

For the past several years, I have been scrutinizing dozens of dark hours—precarious situations, as well as individual lives, spiraling out of control—and how talented men and women refused to be trapped by them. Because personal stories are a lively and effective way to illustrate important points, I chose to examine a wide range of extraordinary individuals from history and contemporary life who overcame seemingly insurmountable obstacles. From these portrayals of people under duress, you'll discover the road maps for negotiating rugged terrain, guides for forging your own bright triumph.

These inspiring and dramatic stories are for people in all walks of life—people who want to be ready when their own lives are on the line and when their actions, large or small, will shape the future of others. As you'll see, our heroes and their vivid portraits are as different as chalk and cheese. Chancellor Joel Klein took on the monumental challenge of trying to overhaul New York City's long-embattled public schools. Coach Bill Snyder descended on another Manhattan—Kansas—to turn around college football's losingest team. Spunky Joanne Boyle not only survived a life-threatening cerebral hemorrhage, but elevated her California women's basketball team from oblivion to national prominence. Similarly, world-renowned scientist and trailblazer Shirley Ann Jackson broke down racial barriers as the first African-American woman to receive a doctorate from M.I.T. and to lead a major research university, Rensselaer Polytechnic Institute. Former Hewlett-Packard chair and cancer patient Pattie Dunn beat the odds to restore her reputation—and her health. Legendary Marine Gen. Chesty Puller, surrounded by overwhelming hordes of Red Chinese regulars, escaped the deadly fog of war at Korea's Chosin Reservoir, so his troops could fight another day. Sacagawea was the lone Indian, the lone teenager, the lone mother on the Lewis and Clark expedition, one of the most foreboding journeys ever undertaken. Equally adventurous, Gary Guller became the first one-armed man to scale Mount Everest, while also leading the largest cross-disability group to its base camp, at 17,500 feet. Retired Navy Commander Scott Waddle fought to remove the stain of the USS *Greeneville*, which accidentally sank the Japanese fishing vessel *Ehime Maru*, killing nine people. Tarnished Time Warner ex-chairman Steve Case plotted his own miraculous comeback through an eclectic array of New Age businesses. Others, though less prominent on the world stage, have demonstrated that a battered heart can still beat strongly.

Because each triumph is situational, I am leery about categorizing these winners. The social world isn't nearly as orderly as the physical world. People—unlike solids, liquids, and gases—are anything but uniform and predictable. But in the course of my research, I found that, however they differed, each had taken one of three paths to secure a bright triumph.

1. *Crusaders*, like Joel Klein and Bill Snyder, took on a seemingly impossible situation and achieved remarkable success.
2. *Combatants*, like Indian guide Sacagawea and the Marines at the Chosin Reservoir, overcame perilous, life-threatening conditions to forge a new tomorrow.
3. *Comeback kids*, like Pattie Dunn and Steve Case, bounced back from personal disgrace to restore their reputations.

Whatever their route to success, these courageous and inspiring men and women prove that taking on a truly hellish situation is not necessarily a death sentence. Within each of their personal stories, we'll examine how you can transcend the darkest hours. We'll also look at actions you can take to overcome potential career-killers. The answers call for very different strategies—all you need are the imagination and drive to aid the process, whether in a company or a community.

As you'll see in the following chart, I've identified six strategies to turn defeat into victory. We'll explore each of these actions in the next ten chapters and amplify them in Chapter 11.

Strategies for Forging a Bright Triumph

1. Learn from Adversity
2. Fashion a New Dream
3. Sell Your Vision
4. Share Your Dream
5. Focus, Focus, Focus
6. Start Now

Life isn't getting any easier. In a world often turned dark and cold, we are seeing more and more instances where talented people—quite often for reasons beyond their control—seem destined to fail. Yet caving in to the dark side is not an option; the costs are simply too high.

In the current Era of the Bailout, blame-mongering runs rampant. The wear and tear of contemporary life has made public lynchings commonplace. This year, for instance, one in seven of the world's largest companies will show their top guns the door. Not surprisingly, there is a significant decline in the ability or willingness of gifted men and women to tackle life's most difficult challenges.

Whether measured by foregone profit, employee turnover, or missed opportunities, dark hours and doomsayers can drain any enterprise of its strength and vitality. Organizational esteem suffers, and even the most confident managers become demoralized. Apparently, no one is immune. Virtually every person I encountered in writing this book had a tale of woe about one or more kamikaze situations. As important, they all agreed that to give up was not acceptable.

The notion that near-impossible challenges exist in can-do America—let alone that they may be on the rise—sounds alien, even heretical. Throughout our history, we have celebrated heroes and underdogs who conquer adversity. We cling to a stubborn belief in capturing the day. It's in our DNA.

The insightful young French nobleman Alexis de Tocqueville first spotted our nation's ebullient personality more than one hundred seventy years ago. "No natural boundary seems to be set to the effort of man," he wrote, describing the average American. "And in his eyes what is not yet done, is only what he has not yet attempted to do." Since then, we have been raised on the ethic that "quitters never win, and winners never quit" and "when the going gets tough, the tough get going." Our national disease, William James pointed out a century ago, was "the exclusive worship of the bitch-goddess SUCCESS."

That optimism continues today despite the swirling vortex of the global economy and rising cynicism about our major institutions. Surveys show Americans are actually less upset than they were a few years ago. Under the new administration, roughly two-thirds of the country feels positive about the future. "Contemporary American culture advertises achievement and accomplishment as the route to ultimate happiness," says Suniya Lothar, a professor of psychology and education at Columbia University. Americans hold out a ray of hope for even the toughest challenge, and see themselves as authors of their fate.

"America is an unlikely place—a country built on defiance of the odds: on the belief in overcoming the impossible," says President Barack Obama. Recalling the lives of America's founding fathers—Jefferson, Adams, Washington, and Hamilton—former Secretary of State Condoleezza Rice agrees, telling recent Boston College graduates that she was "struck by the overwhelming sense that there is no earthly reason that the United States should ever have come into being. But, not only did we come into being, we endured. So, remember, even when the horizon seems shrouded in darkness, the hope of a bright beginning is always in sight."

Mind over matter. That's the message issued by Norman Vincent Peale in his vintage best-seller, *The Power of Positive Thinking*. "You can think your way to success and happiness," he wrote more than fifty years ago, adding that it was every American's God-given duty to face down reality. This ethos of unbridled optimism has nurtured a rescue culture—the notion that any problem can be dispatched—in business, the arts, the military, sports, politics. That's the American dream that still inspires tens of millions of our unshakably optimistic countrymen.

Americans harbor the belief that when confronted with harsh economic realities or an intractable assignment, we will somehow find the sources of superhuman strength to beat the odds. Coleridge's pronouncement that "fear gives sudden instincts of skill" best describes this faith in our determination to rise to any occasion.

Throughout history, the world's greatest leaders have refused to let life's darkest hours prevent them from forging a bright triumph. Despite being imprisoned for twenty-seven years, Nelson Mandela turned around a country mired in the racial oppression of apartheid. Mikhail Gorbachev, as the Soviet agriculture boss, was condemned to seven years of hard labor, yet still managed to become leader of the Soviet Communist Party. Winston Churchill, arguably the greatest personality of the last century, overcame the stain of the Gallipoli disaster and political defeats to rally the Western world against Adolf Hitler's juggernaut. "The vistas of possibility are limited only by the shortness of life," he warned. "Success is going from failure to failure without the loss of enthusiasm." To Churchill, anything was possible: Victory was always at hand. "Never give in!" he told students at Harrow in 1941. "Never give in, never, never, never, never!"

It's worth noting that even the greatest of the greats have stumbled into an abyss. No one illustrates this better than George Catlett Marshall. As important to his country as George Washington, Marshall rebuilt the United States Army in World War II despite extraordinary initial resistance. Later in his career, however, Marshall suffered his darkest hour, failing to squash China's civil war.

In 1945, Mao Tse-tung's Soviet-backed Communists threatened the Nationalist forces of American ally Chiang Kai-shek. With Eastern Europe quickly becoming a laboratory for Marxist-Leninism, the free world could not tolerate the defection of Asia's strongest and most powerful nation to socialism. At President Harry Truman's urging, Marshall came out of retirement to negotiate with these two impassioned strongmen and put the Chinese civil war to rest.

Truman's choice of Marshall as his special emissary to China seemed a safe bet. A superb negotiator and brilliant public speaker, Marshall proved he could manipulate the most stubborn, difficult, and politically astute men of the time, including Roosevelt, Churchill, and Stalin. But Marshall knew full well the risks of this, his first diplomatic assignment. He had firsthand knowledge of China. From 1924 to 1927, he had commanded a garrison in Tientsin, where he acquired a working knowledge of Mandarin. Thereafter, he had made it a point to stay abreast of Chinese affairs of state. Clearly, Marshall knew that the odds were stacked against him.

Readers of history know the unfortunate outcome of the general's first foray into international diplomacy. After arriving in China in late 1945, Marshall found the Nationalist armies engaging, but not defeating, the Communist forces. He soon realized that Mao's greatest weapon was Chiang Kai-shek's dismal record of corruption. In short order, Marshall recommended that all future U.S. aid to the Nationalists be limited and strictly supervised by American officials. This, of course, enraged the Generalissimo. The Communists, for their part, viewed any U.S. support for the Kuomintang as an assault on China's sovereignty. They, too, fell out with Marshall.

Civil war was inevitable. No outsider, however skilled, could have reconciled the monumental differences between the Chinese leaders and their millions of followers. As one commentator said of the assignment, "Talleyrand, Metternich, and Castlereagh could not have pulled it off." Marshall returned home from this impossible mission in January 1947.

From this dark hour, the resilient general quickly rebounded. The architect of the Marshall Plan for rebuilding post-war Europe, he became Truman's steady right hand as secretary of state and, later, secretary of defense. The first soldier to win the Nobel Peace Prize, he was also a hero to the captains of his era. Truman, Roosevelt, Eisenhower, and Churchill all said he was the greatest man they had ever known.

Why, then, does this special breed of bravehearts take on these seemingly impossible assignments? In Marshall's case, "duty, honor, and country" were overriding. When the presidential call came to serve the nation, Marshall had no choice. He would simply do his best—as he had always done. If that required taking on the near-impossible, so be it. Appropriately, Churchill called this American hero "the noblest Roman of them all."

Others possess an overarching belief that you have to seek out the toughest challenges because that's where the greatest opportunities lie. "Man cannot discover new oceans unless he has the courage to lose sight of the shore," wrote André Gide. Those confronting tough times are undaunted risk-takers. Rather than cling to safe havens, these intrepid explorers want to stretch their limits. They are on a never-ending search for higher mountains to climb—literally.

On May 29, 1953, New Zealand adventurer Edmund Hillary and his Nepalese climbing companion, Tenzing Norgay, scaled the world's highest peak. During the ascent, Hillary, then thirty-three, recalled, "each night, when I went to bed, I'd let my mind dwell on likely things that might happen the next day, and think out carefully the sorts of decisions that it might be necessary to make." With proper planning and perseverance, Hillary said, "You can extend yourself far more than you ever believed. It's not the mountain we climb but ourselves." Since then, more than 2,400 mountaineers have reached Everest's summit; another 210 have died trying.

Adrenaline-pumping adventurers like Sir Edmund Hillary are attracted to the flame of risk. For them, risk-taking sits at the top of the hierarchy of needs. "It's the pinnacle," says sports psychologist Matt Grough. Whether braving the highest peaks, exploring unfathomed depths or assaulting treacherous day jobs, chance-taking is a critically important emotional need. But not every person is up to the task. "People need different levels of stimulation," explains clinical psychologist Robert Bailey. "Some need constant levels, some require little." The former represents an intoxicating cult of high rollers who believe that boldness rewards those who take risks.

Risk-it-all personalities expect some dark clouds. During his sophomore year, Michael Jordan was dropped from his high school basketball team; Henry Ford went bankrupt five times; Dr. Seuss was rejected twenty-seven times; and Elvis Presley got an F in music. But winners dare to stumble. They know that, without failure, there would be no bright triumphs—no discovery, no invention, no trip to the moon, no Everest ascents. The challenge, the reaching out, the exploration, lifts us out of our everyday, well-trodden paths into fresh fields of endeavor and fulfillment.

Those who go on to triumph don't equate mistakes with failure. Biographer Victor K. McElheny termed Edwin Land's try-try-again mentality "insisting on the impossible." The inventor of instant photography and founder of Polaroid, Land poured millions of dollars into research projects, rejecting the advice of his scientists that they were all doomed to fail. In another triumph of persistence, Thomas Edison, the Wizard of Menlo Park and the most prolific inventor in American history, who holds the record for patents, came up with 1,600 versions of the incandescent bulb before he got one to work. "Nearly every man who develops an idea works at it up to the point where it looks impossible, and then gets discouraged," he said. "That's not the place to become discouraged." Orville and Wilbur Wright, for their part, were hardly the first to try to build a flying machine, but they tinkered with their design for years, revising each element again and again. For the wings alone, they tested more that two hundred designs in a wind tunnel they built, and each attempt sparked new ideas that would lead to a machine that actually flew.

Where would we be without these dogged optimists? Their spunk transforms the darkest times into victory. Whereas some people are overcome by circumstances—the financial meltdown, Hurricane Katrina, tsunamis in the Indian Ocean—others quickly bounce back after being knocked down. They share a positive outlook when confronted with life's many obstacles: a trait associated with greater resilience.

"Resilience is a reflex, a way of facing and understanding the world that is deeply etched in a person's mind and soul," explains Diane L. Coutu, senior editor of the *Harvard Business Review* and a 2008–2009 fellow at the American Psychiatric Institute. "Resilient people and companies face the reality of staunchness, make meaning of hardship instead of crying out in despair, and improvise solutions from the air." These quintessential men and women reject the cynical smirk that smiles on the dark side.

Even the most da Vincian personalities recognize that failure is not defeat. "Failure is part of the learning process that leads to success," says John O. Whitney, a turnaround specialist and professor emeritus at Columbia Business School. Land, Edison, and the Wright brothers were as stimulated by failure as they were by success. It never took them out of the game. In their minds, failure implied you'd taken a chance. The bigger the failure, the bigger the chance you had taken.

Other experts cite self-efficacy as the distinguishing trait between the stouthearted and those who surrender to adversity. According to Stanford psychology professor Albert Bandura, self-efficacy represents unbridled determination. It represents a deep-seated belief that we really do have the power to achieve our goals. Some of us are born with it, he says. Others acquire it the old-fashioned way: They master a difficult task, mimic successful people, or seek out helpful advice from others. They realize that no one's life is a fairy tale. For them, it's an adventure, a journey through uncharted waters with countless stops and starts. They understand that nobody's perfect: Success is elusive; failure is always lurking. Indeed, fear of failure can be one of the most paralyzing forces than can seize the human spirit. It constricts people's visions of futures that are theirs for the taking.

"All of us have failed to reach our dream of perfection," Nobel Prize–winning author William Faulkner once explained of his fellow authors. "So I rate us on the basis of our splendid failure to do the impossible." Dark hours, when confronted directly, provide opportunities to excel. "Never confuse a single defeat with a final defeat," wrote F. Scott Fitzgerald, who received more that one hundred twenty rejection slips for short stories before his best-selling *This Side of Paradise* was published in 1920. "The anger of rejection motivated me to keep going," he recalled. Like J. K. Rowling, rejection to Fitzgerald was like grains of sand for oysters. By reacting positively, he often wrote sixteen hours a day, churning out up to 8,000 words.

Writers, artists, inventors, and leaders of every stripe are energized by volatile times. They expect some dry spells along the way. They know that it's the rare person who receives traction right away. These are "people who undertake the most characteristic of human endeavors: the pursuit of lost causes," claims *Atlantic*'s Cullen Murphy. They pursue a cause even "when all evidence suggests that it is doomed."

These same miracle workers believe certain causes are worthy of extraordinary sacrifice—winning the war, putting a man on the moon, defeating communism, reforming public education, discovering cures for serious diseases. Marshall, Mandela, Gorbachev, and Churchill all felt that history beckoned them to confront a world turned dark and cold. Robert Oppenheimer worked so hard that he damaged his already precarious health in the course of leading the Manhattan Project, which, fortunately, accelerated the end of World War II.

"The first and last task of a leader is to keep hope alive," wrote John Gardner, the distinguished educator, public servant, and founder of Common Cause. Inspirational types are not constrained by the darkest hours. They are experts at restoring people's faith in the future, especially the faith of talented people who have run into brick walls. In the pages that follow, we'll track ten exceptional men and women—people who turned adversity into bright triumphs.

Remember the U.S. Navy SEALs' favorite saying: "The only easy day was yesterday." Properly scripted, tomorrow *can* become better than yesterday.

part one

CRUSADERS

1

JOEL KLEIN:
Making the Grade

Good ideas are not adopted
automatically. They must be driven into
practice with courageous impatience.

—HYMAN RICKOVER, U.S. Admiral

Against all odds, hard-charging Chancellor Joel Klein has overhauled
New York's long-embattled public schools—with dramatic results.

WANTED: Superhero. Dynamic professional to lead big-city public school system. Must balance anemic budgets, repair crumbling classrooms, transform underperforming students and attract, and retain bright, but underpaid teachers. Must mollify demanding parents, aggressive unions, community activists—not to mention the Boss in City Hall. Be prepared for long hours, protracted legal and political battles and relatively low pay. Must show progress immediately or face termination. Previous education experience not necessary.

WHY WOULD ANYONE take such a tough, thankless job? It's been called the hottest kitchen in America. Yet those who oversee the country's big-city schools occupy one of the most critical positions in any community, with, in many cases, a larger budget, more employees, and more physical facilities than almost any other area business. Despite its importance, this bastion of educational purgatory has chewed up both neophytes and experienced hands.

The Herculean job "consumes all of you—your personal life, your professional life. I was totally exhausted," recalls Gerry House, who held the top post in Memphis and Chapel Hill, N.C., and is now president of the Institute for Student Achievement in Lake Success, N.Y.

Everyone, it seems, has a stake in a city's educational system—teachers, parents, students, business and political leaders—and all look to the superintendent to solve problems overnight, problems magnified by poverty and race. As a result, it has become increasingly difficult for today's big-city school czars to stay in the saddle long enough to make an impact, where school reform typically takes at least five years to show results.

"A keep-your-bags-packed kind of career" is how Michael Casserly, executive director of the Center of the Great City Schools, describes what may be the toughest job in America. But nowhere are the perils of leading the country's urban schools more daunting than in New York City. For years, the Big Apple's schools have been a toxic zone—a land mine of mean-spirited politics aggravated by contentious ethnic and social enclaves. No wonder that since the '60s the shelf-life of New York's educational top guru—or "chancellor" as the position is called—has shortened to a paltry two-and-a-half years.

The all-too-familiar problems of urban poverty, crime, and unfamiliarity with the English language—or the fact that the job may simply be too big (New York has 1,450 schools, 1.1 million students, 83,000 teachers and a $15.4 billion budget)—may make the assignment too difficult for any individual to manage. If Gotham's school system were a corporation, it would rank in the top third of the *Fortune* 500. For years, though, the real killer was the city's Byzantine accountability structure within which chancellors had to operate—a nightmarish mishmash of citywide and local school boards and districts. Despite spending more on each student (almost $12,000 a year), New York City's schools were plagued with struggling test scores, crumbling infrastructure, continual budget problems, and low morale.

When the idea of managing the Big Apple's chronically troubled system was floated by Paul Vallas, the highly respected CEO of New Orleans' schools and the former education chief of Chicago and Philadelphia, he quickly ruled himself out, admitting, "I'd get eaten up there." Why then did Crusader Joel I. Klein, a former federal trustbuster and business executive, decide, at age fifty-six, to take on this incredible challenge?

"Call it my profound love of our public schools," he told me. "I owe my teachers and this city's schools more than I can ever repay." The self-made son of a postman and a bookkeeper, raised in Bensonhurst and Astoria, Queens, is the proud product of Gotham's public schools, before graduating magna cum laude from Columbia University and Harvard Law School. "Next to global terrorism," he contends, "reforming our public schools is the single biggest challenge confronting the nation. We simply have to get it [public education] right!"

This lifelong Democrat, who served in the Clinton Administration, believes that getting it right in America's schools could also serve as an important first step in restoring public confidence in government. "Most Americans—whatever their political party—believe in a role for government, but they also believe that government too often wastes their money, puts special interests ahead of their interests, and doesn't do its job well," he says. "But it doesn't have to be that way."

Klein understands the nation's cynicism with its public institutions. Americans today are no longer shocked to learn that their schools perform poorly and have been losing ground to other industrialized nations. Despite U.S. taxpayers pouring $3 trillion in the last four decades into K–12 education, student achievement continues to lag. Not even one in three American eighth-graders meets U.S. proficiency standards in reading and math. According to educational assessment's gold standard—the National Assessment of Educational Progress—performance levels have barely budged since NAEP began measuring the impact of the school reform movement in 1969. What's more, each wave of education reform has been squashed by teachers' unions and administrative bureaucrats who fear change and reject accountability.

Yet, we know that nothing affects the quality of human capital and living standards more than education. It is crucial to our future prosperity. "The only way to ensure we remain a world economic power is by elevating our public schools," says Carlyle Group ex-chairman Louis V. Gerstner Jr. In other words, we need a bright triumph: a public education system whose students can compete with their counterparts in India, China, and a host of other nations.

Upon entering office in 2002, Mayor Michael R. Bloomberg recognized that this was a defining moment. If New York City—and the nation at large—were to avoid becoming a technological colony of other countries, there was no time to waste. To escape its darkest hour, the goal-oriented "CEO Mayor," as *Business Week* called him, would follow the lead of his counterparts in Chicago, Boston, Cleveland, Washington, and other cities, who wanted—and got—more control over their schools. Today, about a dozen of the nation's seventy-five largest school districts are under mayoral control—an approach the Obama administration strongly endorses. "Mayors fancy themselves as better-trained public administrators," says Michael Kirst, a Stanford University professor of education. "They have the hubris, or the guts, to take this on."

With his businessman's mind-set, Bloomberg displayed the courage to take on the near-impossible task of righting New York City's schools. Likening America's educational system to the automobile industry of the '70's—"stuck in a flabby, inefficient, outmoded production model driven by the needs of employees rather than consumers"—Bloomberg warned: "The choice is clear. It will require a top-to-bottom rethinking of our school system, one that insists on a performance-based culture that is oriented around children, not bureaucracies."

Although every mayor since Ed Koch had tried—and failed—to wrest control over Big Apple schools, billionaire Bloomberg quickly seized power in early 2002, making him directly accountable for their performance. If the schools were not better in four years, "you'll know who to blame," he told the city's eight million residents, most of whom harbored a deeply entrenched cynicism toward public education. With the acquiescence of the teachers' union (in return for a new contract with pay increases of 16 to 22 percent), the mayor convinced the New York State Legislature to abolish the 160-year-old Board of Education, which he derided as "a rinky-dink candy store," and took control of the schools. In its place, an advisory panel—with no real authority—was established to counsel the administration on education issues. The mayor also eliminated the smaller, politically fractious, union-controlled neighborhood school boards and reorganized thirty-two community school districts into ten instructional regions under tight central control. Taken together, these changes gave Bloomberg the unfettered ability to hire and fire the chancellor—and make New York City a test-bed for national education reform.

Twenty years ago, school chiefs were almost always former teachers who became principals and then superintendents. But there was "nothing in their background that would lead you to believe they'd be good managers," argues Frederick Hess, director of education policies at the American Enterprise Institute in Washington, D.C. Exasperated by the lack of progress in school reform, mayors across the country have been desperate for someone—anyone—to jump-start their failing schools. Increasingly, many of them have turned to a new breed of non-educators. Los Angeles hired a retired Navy admiral; Seattle, an ex-banker and public utility official; San Diego, a former U.S. prosecutor; New Orleans, a retired Marine colonel; and Kansas City, a former federal aviation official. "Outsiders have a lot more experience managing these kinds of problems than educators do," Hess explains. They not only bring with them a sense of urgency, but a fresher perspective of big-city governance.

Sensing that his choice of School Superhero was perhaps the last chance for New York's children, Bloomberg searched through a long list of potential candidates. He quickly concluded that he wanted a crusader: a bold, fearless leader with superior management skills. "You have to have an outsider," he said. "You need someone who is willing to shake things up."

Although he barely knew Joel Klein, from all reports the dyed-in-the-wool New Yorker seemed well suited to the pressures of politics, as well as those in the classroom. In truth, Klein was not the first talented outsider to be placed at the head of New York schools. His predecessor, Harold O. Levy, a Wall Street lawyer and Citicorp alumnus, worked furiously to shake things up, but often clashed with Mayor Rudolph Giuliani and suffered from the city's fractious politics. He lasted two-and-a-half years.

Klein, however, seemed destined to score a bright triumph where a long line of predecessors had failed. In addition to his lofty academic accomplishments, he displayed a long-standing interest in educational issues. During a leave of absence from Harvard Law School, he studied at New York University's School of Education and later briefly taught math to sixth-graders at a public school in Queens. After law school, he spent the next twenty years in public and private legal work before joining the Justice Department in 1996. Serving as head of the antitrust division, the hard-charging litigator was best known for prosecuting the government's case against Microsoft. In 2001, he left law and returned to New York to run the U.S. operations of media giant Bertelsmann.

Despite his modest roots, Klein slowly worked his way into Washington and New York's corporate and cultural elite. In the Beltway, he played tennis with luminaries such as Alan Greenspan and Antonin Scalia—and was a regular on the D.C. cocktail circuit. In New York, he could be seen hobnobbing with former GE CEO Jack Welch, current Citigroup chair Dick Parsons, Barnes & Noble chairman Leonard Riggio, Caroline Kennedy, and other bigwigs.

Bringing his golden résumé and sharp mind to the Bloomberg administration seemed like a wild dream to Klein in the summer of 2002. The prospect of running New York City's embattled schools was not in his game plan. "The mayor's offer surprised me," he told me. "And I didn't think I'd get it. But I was really excited when it came, and I honestly believe I'd trained for the job my entire life."

The clever Bloomberg understood that a little trust-busting was exactly what this most creaking of all public monopolies—NYC's public schools—needed. Calling the new chancellor "a true leader who never shies away from the tough and sometimes controversial decisions that are necessary to implement change," the mayor demanded a complete overhaul. His public-spirited partner was definitely on board. "I'm not afraid of breaking glass," Klein the crusader said, adding "I'm prepared to risk failure with this job because I know there's life after being chancellor of education in New York."

As for his lack of the required professional credentials (Klein, like his predecessor Levy, had to receive a waiver from New York State to lead the city schools), the new honcho concedes that the biggest obstacles were "not knowing the people and what the real challenges were at the operational level. But I certainly understand them today," he says, "although I still get criticized for being an outsider." As a non-educator, however, KIein wasn't mired in what was then a chaotic and dysfunctional culture. "I was able to bring a fresh set of eyes and a new perspective to the job," he recalls, "and that's what many insiders were yearning for."

Klein uses a favorite metaphor to describe the self-defeating culture he encountered in his new digs. It involves an elementary school in Manhattan's Washington Heights. Built decades ago, the school building had a leaky roof over the auditorium. Every time it rained, the water dripped through to the wood floor, causing it to buckle. Calls were placed to the central administration to fix the problem. One day, a contractor showed up to repair the floor. When told the problem wasn't the floor, it was the leaky roof, the contractor replied: "I don't do roofs. I do floors!" He then proceeded to replace the floor, leaving the damaged roof in place. With the subsequent rains, the new floor buckled and had to be replaced again.

"That's the problem with education reform," Klein explains. "Ever since the 1983 *A Nation at Risk* report, public school systems have been trying out different flooring under a leaky roof. In many ways, we tried to reform just about everything—curriculum, teacher certification, pre-school, after-school, lunch programs, and everything else in the system—everything but the culture of the system itself. It's a culture that claims to be in the business of educating children, but puts schools—and the people who work in them—at the bottom of the organizational chart at the expense of the kids."

In another stroke of genius, the mayor moved the Board of Education—renamed the Department of Education (DOE)—into the Tweed Courthouse next to City Hall. Symbolically, the move further joined Bloomberg and Klein at the hip, reinforcing the city's high priority on education. Today, both men meet regularly on Mondays, although contact is often more frequent.

Indeed, the first impression one gets after climbing the thirty courthouse steps is professionalism and efficiency. Whether it's clearing security or accessing key personnel, the cadence is decidedly upbeat. There's not a hint of the bureaucratic sclerosis that typically grips most government offices. Here, the revamped facilities sparkle and are well maintained—a far cry from the cluttered mess that one finds in many public-sector buildings. Service-with-a-smile is commonplace, and, in my dealings with the chancellor and his staffers, access was never a problem; calls and e-mails were returned immediately. Simply put, Klein's sanctuary at 52 Chambers Street in Lower Manhattan resembles a well-oiled machine.

Back in 2002, New Yorkers were truly hoping for miracles from the new school czar. Touted as the potential savior of the city's schools, the former trustbuster was well aware of the perils of the job when he took over six years ago. Classrooms were dull, bleak places where kids, who spoke 130 different languages and were overwhelmingly black and Hispanic, were floundering. Only thirty-nine percent of students could read and write at grade level; even fewer met state standards in math. Less than half the high-schoolers graduated in four years. In addition, the system suffered from overcrowded classrooms, run-down facilities, serious teacher shortages (especially in science, math, and special education), and a bloated bureaucracy that stifled reform.

Undaunted, Klein viewed his $250,000-a-year job as an opportunity to shine on the country's biggest educational stage. Even by New York standards, he began sprinting—imposing a dose of culture shock on a system that had chewed up ten chancellors in twenty years. With a brass-knuckles management style and political deftness, he initiated an exhaustive overhaul of what had long been considered one of the nation's worst and most reform-proof school systems.

Unveiling what most observers believe is the most important education transformation in the country, the new chancellor got off to an unexpectedly strong start—and his reforms seem to be sticking. Student performance is rising, social promotions of kids who fall behind have ended, there are increasingly more and better choices for students, schools are safer, and educators are receiving additional autonomy while being held accountable for progress.

The Big Apple's success to date stems in part from Klein's belief in focusing on key elements that can make an impact. He is as inflexible as a chalkboard when it comes to what makes for winning education: decentralization—giving principals a freer hand, provided their schools can meet goals for attendance, test scores, promotion rates, and other criteria. Scholars like UCLA business professor William G. Ouchi, author of *Making Schools Work* and a staunch supporter of Klein's restructuring efforts, argues that decentralization saved American business; it could save the city's schools, too.

Early on, Klein's "Children First" initiative set a goal of establishing more than three hundred small, theme-based secondary schools and a doubling of the number of high schools to four hundred. Since then scores of new elementary and middle schools have opened. He also converted forty-plus elementary schools into K–8 schools and closed twenty underperforming middle schools. In addition, he increased the presence of charter schools, alternative providers, as well as new gifted and talented programs and arts schools. "Giving people choices is always empowering," he says, "and almost always leads to better outcomes for kids."

Recognizing that New York's ultimate success depends on the in-the-trenches work of the principals, Klein has been fighting tooth and nail to transform them from dispirited administrators to businesslike leaders. "We're converting the role of the principal into a CEO role rather than, if you will, a cog in a top-down administrative machine," he says. "We're trying to drive more authority to the school, for the school to become the unit that matters." His strategy is to give principals the freedom to create their own programs, while enforcing accountability for what students learn and when they should learn it. If, at the end of the year, performance is dismal, principals are replaced.

To assist would-be principals and veterans alike in this new, no-holds-barred culture, the chancellor created the New York City Leadership Academy, a $77 million program funded from private sources. But for many of the old-timers, the adjustment has been painful—leading to heavy principal turnover. More than half of the system's principals have left the job in the past five years. "We're demanding much greater accountability," Klein admits, "and I think that leads to greater turnover."

To fill these ranks, Klein has placed a big bet on "kid principals," as union skeptics call them, recruiting outside the profession and taking a risk on twenty-somethings who often lack a decade or more of classroom experience. He defends the practice of injecting selective dollops of high-energy, high-caliber youngsters into school management. "Nobody said Bill Gates was too young for the job [CEO at Microsoft]," he told me. "If you put artificial restrictions on human resources, you're going to lose good people who are up for the job."

Driving a wedge between these Children First initiatives and the unions has made Klein the darling of the corporate and philanthropic communities. For years, affluent New Yorkers largely abandoned and disparaged city schools. Recently, however, many of them feel a special kinship for the feisty crusader. They no longer consider city schools a black hole for outside funding.

Given his flair for high-society schmoozing, Klein has led the effort to lure unusually large amounts of private monies to the city's schools. Early on, Klein created the Office of Strategic Partnerships, with Caroline Kennedy, his wife's former college friend, serving as chief executive. Luminaries such as media moguls Rupert Murdock and Mortimer Zuckerman and actress Sarah Jessica Parker, as well as a host of corporate donors—from Morgan Stanley to Goldman Sachs—have pitched in to renovate libraries, refurbish playgrounds, and accelerate curriculum improvements. Ironically, the ex-Microsoft nemesis snared his largest gift by far—more than $125 million—from the Bill & Melinda Gates Foundation to jump-start the city's small-schools effort.

Among other things, these powerful helpers have allowed the chancellor to tap some of the nation's leading consultants—from McKinsey & Co. to Edison Schools—to fix his ailing schools. "Private funds have been absolutely essential to our success," Klein told me. "They're our R & D dollars, our venture capital. They also give people skin in the game. Donors have a sense that they have more than a civic investment. They now have a financial investment."

The chancellor's multi-pronged makeover features clear pedagogical plans for helping low-achieving minority and poor students. While studies suggest that seventy-five percent of the average student's performance is correlated with his or her parents' socioeconomic status, they have also shown that highly skilled, engaging teachers can eliminate the achievement gap between rich and poor kids. Klein rejects the notion that children raised in difficult circumstances are destined for the educational slag heap. "That argument," he says, "only breeds low expectations and a culture of excuses." Klein has worked feverishly to corral the resources needed to help correct the imbalances of poverty and race. In the last several years, the city has reported impressive improvements from high-poverty, traditionally low-performing schools—and the difference between the performance of black and Hispanic students compared with that of whites is narrowing.

To build on these gains, the chancellor also sought to scrap the arcane funding formulae that left many students—particularly those from low-income and non-English-speaking families—under funded. His "fair-student funding" program, being phased in over the next few years, insures that dollars follow students based on their special needs. "Families can now be assured that, no matter which school their child attends, the resources will follow," Klein promises.

The avowed anti-incrementalist insists that "timidity and tinkering around the edges" won't deliver the results the public has a right to expect. "We've been doing that for at least thirty years," he says. "And it has failed." That's why the Brooklyn native is undaunted in stepping on the toes of those around him who are unwilling to change. Determined to squash the city's huge, centralized education bureaucracy, he reduced the staff to 3,500 (down from an earlier high of 6,300) and transferred approximately $273 million in administrative savings to the classrooms—where education takes place. "We are trying to devolve both dollars and powers to the schools," he says. "As much as we can, I'd like to see the dollars flow first to the schools and then to the outstanding people in those schools."

Defying fierce opposition, Klein also has been skewering bureaucrats, peeling back union rules, recruiting new teachers, motivating top performers, and finding new ways to assist or remove poor performers. One of his biggest challenges has been attracting and retraining sufficient classroom talent. During his crusade, Klein has increased teacher salaries forty-three percent; created $15,000 housing bonuses for those in shortage areas—such as math, science, and special education; and started a Lead Teach program, which provides an additional $10,000 a year to mentor and coach other teachers. In an important concession, he secured a new "open-market hiring system," where more than 3,000 experienced teachers can vie for vacant positions within the system. However, the current union contract—a 204-page tome, with 800 pages of side agreements—still makes it virtually impossible either to fire incompetent teachers or offer merit pay. "Most disappointing," concedes Klein, still determined to rectify these long-standing taboos.

Pushing for more rigorous educational standards, more time in school for students, and better pay for better-performing teachers have only brought ridicule from the powerful United Federation of Teachers (UFT). Its decade-long head and president of the powerful American Federation of Teachers, Randi Weingarten, has acidly accused Klein of "demonizing and micromanaging" teachers. The school chancellor, she contends, "sees teachers as cogs in a factory model, not professionals worthy of respect," adding that he is "anti-union" and wants to cripple the UFT. Klein vehemently denies these charges, pointing out that his father was a member of the Letter Carriers union and, earlier in his career, he represented organized labor.

To be sure, some of his ideas grate on educators. But even his harshest critics acknowledge that his direct, get-it-done management style is delivering the goods and is firing up the system's amazing turnaround.

Klein also rejects the notion that education—unlike every other domain in American life—is not compatible with serious and meaningful accountability at every level. The chancellor, like his boss, is an unabashed metrics junkie. "The mayor wants to know our progress in very, very specific terms," he says. "Give me the data, give me the detail." Klein also insists on details—or "deliverables"—to manage what is often seen as unmanageable. To the nonaligned, this can be confounding and smacks of micromanagement. But slowly, principals, teachers, and staffers discover that once his "new systems thinking" is in place, clarity invariably leads to improved student performance. And with it comes greater autonomy. Without question, his strategy of applying tight, then loose, central controls is contributing to enhanced student outcomes.

"We want to be able to measure how every part of the organization does or doesn't affect student achievement," Klein says. "Based on how well a school does on these evaluations, we make the tough decisions about both replacing principals and closing schools." This high-powered analysis has not come without its critics. The outgoing head of the school supervisors and administrators' union, Jill Levy, called Klein's school report-card system "a sword of Damocles" over principals' heads.

And yet there's no disputing that Klein is reversing the long-running fiasco that gripped New York City schools. His hands-on reforms have begun to show significant progress. The percentage of students at or above grade level standards in math jumped from 37.3 percent in 2002 to 74.3 percent in 2008; in reading, from 39.3 percent to 57.6 percent over the same period. These gains easily outpaced those in the rest of the state and placed the Big Apple in the upper quartile of the nation's big-city schools. Over the years, performance had dropped off as students aged. Now, in defiance of this historical trend, New York City youngsters have been improving as they moved from grade to grade. But the "most important metric" to Klein is the graduation rate, where New York has long lagged the national average of 71 percent. At latest count, this had increased to 58.2 percent—its highest level in two decades. In recognition, the Big Apple won the 2007 Broad Prize for Urban Education, which cited the city's outsize gains in reading and math scores for economically disadvantaged, African-American, and Hispanic students.

"I'm ecstatic," said Klein, when informed of these improvements. "The hard work is really paying off." For his part, Mayor Bloomberg described the makeover as "a dramatic upward trend" over the last six years and reported that New York's public schools were now "in a different league." The state education commissioner, Richard P. Mills, agreed—noting that the city's reforms were "encouraging and exciting," adding that "the schools have delivered."

On balance, most pundits believe that there is light at the end of the tunnel. But to get through that tunnel, Klein knows there are no quick fixes or magic solutions in shedding the dark clouds surrounding city schools. "I see these changes as evolutionary, not revolutionary," he says, refusing to gloat over his impressive accomplishments. He understands the long, difficult journey ahead. "We have a long way to go," he warns. "Too many of our children still are not receiving the education they need to succeed—or even survive—in the twenty-first century."

Finishing his seventh year—well north of the length of service seen by his predecessors, the working-class boy who made good says: "We've made a great deal of progress over the past several years, but the continuing challenge is enormous. The human stakes are too high for complacency or self-congratulation."

As my time with the chancellor came to a close, Klein's ambitious dreams had him on the run—literally. His typical day begins at 6 A.M., scanning e-mails and reading a bevy of newspapers, followed by breakfast (that day with Philip Handy, chairman of the Florida State Board of Education). Then, it was off to City Hall for a session with deputy mayors. An inveterate walker, who religiously avoids lunch, the sixty-two-year-old Klein was able to get almost an hour's worth of hoofing around lower Manhattan before tackling a series of afternoon meetings with, among others, Washington, D.C.'s mayor, Adrian M. Fenty, and the DOE's senior leadership team. Finally, there were evening sessions with various community groups.

Given New York's size, complexity, and immense challenges, maintaining the schools' positive momentum will be extremely difficult. The road to success is always under construction. That said, the situation has changed from hopeless to hopeful. New York's famously cynical citizenry now express warmer feelings about public education instead of the usual doom and gloom.

Although it is too early to talk about his triumphs, Klein is winning hearts and minds. His enthusiasts are even touting him for Gotham's highest elective down the road. "If he fixes the schools," says good buddy Jack Welch, "he can own the city." For now, Joel Klein remains committed to his crusade—giving current and future generations of New York City students the tools to succeed in life. "I wake up every morning feeling like I'm the luckiest man in the world," the school chancellor says, "getting up fighting for the kids in the city I grew up in." Stay tuned!

SHIRLEY ANN JACKSON:

Aim for the Stars

If you want something said, ask a man.
If you want something done, ask a woman.

—MARGARET THATCHER

Rensselaer President Shirley Ann Jackson, shown here cutting a ribbon at the new Experimental Media and Performing Arts Center, sidesteps the critics in leading RPI's remarkable transformation.

FOR AMERICA'S UNIVERSITIES, once the envy of the world, the honeymoon may be over. Survey after survey indicates that they are losing the public trust. Skyrocketing costs, lack of accountability, uneven quality, and poor graduation rates are just a few of the black marks leveled against the academy. More disturbing are reports that the competence of recent graduates is declining. Derided as "compassless" and "underachieving," universities face a cascade of dark clouds—from tighter budgets and declining enrollments to unruly faculty and Congressional oversight.

Gone, too, is the Golden Age of university presidents. Today's college chieftains work 24/7. Few last more than seven or eight years, and the number of presidential meltdowns grows and grows. From the nation's two oldest colleges, Harvard and William and Mary, to two of the youngest, University of California at Santa Cruz and the University of Maine at Presque Isle, recently departed CEOs fill an ever-expanding Rogues Gallery.

Despite relatively high salaries—roughly $350,000 to $500,000 plus attractive perks—fewer and fewer people seek a college presidency. The numbers fluctuate, but, at last count, more than one hundred schools were looking for a chief executive. What was once a plum post has become a position of extraordinary precariousness. "There's no question that the job has become more demanding, and there is a greater accountability expected," adds John DiBiaggio, former president of Tufts, Michigan State University, and the University of Connecticut. "The pressures are far, far greater than they once were." With expectations increasing and resources decreasing, those pressures have made the position frustrating, dispiriting, even dangerous. Exhaustion claimed Harvard's Neil Rudenstine; depression, Mary Washington's William Frawley; suicide, UC Santa Cruz's Denice Denton.

Think about it. A candidate for these hellish jobs must be a visionary, a scholar, an ambassador, a manager—able to handle issues like diversity, student catastrophes, faculty pay and tenure, while increasing the endowment and enrollments. He or she also must have an attractive family and an effortlessly sociable spouse—plus a thick skin. Herman Wells, former president of Indiana University, summed it up brilliantly: "He should be born with the physical strength of a Greek athlete, the cunning of Machiavelli, the wisdom of Solomon, and the courage of a lion, if possible. But in any case, he must be born with the stomach of a goat."

University trustees, therefore, have seen fit to broaden their search for would-be presidents. They are actively pursuing more diversity at the top. Today, 23 percent of U.S. colleges and universities are run by women, up from 10 percent in 1986. Women sit at the top of half of the eight Ivy League schools—as well as the presidencies of M.I.T., Purdue, Case Western, Iowa, and Michigan.

No surprise then that, eight years ago, the trustees at Rensselaer Polytechnic Institute gave nationally renowned physicist Shirley Ann Jackson a mandate to steer their university in a new direction. In short order, she transformed the venerable institution into a showcase campus. But in raising the college to a higher level, Jackson's crusade generated a grab bag of complaints, leading to a faculty no-confidence vote, in academia an action that often precedes a forced resignation—one that, in fact, claimed her predecessor, R. Byron Pipes. Jackson, however, not only survived, but created a bright triumph.

"For me, the world has always been full of mysteries," Jackson told me. "Studying physical properties of matter allowed me to unlock the secrets of the physical world." As a child in the 1940s, she dreamed of unlocking those secrets as a world-famous physicist. Growing up in Washington, D.C., her passion for exploring the unseen blossomed as an eight-year-old with her carefully documented bumblebee experiments—examining their habits and habitats, studiously keeping a detailed log of their behavior.

Her parents encouraged her youthful enthusiasm. "Aim for the stars," her father, a postal supervisor with a gift for math and science, urged her, "so that you can reach for the treetops." Meanwhile, her mother, a social worker, taught Shirley and her three siblings to read before they went to kindergarten. "Looking back, my parents were my role models," Jackson says. "I believe I inherited my father's genes relative to science and technology, but my mother's genes relative to a love of reading and writing. This was coupled with the events of the times."

Those events included experiencing discrimination firsthand. Segregation meant, among other things, that blacks were forced to attend separate, often inferior, schools. During those dark days, the Jacksons refused to let prejudice hinder the intellectual development of their children. Their bedrock determination paid off. A straight-A student, Shirley attended accelerated programs in science and math and graduated from segregated Roosevelt High School at the top of her class. In her valedictory address, she urged her classmates to maximize their potential and "aim for the stars."

In 1964, the brainy eighteen-year-old enrolled in M.I.T. on a full scholarship—one of only two African-American women in her freshman class. She would soon discover just how alone she was. "In class, she found herself surrounded by empty seats," wrote Diane O'Connell, who chronicled Jackson's early years in *Strong Force: The Story of Physicist Shirley Ann Jackson*. "Her classmates would sit anywhere—except next to her. No one talked to her. For the first time in her life, she felt like she had no friends."

Though her classmates were not outwardly hostile, they often ostracized her—from the campus cafeteria to critically important study groups. Craving fellowship, she joined Delta Sigma Theta, one of the country's oldest African-American sororities. But here, too, there were obstacles. No school, including M.I.T., provided black students with on-campus social facilities. So the chapter had to secure rental facilities at a YMCA in nearby Roxbury and at the Negro Professional and Business Women's Club.

During her senior year, Jackson and another African-American woman were visiting the University of Pennsylvania. Driving through Philadelphia the evening of April 4, 1968, they heard on the car radio that the Rev. Martin Luther King Jr. had been assassinated in Memphis, Tennessee. From that point on, Jackson committed herself to making the fallen leader's dream a reality. For starters, she would focus on what she could do to improve conditions for other African-Americans at M.I.T. In short order, she formed the Black Student Association and increased the number of minority students from two to fifty-seven in just one year.

That June, Jackson graduated with honors and enrolled in Tech's doctoral program in physics. While carrying a full course load, she also pioneered efforts to prepare entering minority freshmen for M.I.T.'s rigorous curriculum. "She had the ability to take on hard issues," said Dr. Paul Gray, the school's former president. "She stood out as quite extraordinary."

In 1973, Jackson became the first African-American woman to earn a Ph.D. at M.I.T. Her research on invisible subatomic particles won wide acclaim and took her to the most prestigious physics laboratories in the United States and Europe. Three years later, she joined what was then AT&T Bell Laboratories in New Jersey, where, for the next fifteen years, she built a solid reputation as an outstanding researcher and public-policy advocate. Her work spilled over to her personal life. There, she met and married fellow physicist Morris A. Washington, now a faculty member at Rensselaer. In 1991, she accepted a tenured professorship of theoretical physics at Rutgers University, while continuing to consult with Bell Labs on semiconductor theory.

Four years later, President Bill Clinton put her in charge of the Nuclear Regulatory Commission (NRC), the first woman and first African-American to hold the post. With a $500 million budget and 3,000 employees, the talented trailblazer marshaled a cadre of experts to reform what had been criticized as a commission too closely aligned with the nuclear-power industry. Among her sweeping changes were toughening safety standards on the nation's 110 nuclear reactors, fast-tracking permits for new and existing facilities, and upgrading the agency's professional staff. She also spearheaded the formation of the eight-nation international agency that safeguards the nuclear industry today. As she departed NRC, her colleagues said farewell by presenting her with an "Energizer Bunny," a fitting symbol of her boundless vigor.

Despite these bright triumphs, Rensselaer's choice for the top academic post bucked tradition. Jackson, after all, had never served as a university president, provost or dean, and her teaching stint at Rutgers was a brief four years. But many in higher education had been eyeing her for various leadership positions for some time. Jackson's status as an accomplished African-American female scientist and high-octane administrator enabled her to skip several traditional rungs in her climb to a college presidency. It was obvious to those around her that the subatomic explorer would bring a whirlwind of winning talents to the job: brainpower, energy, commitment, and focus.

Jackson, therefore, seemed to be the perfect fit for a school that touted its long-standing strength in science and engineering, with top-ranked programs in information technology, applied mathematics, civil and chemical engineering, lighting and electronic arts. The feisty female's aggressive, self-assured style suggested she could launch the Institute to greater national and international prominence. The school's trustees, made up of highly respected scientists and business executives, also hoped that she could strengthen campus ties with the embryonic high-tech industry in hometown Troy, New York, and adjacent communities.

"We were looking for change," board chairman Samuel F. Heffner Jr. explained at the time of her appointment. "Dr. Jackson's experience, her perspective, her record of achievement in government, in industry, in science, and in academia provide her with extraordinary qualifications to advance this great university in the twenty-first century."

At her inauguration, Jackson told the campus to "aim for the stars," promising "to bring to Rensselaer a leadership that will be characterized by the development of shared vision, the clarity of that vision, the skill to articulate it, and the perseverance to bring it to fruition." At the same time, the straight-talking scientist, who describes herself as assertive but not adversarial, warned that transforming Rensselaer into "a premier technological university that competes internationally as well as nationally" could ruffle some feathers and create inevitable tensions within the university community. What's more, there would be no dillydallying. "If you know there needs to be change, and you know there's a lot of ground to cover," she declared, "you don't waste time."

In the months preceding her appointment, Jackson had heard all about the litany of problems facing the Institute, including faltering enrollments, shaky finances, and a relatively paltry $500 million endowment. In addition, Rensselaer had run through five presidents in the fifteen years prior to her arrival. Then, too, Troy, situated in New York's frost belt, presented some formidable recruiting challenges.

Three hours north of New York City, the modest city, with only 48,000 residents, sits on the eastern bank of the Hudson River. Legend has it that a local butcher named Samuel Wilson supplied the local militia in the War of 1812, which earned him the title as America's iconic "Uncle Sam." For most of the nineteenth and early twentieth centuries, the city was an industrial powerhouse, producing iron and steel, and, later, highly engineered mechanical and scientific equipment. Troy's prosperity, however, began to fade after World War II. Driving into the city today, visitors discover broken-down factories and ugly brick housing projects juxtaposed with one of the most perfectly preserved nineteenth-century downtowns in the United States—anchored by townhouses, churches, and commercial buildings that look almost exactly as they did one hundred years ago. But when it comes to the first-class amenities that twenty-first-century sophisticates want—restaurants, nightlife, and buzz—Troy falls short.

Rensselaer's leafy, 275-acre campus towers over the city from a hill just east of historic downtown. Billed as the nation's oldest technological university, RPI—as the school is more frequently known—has produced groundbreaking work in a broad range of important areas. It developed one of the earliest university-based business incubators, targeting on high-tech start-ups. It pioneered the use of studio classrooms, where students work in teams connected by computers, and led the revolution in robotics and artificial intelligence. From the bridge builders of the nineteenth century to the engineers of space exploration, from the inventors of the Industrial Revolution to the entrepreneurs of today's Innovation Economy, Rensselaer's graduates have had an important and far-reaching impact. A roll call of distinguished alums includes George Ferris, whose famous wheel debuted at the Chicago World Fair in 1893; Texas Instruments founder J. Erik Jonsson; William Wiley of publishing giant John

Wiley & Sons; astronaut Jack Swigert; and NCAA czar and former Indiana University president Myles Brand.

Despite its famous grads and storied history, the 175-year-old institution had long flown under the radar. Unlike many of its peer institutions, RPI chose to concentrate on a hands-on approach to undergraduate education at the expense of cutting-edge research and graduate studies. Those forces, many argued, removed the college from the national limelight. "We were either drifting or dropping—take your pick," recalls David Haviland, former Vice President for Institute Advancement and a forty-plus-year veteran of the school. What Rensselaer needed, the trustees and Jackson agreed, was someone to lift the school out of the darkness and into the top tier of science and technological colleges.

As the first African-American woman to head a major research university, Jackson had already made history. But could she forge another bright triumph?

People who had seen her work in government, industry, and academia had few doubts. They marveled at her ability to focus, tenaciously bringing clarity to complex issues. In her last assignment at the Nuclear Regulatory Commission, she proved that she was no shrinking violet. In fact, she's more of a steel magnolia, a strong woman raised on Washington's mean streets, who clothed her iron resolve in a veneer of collaboration. That was exactly what Rensselaer needed: a president who could cajole and coddle faculty and staff; a crusader who could push her agenda for change, while finessing a consensus.

From her first day on campus in July 1999, Jackson insisted on "new ideas, new ideals—and bold action." As one of her first acts as the new chief, she began to chart the Institute's strategic blueprint. Over a seven-month period, she met regularly with faculty and administrators to develop The Rensselaer Plan. That road map to the future, approved by the trustees the following year, highlighted the university's multidisciplinary focus on biotechnology, nanotechnology, information technology, media arts, and technological creativity. Beginning with 140 "we will" (not "we should") statements, the plan emphasized personal and unit responsibility for achieving specific goals and establishing metrics to measure progress. Every year, results are assessed against those benchmarks and revised accordingly.

The Institute's blueprint for change targeted an ambitious $1 billion fund-raising campaign, aimed at doubling RPI's endowment, research funds, and the number of doctoral degrees awarded. The plan also emphasized recruiting renowned faculty, while toughening the standards for promotion and tenure. Finally, it placed a high priority on more closely linking town and gown (building what Jackson calls a "communiversity"), as well as improving the first-year experience for students, faculty, and staff.

Even Jackson's staunchest skeptics were impressed by the speed with which the steel magnolia accomplished the key milestones of the plan. On the fund-raising front, she drew on her remarkable collection of friends and powerbrokers. Less than two years in the saddle, she lassoed an anonymous, unrestricted $360 million gift, at the time the largest single donation made to an American university. "It got people's attention that we were serious about what we were doing here," Jackson told me. Since then, her Midas touch has given her a national profile that is much more like a hotshot CEO than that of an ivory-tower leader.

Subsequently, Jackson upped Rensselaer's campaign to $1.4 billion. Research awards jumped from $37 million to $80 million; the school hired 180 new faculty, 73 of them in newly created positions; the number of doctoral students rose from 775 to 886—all since 1999. Before the financial meltdown of 2008, the endowment had reached $828 million.

In addition, the energetic president presided over a burst of capital construction. She freshened up the Troy campus, opened a $200 million Experimental Media and Performing Arts Center, a $100 million Computational Center for Nanotechnology Innovations (housing the most powerful university-based computer), a new dining hall, state-of-the-art fitness center and athletic village, while renovating several student buildings to give the school a more comfortable feel. But this crusade was not about bricks and mortar. Rather, her intent was to create a "top-tier, world-class university, with global reach and global impact."

Understandably, enhancing the school's diversity carried special weight for Jackson. Today, roughly one-third of RPI's students are women; fifteen percent are members of minority groups—triple the numbers of a few years ago. Under Jackson's leadership, the college also secured federal funding for a project that would help more than nine hundred local low-income students receive supplemental instruction in math, science and technology, beginning in the seventh grade and continuing through high school.

After just a few months as president, Jackson established a reputation as a diligent and dogged leader, with skills not often associated with the academy: speed and accountability. She also sent a strong message to prospective students and faculty: It was time for them to step up to the challenge. "If you want to run with the big dogs," she said, "you have to get off the porch."

In 2008, more than 11,200 students applied for admission to the undergraduate program, double the number since 2005, and average SAT scores increased almost twenty points over the previous year. On the faculty front, Jackson increased the number of women and minority professors 46 percent and 100 percent, respectively. From child-care centers to career-development workshops, the former bastion of white male domination has led the way in uplifting the role of these underrepresented groups in science and engineering. Finally, Jackson created a Revitalization Fund for new faculty research.

People were impressed with the hard-charging leader's ability to set an ambitious agenda and get things done quickly. Her initiatives, for the most part, garnered high marks. "I feel very positive about the plan," Joyce R. McLaughlin, a senior mathematics professor, told *The Chronicle of Higher Education*. "But at the same time, not everybody says they're on the train. Many people are enthusiastic, but not everyone."

Despite Jackson's impressive accomplishments, some cracks in Rensselaer's ivory tower began to surface. In April 2006, her accelerated attempts to transform the university were challenged by a faculty no-confidence vote. The halls of ivy were no longer filled with the optimism of a few years earlier.

In ways that only later became clear, Jackson's straight-talking, businesslike approach had alienated some of the people who were most affected by her high-speed changes: entrenched faculty. "Failing to appreciate the importance to the organization of the people already in it is a classic managerial mistake, one that new managers and change-oriented administrators are especially prone to make," says Warren Bennis, noted leadership guru and a former university president. "Organizations only change themselves when the members want to. You can't force them to change, even in a Batman cape."

What evidently sparked the squabble were complaints about Jackson's swift style and an alleged attempt to tweak the university's pension scheme. On April 27, the faculty narrowly voted down the no-confidence motion: 155 to 149.

Message received. Crusader Jackson recognized that there was a clear disconnect between those professors who were committed to reforming RPI and others who were not. According to most observers, the demarcation broke over those high-performers eager to push the plan's agenda forward and others, more entrenched and generally less productive, who felt threatened by change in any form. In any case, the president met with rankled faculty members shortly after the vote to defuse the tensions. She acknowledged that she may have made some mistakes in jump-starting the Institute's makeover. While promising to listen more to the faculty, the unflappable administrator demanded that they afford her the same respect. "You cannot *not* reach out to me while saying I must reach out to you," she insisted. "You cannot hope to get my attention and cooperation by vilifying me or trying to embarrass me publicly."

Jackson quickly worked to shore up the lines of communication. She organized a regular series of dinners with small groups of professors and lunches for entire departments. These sessions, in turn, complemented her monthly "pizza with the president" lunches designed to address potential student concerns. These steps and a subsequent review of faculty governance obviated further strife.

Admitting that she felt the no-confidence vote was "especially wrenching," Jackson nonetheless won the full backing of RPI's trustees. "The board is one hundred percent behind what Shirley has done and is doing. We are on the right track and are moving full-speed ahead," Chairman Heffner said at the time. "The circumstances of dramatic change create challenges for all engaged. Anytime you do something of this magnitude, you're going to have issues with people who don't like change. The facts are undeniable. The naysayers have very few legs to stand on."

Not every Rensselaer alum shared this opinion. "Sad that the trustees can't see that they have a problem when half their faculty votes no-confidence," said one anonymous grad. "They need to take an honest poll of the alumni to see what they think of Dr. Jackson and the plan. Then they'll see some 'against' members."

Undeterred, the trustees steadfastly endorsed Jackson's dynamic leadership, rewarding her with a new five-year contract after the faculty vote. Today, her highly publicized pay package—$1,326,774, which includes contributions to a deferred compensation account—provides further ammunition for critics of presidential pay. Then, there are the related concerns about her participation on corporate boards. Although fewer than six percent of college chiefs serve on three or more for-profit boards, Jackson sits on six: FedEx, IBM, Marathon Oil, Medtronic, The New York Stock Exchange Euronext, and the Public Service Enterprise Group. For her efforts, it is estimated that she receives more than $400,000 annually, excluding restricted shares and stock options. While these activities have greatly enhanced her ability to solicit funds for the university, as well as raise its national and international profile, Jackson's opponents not only view her total compensation as excessive, but also complain about her time away from campus.

Complementing her corporate directorships is her service on boards of some of the nation's most prestigious nonprofits: the Smithsonian Institution, Brookings Institution, M.I.T. Corp., Georgetown University, and the Council on Competitiveness—among others. Here, too, critics argue that these commitments, while beneficial to the university, detract from her presidential responsibilities.

Taken together, the time constraints and pressures of leading RPI and meeting multiple corporate and nonprofit boards are daunting. Jackson admits that all these activities keep her days, and sometimes her evenings, fully occupied. "But," she argues, "I have a lot of energy. I sleep only four or five hours a night—and I get bored easily."

Indeed, Jackson's incredible stamina and ability to contribute to the national debate on a wide range of important issues are exactly what Rensselaer's governing body wanted from the school's eighteenth president. As past head of the American Association for the Advancement of

Science, the world's largest scientific society, Jackson first identified the "quiet crisis" of projected shortages in the science and technology work force that is threatening the U.S. economy. In large part, it stems from the apparent lack of interest in young Americans toward math and science.

Compounding the crisis is what Jackson calls the "underrepresented majority": women and ethnic minorities. "They make up the majority of the U.S. population [and are] a relatively untapped talent pool. The basic message is that innovation is rooted in people. We don't know where the next breakthrough will come from. If we want to maintain our standard of living, preserve our security, and remain the world's strongest economy, as a culture we need to value science and engineering and those who do it."

Similarly, Jackson is hell-bent on eliminating the image of engineers and scientists as nerds or geeks. Recognizing that globalization and technology are the two most important forces of our time, she insists that Rensselaer's engineering students, who account for sixty percent of the undergraduate program, acquire greater balance by spanning the globe. Under a recent initiative, the school's engineers will spend at least one semester overseas. In exchange, partnering institutions—today, two, but eventually ramping up to twelve to fifteen—will send their students to the Troy campus.

"This is a big change for people studying math, science and engineering," says Alan Cramb, RPI's dean of engineering. The administration believes that this ambitious effort, to be phased in over several years, will give the school's techies a quantum leap in developing the diversity of thought needed to compete globally. At the very least, Jackson contends, going overseas and experiencing another culture should provide them with "the intellectual agility to live a purposeful life."

For her advocacy of these and other groundbreaking initiatives, RPI's tenacious CEO has won numerous plaudits, including forty-three honorary doctoral degrees and a place in the National Women's Hall of Fame. What the 5-foot-3 leader and avid hiker lacks in size, she makes up in accomplishments. By every measure, she has cut an imposing figure in the rough-and-tumble world of college presidents. Her good friend, Secretary of State Hillary Rodham Clinton, calls her a "true pioneer."

Some wonder whether the challenges at Rensselaer will be enough to hold her attention. For now, the sixty-one-year-old crusader remains committed to RPI's tradition of putting quality education within reach of anyone willing to strive. "Our progress has been transformative and exceptional," she says, reflecting on the last eight years. "We are steadily building national and international stature, standing, and recognition. But," she adds, "we're not done yet."

Jackson's quest to "aim for the stars" will continue to inspire future generations of America's scientists and engineers. Always mindful of her early struggles, she constantly urges others, especially young minority women, to follow their dreams and take the road less traveled. Speaking at a recent University of Rochester commencement, she exhorted graduates to always think positively: "I'm an optimist. I'm short, and short people only see the glass as half full. So optimize who you are and what you are. Optimize others. Optimize your opportunities. Seize them—and do meaningful things."

3

BILL SNYDER:

Miracle in Manhattan

If you're not tested, you're not living.
It's the test that challenges your character.
The tougher the job, the greater the reward.

—Hall of Fame Coach GEORGE ALLEN

Now in his second stint, Coach Bill Snyder strives
to create another "Miracle in Manhattan."

WHEN NEWT GINGRICH WAS ELECTED Speaker of the House, one of his first tasks was to call legendary Penn State football coach Joe Paterno for advice on how to gracefully replace the old guard on the Hill with fresh blood. Gingrich was seeking Paterno's advice because the crafty coach was known for reinvigorating his team each year.

In 1988, Kansas State University's president, Jon Wefald, sought similar counsel. His football team had crashed, burned, and was rusting in pieces. Stan Parrish quit as the team's coach four days into the season, unable to endure what eventually became the 0–11 finish, a school record 30-game winless streak, and a 1–36–1 stretch at the close of the 1980s.

The first major college football program to lose 500 games, the Kansas State Wildcats—a.k.a. "Mildcats"—were a national laughingstock. *Sports Illustrated* proclaimed "Futility U"—with its horrific play before near-empty bleachers—the worst program in the country. "The losing atmosphere was palpable to anyone who came in contact with it," wrote Dennis Dodd of the *Washington Post.* "The ugly purple uniforms, the ancient facilities, the pittance of fans. Players' self-esteem was lower than the team's place in the standings—which was usually last." So noncompetitive was K-State that there was a serious move afoot to kick them out of the football-frenzied Big Eight (now the Big 12) Conference.

The program had hit rock bottom. "The morale of the players and coaches was terrible," says former captain Rob Goode, recalling the bad old days. "Being a football player at K-State wasn't something to be proud of. It was common for players to arrive late to team meetings and practices. There was no discipline on the team. No one believed we could win."

Achieving any modicum of success back then would have seemed miraculous. More than that, pure fantasy. But fantasizing about K-State football had always been rare, and Wildcat fans had never been an especially large or passionate gang. Attendance barely cracked 20,000 per home game—less than half of capacity—in the team's creaking, rusty stadium. Folks in the isolated college town of Manhattan, known as the Little Apple, were more likely to root for in-state rival Kansas University or any other Big Eight team as they were for the team in their own backyard. Back then, Kansas State was everyone's second favorite.

The skeptics felt it was time for the university to withdraw from collegiate competition, as Wichita State had done, and leave Kansas as the only major college football program in the state. "I don't believe, as much as you could write about it, you know how bad it was—the facilities, the players on scholarships, the budget," recalls Bob Stoops, head coach at Oklahoma University and a former K-State assistant.

Dr. Wefald, who became Kansas State's twelfth president in 1986, knew he had to put some bite back into the Wildcats. He understood the symbiotic relationship between football and academics. The gridiron, he argued at the time, "provides an opportunity to look forward to six or seven weekends each fall when the trees are turning and the crops are being harvested. It's the tail that wags the dog. It's far too important. Athletics is our window to the world. Like it or not, sports in America are important in determining the reputation of a university."

Yet the distinguished historian, whose interests range from Gen. George Custer to Genghis Khan, knew that turning around his failing football team would be no small accomplishment. He needed a crusader. "There weren't five people in the Western world who thought we could do it," Wefald recalls. He charged his then athletic director Steve Miller with finding a miracle worker. Eighteen candidates were interviewed, most displaying "monumental indifference," says Wefald. Jim Epps, Kansas State's senior associate athletic director, suggested Miller look at Iowa University, which had rebuilt its program in the early 1980s. Thumbing through an Iowa press guide, they stumbled on the name Bill Snyder; he had served as the Hawkeyes' offensive coordinator from 1979 to 1988. Epps called Snyder, who agreed to listen.

Bill Snyder, then 49, had experienced transformations firsthand. He was part of Iowa's makeover, from nineteen consecutive non-winning seasons to eight consecutive bowl appearances, including three Rose Bowls. A notorious workaholic, Snyder had gained a solid reputation as an offensive genius. His passing attacks had wreaked havoc on Big Ten opponents. When Miller called coach Bo Schembechler of Michigan to ask about Snyder, the crusty Schembechler hollered, "Hire him, get him the f_ _ _ out of this conference!"

Don't think the savvy Snyder was unaware of the risks. In the win-at-all-costs world of big-time sports, he knew football-barren Manhattan was one of the game's deadliest addresses. Athletic director Miller leveled with him: "Kansas State is flat on its back. You must have heard it's one of the toughest jobs in the country. It's not. It's *the* toughest."

Friends also warned Snyder that Kansas State was a lost cause—a professional black hole—and pleaded with him not to take the job. Previously, the program had fourteen different coaches with an average tenure of just under four years. In addition, none of the four head coaches who immediately preceded him, dating back to 1967, ever became a college head coach again. Still, Snyder wanted to breathe life into this moribund program and forge a bright triumph.

But why? "A diminutive IQ," Snyder now quips, from his newly decorated office in the Vanier Football Complex. "More seriously, I was impressed with the quality of people I met. They meant a lot to me. It was their genuine interest in developing K-State, not only the athletics department or the football program, but all aspects of the university. People like Jon Wefald, [vice president] Bob Krause and Steve Miller had a very strong impact on me. There was a genuine, sincere and honest commitment to move K-State in a better, more positive direction. Also, I'm future oriented, and I wasn't concerned with all the history that went with Kansas State football."

On November 26, 1988, Snyder signed a five-year deal calling for $85,000 for the first year, which he bargained up to $90,000—peanuts compared to the $1.5 million package he would receive at the end of his first head coaching stint. Arriving on campus a few days later, the new sheriff surveyed the losing landscape before him and told his players,

"We have an opportunity to create one of the greatest turnarounds in college football. I have no idea how long it will take. I just know it will get done." And that is precisely what K-State did. Over the next seventeen years, Snyder engineered a bright triumph, the so-called "miracle in Manhattan"—converting a program that had gone winless in the 27 games before his arrival and molding it into a national power. He took the Wildcats to 11 straight bowl games and the Big 12 title in 2003. In gratitude, when he retired in November 2005, the school affixed his name to the stadium.

A simple alpha-to-omega summary of Bill Snyder's career misses the mark. His life has had more gyrations than the stock market. Genesis is easy enough. Born on October 7, 1939, Snyder spent most of his childhood in the northwest Missouri city of St. Joseph, raised by his divorced mother, Marionetta, who worked as a sales clerk and buyer at the local department store. Living conditions were difficult. Snyder's mother slept on a rollaway cot, with son Bill occupying a Murphy bed next to her in their cramped second-floor apartment.

"I was never embarrassed by how we lived," Snyder says. "I was proud of it. My mother worked hard. We didn't have much, but she provided me with all that she could. If my work ethic came from anyone, it came from my mother. She taught me what the Lord gives you is time, and twenty-four hours a day is all you get."

Coaches are usually former stars who understand greatness in their bones or marginal players who understand the intellectual nuances of the game. Bill Snyder was the latter. He played five sports at Lafayette High School before matriculating to William Jewell College in Liberty, Missouri, where he performed as a "pretty nondescript" defensive back. If coaching were to be his chosen profession, he would have to learn how to recruit, find and mold stronger, more talented athletes than he had been, all in new and different ways.

Snyder began his carrer in 1962 as an assistant coach in Gallatin in northeast Missouri, moving to Indio High School in California's Coachella Valley in 1964. That year, he also got married. Two years later, he received his first collegiate experience, serving as a graduate assistant under legendary John McKay at the University of Southern

California. The following year, it was back to Indio High, this time as head coach.

"I went back there thinking I was John McKay, and I wasn't," Snyder laughed. "I planned to outwork everyone, and I flat wore out my coaches." Two years later, he took on the top job at the much bigger Foothill High School in Santa Ana, California, where he coached for four years. In 1974, Snyder packed his bags again, moving to Sherman, Texas, to become the offensive coordinator at tiny Austin College. "There were no scholarships there, and everyone coached or played for the love of the game—something I really didn't understand until I was gone," he remembers.

Two years later, Snyder began a seventeen-year association with Hall of Fame coach Hayden Fry, joining the University of North Texas staff and helping engineer an impressive turnaround. "He was a workaholic," Fry said of his new coach. "He was the first guy in the office and the last guy to leave the building." But the pressures of college coaching came at a high price. Too many late nights at the office followed by early mornings; too many crises and too little time—all took its toll on the family. In 1978, the Snyders (then with three children: son Sean and daughters Shannon and Meredith) separated and divorced the following year. "I was simply a bad husband, that's all," Snyder told *Sports Illustrated*. "I was a faithful husband, but a bad one. You could certainly say that football was part of it."

Snyder, nevertheless, refused to throttle back when, in 1979, he and Fry moved in tandem to the University of Iowa. There, he served as the Hawkeyes' offensive coordinator for the next ten years. "He's the greatest," Fry said of his talented assistant. "He's extremely intelligent and organized. He's fundamentally the best coach I've ever seen."

It was during his Iowa days that Snyder married Sharon Payne, an elementary school principal. Her son, Ross, went on to play for his stepfather at K-State. Bill and Sharon had a daughter, Whitney, who now rides on the Wildcats' nationally ranked equestrian team.

Snyder's bright triumph at Kansas State is a story for the ages. It is also a testament to the sad, stubborn imbalance in big-time college sports that a virtual outsider could make his way into football's top echelon. Over the past twenty-five years, perennial powerhouses—Texas,

Ohio State, Southern California, Miami, Notre Dame, Alabama, Oklahoma, and Florida—have dominated the game. "It's caused by a lot of factors, central among them the tradition of winning counts enormously," explains Douglas Looney, a longtime sports columnist for *The Christian Science Monitor* and *Sports Illustrated*. "Players want to be seen on television, so they go to the traditional powers that surface almost weekly on the tube, which allows the same teams to be on TV more and more, which attracts better players. So if you're at Kansas State, you assume your humble position at the bottom of the heap far from the glare of TV lights and scavenge for crumbs."

Crusader Snyder would have none of that. His spunky Wildcats would take on football's blue bloods and thump them soundly. Clawing and scratching, poor little K-State joined the elite programs of college football. In retrospect, sculpting the Wildcats into a national power seems like a far-fetched dream. "The construction project Bill did at Kansas State is unsurpassed in my memory in terms of developing a program," says Chuck Neinas, the founder of the College Football Association and the former commissioner of the Big Eight Conference. Barry Switzer, whose last three Oklahoma teams (1986–'88) had run up 185 points on the Wildcats, agreed that Snyder's efforts at K-State were unparalleled. "Bill Snyder isn't the coach of the year, and he isn't the coach of the decade," he proclaims. "He's the coach of the century."

Even the National Football League took notice of Snyder's skill, dedication, and leadership. "To me, the best football coach in the country is Bill Snyder," says then Kansas City head coach Dick Vermeil. "I don't care if it's pro football or college football. He's the best."

So how did Snyder do it? "The major task was to get our youngsters to expect more of themselves than what they actually expected," he explains. Translation: Snyder had to create a winning tradition by fanning dreams and by simply getting better every day. It's hardly the sort of blueprint you might expect, but it worked quite nicely in Manhattan.

Soft-spoken Snyder injected self-esteem into this school of a little more than 23,000 nestled in a windswept prairie town in the rolling Flint Hills of northeast Kansas, where buffalo once roamed. With its roots as an agricultural institution—and derisively known as "Silo U" or "The Cow College"—K-State had always lived in the shadow of near-by Kansas University. Not anymore. From Day One, Snyder focused on winning. Anything less was unacceptable. His attitude rubbed off on his players. Working twenty hours a day, the hyperkinetic coach looked for ways to motivate his gridders, introducing a slew of invectives to get his team to play harder.

"Some people try to find things in this game that don't exist," legendary coach Vince Lombardi once observed. "But football is only two things—blocking and tackling." This philosophy meshed nicely with Snyder's belief in the basics. Among his favorite ditties:

Little things are trifles;
Trifles make perfection;
Perfection's no trifle.

Outstanding coaches have high expectations of everyone, while maintaining a positive environment. The expectations extend to players, assistant coaches, and supporting staff. "The great coaches have demonstrated personal drive, expertise and knowledge," Hall of Fame coach Bill Walsh noted. In return, great coaches expect dedication and concentration. With that ethos, Snyder set about reversing the fortunes of Kansas State football. The result would be a near-dynasty: a bright triumph.

K-State's arrival among the perennial pigskin powers is mind-boggling given the state's limited population and its relative paucity of blue-chip players. In those dark early years, high school superstars wouldn't return his calls. "Blue chippers wouldn't even talk to Kansas State," Neinas recalls. "Only one of Snyder's recruiting classes was ranked in the top 20. So Bill and his staff had to be so very, very careful to find kids they could mold into good players." They were forced to develop an uncanny knack for sizing up a young athlete's potential. To find players who could flourish in his system, Snyder diligently evaluated players beyond their physical abilities.

Wildcat rosters typically were stocked with undersized overachievers—the anonymous castoffs of elite programs. From these cracked bricks, the new coach built teams that began to produce handsome results on Saturdays and brought fans to their feet. As they started winning, blue-chip players started paying attention to them. K-State not only began to win the recruiting wars in the Sunflower State, they enjoyed profitable harvests in the bastions of high school football: Texas, Florida, and California.

To supplement his high school recruits, Snyder worked feverishly to obtain a stream of junior college veterans. He admired their football savvy and winning instincts. By milking the JCs for seasoned players, Snyder brought big-time talent to small-town Manhattan. "Basically, what he did was take a bunch of misfits," says Quentin Neujahr (hometown: Surprise, Nebraska), who played center at Kansas State from 1990 to 1993 and later the Baltimore Ravens. "He took a bunch of people nobody wanted and made them play together."

Blending this mishmash of talent was just one element in Snyder's Manhattan Project. He told the Kansas State hierarchy what needed to be done to win—pay your coaches, build first-rate facilities, be proud, don't be afraid to fail. He then set a workaholic example, sometimes eating only once a day—at 1 A.M., after finally turning off the projector.

"He was so damn focused," former athletic director Miller remembers. "He was an AD's dream, because he worked so hard, and an AD's nightmare, because he wanted things. That first year, any time Bill came into the building, Jim Epps and I would just about hide under our desks, thinking, 'Oh, jeez, what does he want now?'"

Snyder wanted his assistant coaches' salaries almost doubled, to be competitive with the top Big Eight schools. He wanted better facilities and a bigger recruiting budget. "His middle name was 'Demand'," says President Wefald. "All of this was difficult, because we were not only broke, we were in debt," adds Epps. "We had no collateral. None, zip, zero. We couldn't say, 'If we default on a loan, you can have this.' It was people willing to believe in us and take a huge personal risk."

For starters, Crusader Snyder offered to cough up $100,000 from his own pocket to overhaul the decrepit football complex. "I didn't have that kind of money," he tells me. "But I thought somehow, some way, I could probably borrow it." Embarrassed, the athletic department turned to Kansas rancher Jack Vanier, who donated funds for the renovation.

Later, Dave Wagner of Dodge City, Kansas, won $37 million in a 1991 national lottery and contributed $1 million to buy new artificial turf for the field named in his honor. During the Snyder years, more than $15 million, all in private donations, were pumped into football facilities. Much of the credit goes to the football-cum-fund-raising fanatic Wefald. "The president cared about athletics and really supported us," says Snyder.

The new coach's arrival charged the air in Manhattan. He immediately whipped up the team's energy level. In short order, he had them believing there were no limits to what they could do. His intensity and fanaticism for perfection came to life on the practice field in the searing summer heat. If you stood behind the huddle in practice, you could see his control over the team. With a serious mien and studied calm, he moved, watching from different angles, talking to his players. A stickler for detail, he broke down every minute aspect of the game, insisting on meticulously timed repetitions and drills. As a play unfolded, the calm, but forceful field general would often erupt into a cacophony of praise or condemnation of a single player or the unit en masse.

Bill Snyder's system was not revolutionary. "It certainly wasn't brain surgery," says professor Robert Shoop, who directs K-State's Leadership Studies Program. "He believed in continuous, incremental improvement—individually and then collectively." Above all, the new coach stressed discipline. He demanded total concentration. He believed a point is best learned by repetition. Hence, the Wildcats practiced longer than almost any team in the country. "Oh, my God," says Barrett Brooks, who played for Snyder from 1991 to '94 and later professionally. "Three hours. Three-and-half hours. Every day. He'd kill us."

When the Wildcats did something, Snyder the perfectionist made sure they did it thoroughly. Leading up to a game, he spent hours and hours alone watching game films of opponents—over and over. Like some mad swami, he studied key players: Their strengths and weaknesses—not apparent to other coaches—set off alarm bells, and he analyzed the best ways to stop them. He then educated his players, who, by game time, were well prepared for what they would face. A Bill Snyder–coached team knew their opponents better than themselves.

"I tried to derive from game action fundamentals that will support the next game action," Snyder says. "I had teaching methods, ways to derive fundamentals, ways to practice. It's the methods I loved. My only burning focus was to get better every day. If that made me a perfectionist, then so be it."

Perfection was always Snyder's game. "It's an obsession," says his wife, Sharon. "When things don't go right, it upsets him terribly." No doubt, the coach's idiosyncrasies caused some of his players grief, at least initially. But for the notorious nit-picker, there was no such thing as "about right."

Instilling a military-style efficiency in his troops, Snyder showed how to win with modest talent. The Wildcats may not have been as gifted as their opponents, but they almost always made fewer mistakes—fewer turnovers, penalties, and misalignments.

As with any bright triumph, there was also a clever plot. Besides tapping the nation for high-achieving players and running arduous practices, Kansas State would beef up on a diet of non-conference cupcakes. Snyder hoped to get the Wildcats off to a fast start against the likes of Temple, Akron, and Northern Illinois. Granted, these were hardly heavyweights in college football, but K-State was playing the same level of opposition in the late '80s when it put together a record of 1–31–1 over three years. "It just didn't make sense to jeopardize ourselves playing the elite teams in the country early," Snyder contends. "Our goal was to achieve continuity and gain momentum early in the year—a practice now endorsed by just about every major college program."

The Wildcats went 1–10 in Snyder's first season, but that win— a 20–17 squeaker over North Texas State—snapped a 30-game losing streak that was closing in on Northwestern University's 34-game mark. On the last play of the game on September 30, Carl Straw rifled a 12-yard pass to Frank Hernandez in the left corner of the north end zone of KSU Stadium with no time remaining. When the game ended, Wildcat fans stormed the field and, given their losing tradition, needed time to figure out how to tear down the goalposts. They reached out to Coach Snyder as he was lifted high, transported like a king on the shoulders of two mammoth linemen. The marching band played the K-State fight song to the joy of 7,000 faithful followers. The symbolic victory, the 300th in Kansas State history, would be the first in the Snyder era.

Snyder was able to stir the hearts and minds of the local populace, after years of their being the Conference doormats. The next year, the Wildcats produced five wins, turning heads with much-needed victories over Big Eight foes Oklahoma State and Iowa State. That effort earned Snyder Conference Coach of the Year honors. In 1991, the Wildcats went 7–4 for their first winning season in nine years, with all the losses to nationally ranked teams. "We had become a better football team by first being individually better, and then collectively better," the coach explains. Two years later, K-State went to a bowl game for the first time in school history. Again, Snyder was named Big Eight Coach of the Year.

The Wildcats were no one- or two-season flash. Combining deep, veteran squads that mixed hellacious defense with a balanced offense, K-State continued to inch closer to the elite programs in college football. The gridders won at least 9 games in each of the next 8 years and 10 of the next 11; they advanced to 11 consecutive bowl games; they defeated every Big-12 team, including runs of 13 in a row against Missouri, 11 against Kansas, 10 against Iowa State; at one point, 5 against Oklahoma and 3 against Nebraska—both national powerhouses.

Did someone say "Grrr"? The Wildcats were "Mildcats" no more. Snyder's quiet, unspectacular efficiency helped the program stay aloft for a long time. The unexpected transformation—impossible as it seemed— stunned even the university's staunchest supporters. "To think," recalls former Athletic Director Bob Krause, "all we wanted to do was hold our heads up high and be competitive—to win maybe five or six games and occasionally go to a bowl game." The team's metamorphosis was proof that the sport didn't belong solely to the football factories: A small-town program could make a big-time impact.

Plaudits came at every turn. But it was the giddy homegrown fans who most appreciated the coach's crusade. "Bill Snyder lifted the cloud of losing," recalls Ned Seaton, general manager of *The Manhattan Mercury*. "He allowed us to care, and to have the sheer ecstasy of seeing our tribe win when we care. He was the father of the Wildcat Nation. The chief of the tribe."

During his successful tenure at Kansas State, Bill Snyder delivered a consistent message to every student athlete: "We want you to be better today than yesterday, and better tomorrow than today." In addition, he counseled them to ask three questions when faced with a life-changing decision: "Will it make you a better person; will it make you a better student; will it make you a better player?" His message definitely got through to his players. "You're a fool if you don't put the things he teaches in your back pocket and continue to use them," says former linebacker Josh Buhl.

Bill as teacher seems an appropriate fit. In a game filled with flamboyant coaches, vociferous fans, and gigantic players, Snyder seems slightly miscast. No Greek god, he is of medium height, wears neat, conservative clothes (coat-and-tie the norm) and is genuinely content to allow the noise and hoopla of big-time sports swirl around others. If anything, Snyder resembles an Oxford don, reflecting his chessboard approach to the game. In fact, President Wefald recalls his first interview with him: "It was like talking to a history professor, a political science professor."

Looking every bit professorial, Snyder stood in sharp contrast to the slick, glib coaches who often infest collegiate athletics. Persistency was perhaps his most endearing quality. "You never had to worry about what he was thinking, because he's a constant man," recalls Jerome Clary, a former K-State player. "Whether winning 11, 12, going to a bowl, he's the same man. He doesn't change from week to week. His idea is to stay steady, stay stable and let us feed off that."

Snyder spoke with unvarnished eloquence—coining simple platitudes not only for his players, but also for himself. Among his pet phrases: "Keep rowing the boat, keep on keeping on, keep chopping wood." Indeed, one of his heroes remains Geppetto, the carpenter in *Pinocchio*, the coach's favorite movie. Snyder has bought dozens of copies of the videotape and sent them to his children and family friends. "Geppetto had such a tremendous passion for children," he says. "He goes though disappointment, yet he has the compassion to stay with it."

For Bill Snyder, life has been all about challenges—overcoming dark days through perseverance. His success at Kansas State was much more dependent on preparation, attention to detail, and old-fashioned hard work than to revolutionary offensive or defensive schemes. Over the years, visiting coaches often traveled to Manhattan to discover the secret of The Miracle. "They expect me to reach into my top drawer and pull out a sheet of paper with a blueprint," Snyder said in a *Sports Illustrated* interview. "I'm flattered, but there's no piece of paper. We just got a little better each year . . . until here we are." Perseverance was the key: Snyder never wavered from his philosophy of getting a little better every day—to keep chopping wood.

So driven was Snyder to succeed that he scarcely found time to eat or sleep. Chewing, he reckoned, was a distraction—something that might take his mind off the game. During the season, he ate just once a day, when he got home, usually well after midnight. As for snoozing, Snyder once consulted a hypnotist to see if he could get by on less sleep. Eventually, he settled on four or five hours a night before driving back to the office, a five-minute drive from home. Even when squeezing in some exercise on the stair machine in his office, he insisted on viewing tapes of an upcoming opponent. That's the effort Snyder felt was necessary to turn around the country's worst football team.

Coach Snyder's demanding, seemingly tireless nature affected players and coaches alike. Even among big-time coaches, he stood out for his obsession with control. He had complete command of play-calling, even pre-game instructions. He changed the school logo from Willie the Wildcat to the Powercat, upgraded the players' uniforms (even selecting the color of their shoestrings), and decreed the number of pats of butter at team meals.

All practices were closed. K-State players had to wipe their feet before entering the athletic complex; they weren't allowed to wear caps or earrings; their facial hair had to be neatly trimmed; and navy blazers were required garb for all road trips. Snyder refused to discuss injuries with the press, and tightly limited access to his players. He never wanted anyone to outwork him, and he never wanted any reporter to undermine his secret plans.

As for his assistants, Snyder insisted on long hours, on laboring in the trenches and finding happiness in the detail. Every subordinate was required to show him their scripts for daily position meetings. Despite his demands, Snyder remained a source of strength to his colleagues in difficult times. In 1996, assistant coach Bob Cope was battling advanced stages of cancer. Snyder made daily visits to the Cope home, and unbeknownst to anyone, personally financed his assistant's trip to Mexico City for experimental cancer treatments. But to no avail. Cope died the following summer.

Tragedy struck again two years later, when defensive coordinator Phil Bennett lost his wife, Nancy, to a summer-morning lightning strike while she was jogging the streets of Manhattan. "He was my clear thinker," Bennett said. "In this business, you need a strong boss, and we had one."

No stranger to dark hours, in February 1992, Snyder learned that his daughter Meredith, then a senior in high school, had barely survived a car crash in Greenville, Texas. She suffered a broken neck, shattered vertebrae and a crushed spinal cord—leaving her paralyzed from the neck down and breathing on a ventilator. The prognosis was that she would probably never walk again.

Miraculously, Meredith recovered, graduating from K-State six years later, with her father accompanying her across the stage arm-in-arm. "It was the highlight of my life," says Snyder. Today, Meredith credits her father's weekly hospital visits and active participation in the rehabilitation program with her recovery. "I can't tell you how much his encouragement meant to me," says the now thirty-seven-year-old mother of two. "He has so much discipline, and he's instilled some of that in me."

No surprise then that Snyder likens a team to family. "I always took personal responsibility for everyone in our program," he explains. More impressive to him than his tenure or win-loss records was the esprit de corps that he instilled in his charges. An outstanding mentor, he groomed a number of standout head coaches. The list of graduates of the Bill Snyder Academy of Coaching includes Mike Stoops at Arizona, brother Bob at Oklahoma, Mark Mangino at Kansas, Jim Leavitt at South Florida, Bret Bielema at Wisconsin, and Phil Bennett, formerly at Southern Methodist. The master left lasting impressions on all of them. "Bill Snyder taught us how to coach," said Arizona's Stoops. "His legacy will always be a relentless work ethic and unquestioning loyalty."

Charting K-State's come-from-behind victories in sports and learning required President Wefald to take risks. In 1988, his choice of Snyder, an assistant with no college head-coach experience, certainly paid off. His down-home honesty forged a special bond between the two men. "When we came here, we were promised the full backing of the university, and that is exactly what we got," Snyder told me. "Everything on this campus has been enhanced since Wefald got here. He's provided us with the opportunity to do the things we wanted to accomplish."

The president, for his part, admits that he and the coach "were joined at the hip." Working together, the co-leadership tandem of Wefald and Snyder propelled the university's ascendancy in academics and athletics. "Bill Snyder's philosophy about building a football program in terms of every individual within that program working to get better every single day is very similar to Wefald's philosophy for the university," says provost emeritus James Coffman. "They're complementary, and that's how you build anything."

Snyder's loyalty to Wefald and Wildcat football were just two of the three factors that rooted him to Kansas State. The other was the contentment that he and his family found in bucolic Kansas. Rich in history and steeped in tradition, Manhattan has become a popular regional center for education, health care, entertainment, and communication. Founded by westward-bound pioneers in 1855, the city planted its roots in the native tall grass prairies of the Flint Hills. (The hills are named after flint-like chert, a native stone that Indians used to make tools.) Affectionately known as the Little Apple, residents have always emphasized education and family. With K-State as its magnet, Manhattan has grown to 49,000 in recent years. The university campus, considered one of the country's most attractive, peacefully coexists with a community known for its small-town hospitality.

It is understandable, therefore, that the Snyders remained content to spend their days in this comfortable Midwestern setting. Over the years, Bill received offers to move on to bigger, marquee programs, and close friends counseled him to jump on the coaching carousel. UCLA, LSU, and Minnesota made advances, and many considered him the front-runner when his mentor Hayden Fry retired from the University of Iowa in

1998. But Snyder opted not to leave. "The more I thought about it, the more I realized, I had a great job at Kansas State," he says. "And I realized there was no better program than what we had here, mainly because of President Wefald, along with Bob Krause, Jim Epps and Steve Miller."

Success is one of the most seductive lures imaginable. And yet, much of the time, we allow the terms of success to be determined by others. Albert Einstein offered priceless counsel on this subject: "Try not to become a success," he said. "Try to become a man of value."

In an era of galloping egos, especially in his profession, Snyder put quality of life before conventional notions of success. He weighed ambition against the status quo and found ambition wanting—as wise people usually do. He had a good life, a happy family, a wonderful working environment and the respect of his peers. In effect, Snyder downshifted before the term became popular. He bent his goals around his life, and not the reverse. He defined success on his own terms.

On November 15, 2005, Bill Snyder decided to end the Manhattan Project. In a teary news conference in the Vanier Complex at K-State Stadium, he announced his retirement. "I think the time is right because, first and foremost, it's best for the university," said the coach who had orchestrated 136 wins—two more than all of K-State's prior coaches since 1937. "I think because of the nature of the profession that we are in, it becomes a difficult thing to follow a great deal of success."

Saying he wanted to spend more time with his family, Snyder acknowledged the rigors of his schedule—the long hours spent at the office breaking down film and preparing game plans from predawn to late at night—which had taken a toll on his home life. "I've not been the kind of father that I should have been, and the kind of husband," he admitted.

After winning the Big 12 Conference in 2003, the Wildcats stumbled to a 9–13 record the next two years—marking the first time since 1991–'92 that KSU had missed bowl games in consecutive seasons. No doubt, the pressures that come with back-to-back losing records weighed heavily on the sixty-six-year-old grandfather. "Some of the glow is off the program," Snyder conceded. "But this will continue to be a very strong program. The foundation is there."

In exiting big-time coaching, the miracle worker would sidestep the recruiting wars, glad-handing boosters, call-in shows, reality-deprived expectations, nonstop travel, and acrimonious Web sites. "With the rise of blogs, message boards, and radio talk shows, the pressure on coaches is just incredible, very different from what it was even a few years ago," says Arkansas chancellor John White.

Less successful, however, was Snyder's replacement, Ron Prince, a young assistant from the University of Virginia with no college head-coaching experience. After only three seasons on the job, Prince was fired for failing to build the Wildcats into a Big 12 contender. So it wasn't a great surprise to many K-State insiders when, last November, the sixty-nine-year-old Snyder decided to jettison retirement and reignite the program he had once turned around. Citing his desire to "calm the waters" in Manhattan and restore harmony to the "Kansas State family," the three-time national coach of the year was re-energized to get back to work. No one was more pleased than Wefald. "He's in great shape," the now retired KSU president said of Snyder. "And his mind is as sharp as a tack."

Will the revered coach re-engineer another bright triumph—a sequel to the Miracle in Manhattan? Whatever the outcome, he'll remain a deity in central Kansas. From its darkest hours, Bill Snyder transformed a perennial loser into a national championship contender with average athletes who were coached to their utmost potential. That ability has made him one of the greatest and most respected coaches in history.

4

JOANNE BOYLE:

Hoop Dreams

*When life kicks you, let it
kick you forward.*

—KAY YOW, Hall of Fame
women's basketball coach

Spunky Joanne Boyle survived a life-threatening cerebral
hemorrhage to lead the University of California's women's
basketball team to national prominence.

THE OCCASIONAL TREMORS remind Joanne Boyle that being a head coach isn't so tough. The fourth-year honcho of the University of California's women's basketball team is almost eight years removed from life-saving brain surgery to correct an aneurysm. But tremors in her hand are a constant reminder that a game—or life—can turn in a second.

November 28, 2001: That's the day a near-death experience transformed an unassuming assistant coach at Duke to one of the nation's rising stars in women's basketball. Boyle, thirty-eight at the time, had finished her regular run on the Duke Golf Course. Perfectly fit and training for a marathon, she had just taken a shower in the locker room and was blow-drying her hair, when she felt a searing pain in the back of her skull. "It was like a knife going through my head," she recalls. "I looked behind me to see if someone was stabbing me." A strange sensation overcame her; her body tingled. "I felt like I was having an out-of-body experience."

The sensation didn't pass, and Boyle knew something was terribly wrong. She hoped that she would find help in the hallway on the way to the elevator, but there was no one. As she stumbled to the elevator, she thought she was going to pass out. "The elevator is usually never there," she recalls. "It's almost always a five- to seven-minute wait." Not this time. When the elevator doors opened, she somehow made it to her fourth-floor office, where Gale Valley, another Duke assistant, immediately called for an ambulance. By this time, Boyle's stroke-like symptoms—slurred speech, nausea, and an excruciating headache—were evident.

Fortunately for Boyle, she was just a five-minute ambulance ride from the renowned Duke Medical Center. An initial angiogram was inconclusive, because so much blood had pooled in the back of her head.

Although doctors quickly stopped the bleeding, the medical staff was concerned about her survival.

In the meantime, Boyle was incapacitated. "It was my left cerebellum and it affected my motor skills, speech and balance," she says. Her first two days were spent in intensive care, where she wondered: "If I go to sleep, will I wake up? I didn't know if I was going to make it, and there were people who thought that I'd be a vegetable if I did survive." Boyle's mother, Joan, remembers: "When we went into the hospital and saw she couldn't move or talk, I thought it was over—that she would never be on the bench again."

In another twist of fate, Dr. Allan Friedman, a top-flight neurologist at Duke (who operated on Sen. Edward M. Kennedy in 2008), and an avid basketball fan, would come to the rescue. He had been on his way to the Raleigh-Durham Airport when he was recalled to consult on the case. Dr. Friedman sensed that Boyle had a neurological arteriovenous malformation (AVM), a genetic defect of the circulatory system that affects about 300,000 Americans, according to the National Institute of Neurological Disorders and Stroke. In Boyle's case, the AVM had produced an eruption of blood vessels, causing the stroke-like symptoms. After ten days in the hospital, she had made little progress. The vertigo and nausea continued, and she was sensitive to everything, especially light and noise. On December 8, however, a second angiogram confirmed AVM.

"Thank goodness, they found something," Boyle exclaimed, hearing the news while awake during the procedure. Immediately surgery was scheduled, a delicate four- to six-hour operation in which doctors removed an abnormal cluster of blood vessels. The procedure eliminated any chance of another hemorrhage and jump-started her recovery.

Forty-eight hours later, the strong-willed coach was making tremendous improvements. "After the operation, the doctors told us to go to her room," Joanne's mother remembers. "She was talking away. You could see her speech coming back. Her hands and feet were moving. She had no doubt she was going to get better." Adds friend Andrew Schuler: "Before, we were running on faith. After the surgery, it gave us physical evidence that things were really going better."

Boyle credits her faith and the prayers and messages of family and friends with her recovery. "The biggest thing in my life is my faith," she says. "I rely on God a lot for the things I do. You have to find your own peace and solace because it's a hectic world." Certainly, her love of the game also helped. "It goes back to sports," she explains. "That competitive element of my life was part of who I was and it definitely helped get me through things."

Dr. Friedman, however, wasn't sure whether Boyle would recover to the point where she could ever coach again. He saw his patient leave the hospital a few days later with the aid of a walker, a metal plate in her head and a scar snaking up from the base of her neck to the left side of her scalp.

Against all odds, Boyle had survived extremely difficult surgery. Now began the task of rehabilitation. The former Division I athlete stayed with her parents for about three weeks; she continued excruciating rehab as an outpatient for six months, regularly making two visits a day. "I was fighting just to be normal again," she says. Three to four months after the surgery, however, she was walking and speaking as before. "She could have been left with a permanent deficit," says Dr. Friedman. "We were fortunate."

In short order, Boyle returned to her beloved Duke Blue Devils. At first, she attended practice and a few games, but didn't play an active role. In December, she was coaching half days and, by February 2002, she was back full-time. "Everybody was a little surprised [at her quick return]," says Duke then head coach Gail Goestenkors. "She was a tremendous inspiration." By the middle of March, Duke was on its way to the NCAA Final Four tournament in San Antonio, with the resilient assistant coach traveling along.

No doubt, Boyle's steel-town roots contributed to her ability to cheat death. A former tomboy, who at age ten moved from Philadelphia to Monroeville, a suburb of Pittsburgh, Boyle honed her competitive attitude growing up with four brothers and sisters and their athletic parents. "I did everything [in sports]," she says. "That was my niche. Not only did I enjoy the competition sports provided, but it helped me develop self-esteem and confidence."

It wasn't until the summer following her junior year at Gateway High that the gangly, six-foot teenager realized that basketball would be a big part of her life. "I was playing basketball just for fun," she says. "I was a great athlete, but not a great basketball player."

That changed at a summer basketball camp in Philadelphia where the youngster began to show the traits that define her today—hard work and competitive fire. She was chosen the most valuable player out of 400 teens. Her performance sparked the interest of college coaches, and Duke came a-calling. Initially, the independent-minded Boyle balked at the Blue Devils' approach, primarily because it was her parents' choice. But she changed her mind once she visited the Durham, North Carolina, campus and was invited to join Duke's first women's scholarship team in 1981.

A four-year letter winner, Boyle ended her playing career ranked among the leaders in assists and steals. In 1985, she graduated with a degree in economics and, four years later, received a master's in public health from the University of North Carolina. Her plan had been to go into the Peace Corps after grad school, but when she was offered the chance to play professional basketball overseas, she jumped at the opportunity. Initially, she played for Ettlebruck in Luxembourg and then went to Osnabruck, a German Elite Division team. The three-year experience of living and working abroad was frustrating and exciting at the same time. "When you play professionally, it becomes a business," she says. "When the team is doing well, it's a team win. When you're losing, it's always the American's fault because the American is getting paid."

Playing in Europe made Boyle realize how much she missed college basketball, as well as the competition and camaraderie that comes from participating in collegiate sports. During a visit home in the summer of 1993, she met Gail Goestenkors, who had just been tapped as Duke's head coach. "We had a conversation about her vision for the women's program," Boyle recalls. "Gail believed that the women's team could be as successful as the men's team at Duke, and she was driven to get there. Gail exuded the same passion that I felt for the game." Sharing Coach Goestenkors' belief that the Blue Devils could become a powerhouse in women's hoops, Boyle accepted a restricted-earnings coaching position for a meager $12,000 a year. "After three months, I knew that coaching was my calling," she says. "I really loved it."

It wasn't long before Boyle moved into an assistant coach slot, and the team began to show progress. Two seasons into her stint in Durham, the Blue Devils notched 20-plus wins for the first time in ten years and advanced to the second round of the NCAA tournament. "We then started getting top recruits. It was obvious the program would go far," Boyle said at the time, in an interview with *Richmond* magazine. "It was important for me to see us go from the bottom of the Atlantic Coast Conference to being in two Final Fours—to see what it takes to get to the top and stay on top. That was invaluable."

During her time as a loyal assistant, the Blue Devils garnered eight straight NCAA berths, reached the 20-win plateau seven times, twice amassed at least 30 victories and were ranked in the top 10 four straight years. Fueling Duke's rise on the national scene were several Boyle-led, top-five recruiting classes. "Joanne makes a tremendous first impression, and she comes across very well to both players and parents," Goestenkors says. "She is so personable. During her nine years as an assistant coach, she became more competent and comfortable in situations where she needed to be in charge. Like anyone, she had to work her way into that."

Boyle, for her part, credits Goestenkors with sharpening her skills. "Gail forces you out of your comfort zone," she explains. "She forces you to sacrifice, to grind it out every day. She definitely prepares you for head coaching. I couldn't have had a better mentor."

Coaches are presumed to live on a career ladder, climbing as they work, always seeking a better job, until they reach the top rung of success. Fresh-faced graduate assistants vie to become assistant coaches, assistants to become head coaches, who then go on to more powerful schools. After nine seasons as Goestenkors' second banana, Boyle had settled into a comfortable routine at Duke. She seemed reluctant to climb the proverbial ladder. She found a home at her alma mater, working for a coach she greatly admired and a school committed to athletics and academics.

Not that there weren't opportunities to advance. In recent years, St. Joseph's University in Philadelphia and East Carolina University had made overtures—but Boyle's heart wasn't in it. Privately, she wondered if she hadn't become too complacent—until her horrific medical episode. "The sickness forced me out of my comfort zone," she says. "I said to myself: 'If I can overcome this, the next challenge in my life can't even compare.'"

That challenge came less than four months after her release from the hospital, when University of Richmond athletic director Jim Miller offered her the head coaching job without a formal interview. Earlier, they had met in Richmond after an NCAA tournament game. "That was the interview process," Miller admits. "It wasn't the normal routine. But we both had the immediate conviction that Richmond was a great fit for her and us."

Breaking out of her cozy cocoon didn't come easily, though. "I could have stayed at Duke for the rest of my life," she reflects. "But something inside me kept saying, 'Don't be complacent. Challenge yourself. Put yourself out there.' I didn't want to live avoiding failure. But I figured if you fail at basketball, big deal. You're still alive."

Boyle began her Richmond crusade in April 2002, inheriting a forlorn team that had posted a 14–16 record the previous year and hadn't enjoyed a postseason appearance since 1990–'91. In her inaugural season, she engineered a 21–11 mark and a spot in the Women's National Invitation Tournament. Her peers quickly took notice. "Anytime you are facing Joanne, she has her team thoroughly prepared," says Cindy Griffin, head coach at conference rival St. Joseph's. "She understands what it takes to play at the next level. You know her teams are going to compete. She puts everything into her job and her kids."

With a positive outlook that is contagious, Boyle guided the long-suffering Spiders to three consecutive 20-win seasons, an overall record of 67–29 and its first NCAA Tournament bid in fourteen years. In January 2005, the program received its first-ever national ranking. While at Richmond, she also met her lifelong goal of running a marathon.

In the meantime, the personable Boyle's stock as a big-time head coach was soaring. Any major college program prowling for a true crusader was bound to consider her. Although she had just signed one of the nation's best recruiting classes, Boyle sensed that it was time to move on. "I was feeling complacent again," she says. "But in a different way."

Boyle's remarkable rescue of the Richmond program got the attention of first-year California athletic director Sandy Barbour. "I had known about Joanne through my associations with Duke, and I watched her succeed at Richmond," she says. "She had character. She appeared to be a good academic fit here, and she had been involved or directed programs that had reached levels we aspire to. There was also no doubt that her earlier life-threatening experience really affected Joanne's approach and attitude. More than anything, it helped spur her to go for it."

The two met in the spring of 2005 at the women's Final Four in Indianapolis. "I remember distinctly what Sandy said to me: 'I want to partner with you and win a national championship,'" says Boyle. Within a week, she was on the Berkeley campus, checking out the athletic facilities, meeting possible future colleagues and looking at temporary rentals. "She called me on her cell from the Claremont Hotel," recalls Lindsay Gottleib, Boyle's top assistant at Richmond. "She said, 'This place is amazing!' I knew right then and there we'd be coming to Berkeley."

Yet, the quick-talking Boyle, who still retains a Pennsylvania accent, didn't come easily. She knew that Cal—like Bill Snyder's Kansas State—was long considered to be a coaching graveyard and a university where more students showed up to watch water polo than women's basketball. By all accounts, the program was in dire need of an overhaul. To beat the odds, the savvy Boyle insisted that "certain things would have to be in place." They included: a strong academic reputation, an administration and athletic director committed to excellence, favorable admissions standards for recruits, a strong, but winnable, conference, and an ability to compete at the highest levels. After long and careful analysis, Boyle concluded that the University of California had them all.

Athletic director Barbour, for her part, landed one of the nation's hottest coaching commodities, inking Boyle to a five-year contract. When Duke coach Goestenkors learned of her former assistant's career move, she felt success at Cal was imminent. "I thought they got a steal," she said at the time. "I thought it was a perfect fit for both Cal and Joanne. I knew Joanne was going to be a shining star in our profession."

Legendary Tennessee coach Pat Summitt, the winningest basketball coach in NCAA history, concurred with that assessment. "Obviously she did a great job at Richmond," Summitt said. "And I know she had a big impact at Duke. She has proven herself to be a successful coach on the Division I level, and I know this is a great move for Cal."

Boyle, too, had every reason to be confident. At every step along her ascent of the coaching ranks, she had helped teams rack up wins. But she would need more than a few coaching tricks to resuscitate a California program that had struggled for years. Although rich in history (the Golden Bears played the first documented intercollegiate basketball game for women against Stanford in 1896), the team recently had suffered through twelve consecutive losing seasons. The incoming coach took over a dispirited program that had gone 52–91 in the previous five years under fired coach Caren Horstmeyer. The departing Horstmeyer, however, had left Boyle with a much-heralded recruiting class, which included a quintet of homegrown freshmen (Oakland-based McDonald's All-Americans Alexis Gray-Lawson and Devanei Hampton, Modesto's Ashley Walker, San Francisco's Jené Morris, and Fairfield's Shantrell Sneed). "A gold mine waiting to happen," Boyle described her frosh recruits.

She would discover that many of Cal's players came from backgrounds more diverse than those at Duke and Richmond. "That really appealed to me," she says. "Because when you talk about having a purpose in your life, is it winning basketball games? Honestly, am I going to leave this Earth saying, 'Oh, I won 200 games, great for me'? No, it's what you do on a daily basis to make an impact on somebody's life."

In April 2005, Boyle stepped into the locker room at Haas Pavilion to address her team for the first time. From the get-go, she demonstrated a firm hand—outlining her plans for the future and how her success at Duke and Richmond could be replicated at Berkeley. "It was important to let the team know what it takes to be a winner," she remembers. "You don't just walk on to the court for two and a half hours and think that's enough. It's weights; it's individual workouts; it's pushing the envelope; it's eating right; and it's representing the university properly."

Boyle walks, talks, and moves so fast it's generally hard to keep up with her, and she expects that same high energy from her hoopsters. Yet, in preseason practice, the task of organizing her new players would take its toll. Those who didn't buy in, wouldn't play.

"That first year created special challenges," recalls associate head coach Lindsay Gottlieb, who followed Boyle from Richmond and now serves as head coach at the University of California, Santa Barbara. "We had to blend two very different groups together: upperclassmen, who were mired in a culture of mediocrity, and talented freshmen, who lacked experience and discipline. Each brought their own passive-aggressive, show-me attitudes to practice. Getting these groups to trust each other—let alone buy into the team concept was no easy feat."

Nonetheless, Boyle quickly established a winning attitude. Though her message had been recited in the past, now it had a lasting impression on the team. "She really had something about her—a winning mentality in her voice," senior Krista Foster explains.

Unlike many coaches who bellow at their players, Crusader Boyle bows to restraint. She grimaces, shifts her gaze downward, holds her head, but you'll seldom hear her raise her voice at her players. A lot of coaches can be cutthroat, but she goes out of her way to know the person outside of basketball. "We know she cares," says point guard Alexis Gray-Lawson. "Coach Boyle is always around to help me with things—relationships, school—you can talk to her about anything."

Never stingy with compliments, Boyle thrives on recognizing what a person can do well and developing those abilities to the hilt. With a face that often contains an impish expression, her openness and velvet glove soon won over her players. However, people who meet Boyle shouldn't be confused by her laid-back demeanor.

"I am intense," she says. "Off the floor, you don't see it. But when I step on the floor, I'm all business. I'm not a big talker, and I expect the kids to get it the first time." Clearly, her style at practice is more boisterous than during a game. "Practice is my favorite part of the job. That's when it's real. You are with your team and you are trying to teach. That's when you can have your biggest impact."

That impact was evident her first year. The adrenaline soon rushed a little faster around Berkeley. As the season wore on, once-downtrodden players seemed to develop a special bond absent in earlier teams, while showing the grit and determination that are a hallmark of Boyle's teams. The new coaching staff, in turn, allowed Cal's hoopsters to run more, taking advantage of their athleticism, as well as the open-court skills of Gray-Lawson. But the looser, high-octane offense was complemented by fierce, in-your-face defense and unselfish team play.

In no time, the bad old days of nearly empty stadiums and fan ennui gave way to moderate frenzy as Boyle led her talented, freshmen-laden Golden Bears to an 18–12 record and the NCAA tournament. Cal's first winning season and first NCAA tournament bid in thirteen seasons "put us on the map, put us on the national scene," recalls the proud coach.

The next year saw continued progress in play and attendance. The Bears improved to 23–9, earning another trip to the NCAAs. The school's biggest win of the season, however, was a 72–57 triumph over archrival Stanford on February 4 at Maples Pavilion. The victory snapped the Cardinal 17-game overall winning streak and 50-game, home Pac-10 winning stretch. "The biggest win in our program's history," declared Boyle at the end of the game. "When people talk about a rivalry, you have to win some of them. I hope we're creating that environment."

The win put an exclamation point on the program's best-ever conference season. Fighting suspensions of star players, a thin bench, a slew of team injuries, and emotions connected with her father's cancer, Boyle led the Bears to a top-25 ranking—and was named Pac-10 Coach of the Year ("icing on the cake," she called it).

The following year, the Golden Bears were neck-and-neck with Stanford for the conference title for most of the season, but could not overcome the Cardinal. Nonetheless, the hoopsters again returned to the NCAA tournament, recording a top-20 ranking.

Under her tutelage, the irrepressible coach transformed the Golden Bears from a laughingstock to national prominence. Discounting her team's newfound swagger, Boyle concedes that the team is still a work in progress. Long-term success, she believes, depends eventually on winning the deadly serious recruiting wars. To lure top talent to Berkeley, Boyle has expanded her recruiting arsenal far beyond the traditional hubs of California and the West Coast. Her 2009 incoming class is ranked second in the nation.

In a profession full of quirky workaholics, Boyle brings the same tireless passion to every element of coaching—from recruiting to scouting opponents. "I think she really appreciates her life every day—and this job—as if you can't take anything for granted," observes UCSB's Gottleib. "She doesn't just say, 'I had a life-threatening illness and now I'm going to embrace every day.' I think she really does attack and approach every single day like that. She'll always get the job done. She'll do whatever it takes—even to the exclusion of other things in her life."

In many respects, that's the kind of resilience and steely resolve needed to thrive in the ever-changing world of women's basketball. While the ladies' game has come a long way in a relatively short time, it still doesn't have the cachet that the men's game has. Perhaps therein lies its special charm. In the testosterone-infused world of male sports, there's a sense of entitlement often associated with young athletes. High school prima donnas, used to having even their mistakes praised, can be petulant, defiant of authority, and especially difficult to mold into the all-for-one team concept.

Women may, in fact, be easier to coach. That's the conclusion of some pundits. "Men have this macho thing going on," says Teresa Edwards, the veteran guard who played in four Olympic Games. "Women have a much better comfort zone with each other than men do." Perhaps the stepchild status that still confronts women's sports contributes to team unity. Vince Goo, who coached the University of Hawai'i's successful women's basketball program for many years, thinks the idea makes sense. "Women *are* more coachable than men," he argues. "They're more open and more receptive to teaching and criticism."

The embryonic and struggling stage of women's professional basketball also makes it far less tempting for youngsters to leave school early—a dilemma that haunts men's college programs. "One of the qualities that makes the women's game appealing is a sense of the basics, of staying in a program for four years, of maturing," says William Rhodes of the *New York Times.* "Some players build on an already solid educational foundation. Others use athletics to discover education." Rather than pushing a fool's dream of playing professionally, female student athletes often find that the college experience is the highlight of their young lives. Former Temple University star Claudrena Harold, now an assistant professor of history at the University of Virginia, recalls that basketball was "a ladder to climb to a successful career rather than a ladder to descend into delusion."

Women's sports—at this stage in their evolution—may also be under less pressure to generate significant revenues. As a result, the pressure to win year after year may also be somewhat less. "Women's athletics aren't quite like men's programs," says Candace Putnam, a sportswriter for the *San Jose Mercury News.* "If a coach has a losing season, they're not immediately shown the door." But make no mistake: More and more schools are taking their hoops seriously.

Increasingly, women's basketball is becoming a super competitive, high-stakes enterprise that mirrors the men's game: three-hour practices, weightlifting, study halls, and outside shooting workouts—with almost no time for other extracurricular activities. The pressure to win and the time demands on coaches and their players are enormous.

"Being competitive in women's basketball today requires a huge commitment," says California's Barbour. "And with the resources schools are pouring into programs [the average Division I team's budget has tripled in the last decade], there's no excuse for not winning." At Pac-10 rival Arizona State, women's basketball coach Charlie Turner Thorne agrees: "It's not OK not to win. Too much money is being spent."

A large chunk of that spending is going into escalating coaches' salaries. Pat Summitt was paid $8,900 when she was hired to coach Tennessee women's hoops in 1974. In May 2006, she became the first woman to earn more than a million dollars annually when she inked a six-year, $7.8 million deal. Elite programs today demand high six-figure and, increasingly, seven-figure salaries. The number of million-dollar coaches should continue to swell as a new wave of coaches replaces longtime veterans, predicts Beth Bass, chief executive officer of the Women's Basketball Coaches Association. "I think you're going to see a growth spurt," she says. Indeed, Boyle's mentor, Gail Goestenkors, became the latest member of the million-dollar club when she left Duke in 2007 to lead the University of Texas women's program, where she replaced retiring Hall of Famer Jody Conradt.

Ironically, as women's athletic programs soar, the coaching ranks are increasingly becoming a male domain. In a variety of sports, women are either leaving intercollegiate coaching or never entering it in the first place. "I find fewer and fewer females who want to enter coaching," says Jim Livengood, athletics director at the University of Arizona, where men coach nine out of eleven women's teams.

In women's basketball, nearly eighty percent of the teams were coached by females three decades ago, compared with sixty-one percent today. No doubt, women today have many more options—many of them in less demanding, more family-friendly environments. But most observers believe that as coaching women has become more lucrative and more prestigious, it has attracted—and will continue to attract—more men.

Clearly, the pressure cooker demands of women's basketball are taking their toll. In May 2007, Washington State coach June Daugherty suffered a serious heart attack. (Fired by Washington despite a winning record, she was hired just a month later by the in-state rival Cougars.) About the same time, Mickie DeMoss left the University of Kentucky. "After thirty years of coaching," she said, "I wanted to step back and reassess what I wanted to do for the rest of my life." Less than a year earlier, she had signed a five-year deal with the school. What changed? It's hard to say, but earlier in her career, the highly respected coach had stepped away from head coaching. She ran the Florida program from 1979 to '85, and then downshifted to serving as an assistant two seasons at Auburn and eighteen at Tennessee before taking over at Kentucky. (DeMoss is now an assistant coach at Texas.)

While the coaching carousel continues to pick up speed and more and more demands are placed on women's sports, the relentlessly optimistic Boyle has no regrets about going West. The lure of Northern California and one of the world's great universities was a major factor in her decision to accept the California challenge.

In the heart of the vibrant, diverse Bay Area, Berkeley sits twelve miles from alluring San Francisco. Just an hour's drive south of the campus is Silicon Valley, home to many of the world's leading high-technology firms. The university also lies within easy driving distance to the high Sierra resorts of Lake Tahoe and Yosemite, scenic Monterey Peninsula, Napa Valley wine country, and the spectacular Mendocino Coast. With a population of 103,000, Berkeley is an interesting study in contrasts: a small town with a big-city flavor, where Nepalese restaurants and Philadelphia cheese-steak shops coexist with second-hand book stores and martial arts studios.

One building that can be seen from San Francisco on a clear day is the tall, granite bell tower called the Campanile—a favorite subject of photographer Ansel Adams. In the 1960s, the famous bell tower served as a rallying spot for Berkeley's infamous Free Speech Movement, which pitted students and faculty against the university administration. Nowadays, student protests are not what they used to be. College Avenue, the town's main drag, is packed with more hipsters with BlackBerrys than hippies with beards. Many of the most fervent activists live off campus, having long ago reached middle age.

Today, the University of California at Berkeley ranks as one of the world's premier institutions of higher learning—the American equivalent of a Grande École. Ranked as the nation's top public university by *U.S. News and World Report* and second only to Harvard among global universities, UC-Berkeley offers students and scholars one of the world's most beautiful and productive academic settings.

By any measure, the California faculty, which numbers 2,028, is one of the most distinguished on the planet. At last count, it included eight Nobel Laureates, three Pulitzer Prize winners, sixteen MacArthur (genius) Fellows, 83 Fulbright Scholars, 128 members of the National Academy of Sciences, and more Guggenheim Fellows (1,398) than any other university in the country. Like the faculty, the Golden Bears' student body represents the best and brightest—attracting what many believe to be the finest applicant pool in the United States. One indicator: The University of California is unmatched in the number of its undergraduates who go on to earn a doctorate. In addition, Cal has produced more Peace Corps volunteers (3,000 plus) than any other university. Then, there are its illustrious alums—among them: actor Gregory Peck, author Jack London, and Chief Justice Earl Warren.

Impressive, too, are California's student athletes, who have enjoyed their own measure of success. The university's 27-sports program—with a $48 million annual budget—consistently finishes among the leaders in the Director's Cup standings, which rates overall performance of the country's athletic departments. In recent years, rugby, men's water polo and men and women's crew have captured national championships, and six individuals have claimed NCAA titles. Typically, 175 student athletes will earn all-conference academic honors every year. By every indicator, Golden Bear coaches are blessed with a deep pool of extremely bright and talented young men and women.

"What exists here is that perfect, but rare, combination of academic excellence and top-flight athletics," says Boyle. "Our players are not your normal student athletes. They're well prepared and, for the most part, high achievers. Similar to my days at Duke, there's no babysitting around here."

Boyle takes enormous pride in being part of a great and prestigious university. Cal is, in fact, populated with truly exceptional people at all levels: students, faculty, administrators, coaches—you name it. Throw in the geography—the weather, physical beauty, economic and cultural vitality—it is no wonder that dyed-in-the-wool Berkeley types remain deeply rooted to the university.

Boyle cherishes the magic the Berkeley name conjures around the world. "There's an intimate, special feeling about this place. But for me, the attraction always comes back to academics. Professors here are committed to teaching in a high-profile academic environment. Plus we have access to the Bay Area—San Francisco, the beauty, the hills, the shopping, the restaurants," Boyle told me over lunch at Berkeley's tony landmark, Chez Panisse, on Shattuck Avenue. "What better place to build a career!"

Anything but immobile, Boyle could have almost any coaching job in the country. In 2007, the rumor mill had her leading a similar crusade at top-ranked Duke or high-profile Florida (the latter, coming off national titles in football and men's basketball). But, instead of bolting for greener pastures, this rising star said no thanks to both schools and agreed to a seven-year contract to coach the Bears until 2014. Turning down the Duke job, in particular, was no easy decision ("my toughest yet," she confesses). After all, it was Boyle's alma mater. She had family there. And she would have inherited one of women's basketball's greatest teams, with four recent appearances in the NCAA Final Four. She opted, however, to stay put—signing a long-term contract to stay at Cal.

No doubt, it will take a truly unusual opportunity for her to abandon Berkeley. She strongly believes in the California model with its special attraction for youngsters who are gifted academically and athletically. As important, Boyle contends: "We're on the cusp of something. We're definitely making significant progress. Plus my heart is at Cal. And you've got to follow your heart."

If and when Boyle packs her bags, it most likely will be for a life outside basketball. "I don't think I'm a lifer," she says of coaching. "These jobs take 100 percent commitment. They're extremely demanding, and it's very, very hard to have a life." Sitting on a couch in her Haas Pavilion office overlooking Spieker Pool, she finds herself thinking more and more about "her purpose in life"—a life beyond the world of Xs and Os. Sensing the full range of opportunities available in the Bay Area, the prospects of eventually breaking ranks and venturing into a totally different field sound appealing. But, for now, Boyle soldiers on—happily—at California.

Every day, though, she continues to reflect on life's slings and arrows. Almost eight years after her near-death experience, she still has some lingering effects—the tremors in her left hand, an occasional slur of speech, and the inability to play basketball. But, to Boyle, these annoyances don't hold her back. "It's hard to say, but I'm really glad this happened to me," she says. "It changed my life—all to the good. It made me re-evaluate who I am and what I want to be."

part two

COMBATANTS

5
GARY GULLER:
Shattering Stereotypes

To climb Everest is an intrinsically irrational act—
a triumph of desire over sensibility. Any person
who would seriously consider it is almost by definition
beyond the sway of reasoned argument.

—JON KRAKAUER, *Into Thin Air*

The loss of an arm never prevented Gary Guller from scaling the world's highest peaks.

MOUNT EVEREST HAS ALWAYS LOOMED LARGE in the minds of mountaineers. The jagged Himalayan peak, called Chomolungma (Goddess Mother of the Universe) by Tibetans, presents an incredible challenge for any experienced, able-bodied climber. Gary Guller had always dreamed of meeting that challenge. But, in 1986, he suffered a serious climbing accident that took his left arm. Undaunted, seventeen years later, he became the first person with one arm to scale the 29,035-foot peak. In the process, he led the largest cross-disability group to reach Everest's base camp, at 17,500 feet.

Not allowing the tallest mountain in the world to stand in his way, Guller's accomplishments seem the stuff of myth. In the face of adversity, he shattered the stereotype that having a disability diminishes a life. This courageous combatant reminds us that bright triumphs can emerge from the darkest hours—even if they come one determined footstep at a time.

Born on September 7, 1966, the son of a British mother and a U.S. airman stationed overseas, Guller spent his early years in England. After his father mustered out of the military, the family relocated to Georgia. Shortly thereafter, his mother was forced to abandon an abusive marriage, moving seven-year-old Gary and his brother Richard, ten, to North Carolina. There, she subsequently met and married Jeff Guller, a successful attorney, who adopted the two boys.

As a youngster, Gary excelled at junior tennis, attempting to emulate his idol, Bjorn Borg. But more than sports, he loved the outdoors—exploring the Carolina countryside. During the summer of 1979, family friends invited him on a camping trip through the Rocky Mountains.

"That trip," he says today, "introduced me to forces that would set my direction: the irresistible pull of high mountains, wild places, other lands, and the addictive weightlessness of nomadic life."

From his early teens, Guller dreamed of pursuing a career reconnoitering the pinnacles of the world. He dedicated himself to learning the craft of mountaineering and mastered various climbing schools—including the rigorous National Outdoor Leadership School—where he was taught the basics of roped glacier travel, self-arrest, and rock climbing. He also learned when to avoid unnecessary risks. In the climbing game, the difference between life and death is narrow. As he took on technically more difficult ascents, Guller understood the perils of making the wrong move. With an almost relentless efficiency, he began ticking off some of the most formidable heights in North America.

Piling up climbing feats in a short span of years, Guller set his sights on even bigger challenges: the larger, more exotic and distant peaks of South America. In 1986, the twenty-year-old adventurer convinced three college friends, all experienced climbers—Dave Cianciulli, Jerry Webster, and Steve Brown—to join him in attempting to scale Pico de Orizaba, Mexico's highest peak. After a "tequila-soaked trip" from Nogales, Arizona, to the village at the base of the mountain, the fearless foursome were mesmerized by the harsh beauty and isolation of the ice-sheathed pinnacle, white and dreamlike.

Orizaba was considered a long, but not technically difficult, feat. "Laughably simple," Guller had described the climb. The 18,800-foot mountain, however, was not a place to make mistakes. Just two weeks earlier, two German climbers had fallen to their deaths.

The ascent began blissfully uneventful, although Brown dropped out because of altitude sickness. That morning, Guller, Cianciulli, and Webster pushed off in darkness, in clear weather with little wind. Disaster struck at 6 A.M. Just 100 feet from the summit, Cianciulli, in the lead position, lost his balance, slingshotting the entire team—tethered together—down the icy, boulder-ridden face.

For mountaineers, the technical term for a long, scary fall is a "whipper." Detailed contemplation of a whipper is called "being gripped"—as in gripped by fear. For experienced climbers, self-arrest is the preferred survival strategy. The idea is to get the ice axe underneath your body, lie on it with all your weight, hold on to the head and try to dig the pick into the slope, as a brake. But before Guller could get the desired traction, he was airborne, jerked downward by the force of Cianciulli's fall on their climbing rope.

The harrowing, 1,500-foot plunge saw the three men plummeting at forty miles an hour, roped together, helpless. "I remember going down the ice so fast," Guller says. "I could see the rocks below and thought to myself, 'Surely I'm going to stop soon.'" Ricocheting against a cascade of rocks at ever-increasing speed, the badly battered threesome finally came to a miraculous halt at the very edge of a steep cliff. The long, violent tumble had grotesquely twisted Guller's body—crushing his spine, damaging his nerves and almost severing his left arm, which then had no feeling. "It was no longer part of me," he recalls of his inert limb. "It obeyed no commands and dangled like an unwanted pest."

Drifting in and out of consciousness during the day, Guller clung to his best friend and climbing partner, Jerry Webster, for warmth as nightfall approached, and the air turned frigid. Exhausted, traumatized and unprotected from the elements, they talked about their injuries in quavery voices. "Neither of us would let the other die alone," they promised each other.

After a night in half-conscious limbo, Guller awakened to find Webster dead: "His battered face looked cleansed, his suffering and his spirit gone." Later that morning, Guller and Cianciulli, also badly hurt, made contact, managing to persevere in the brutal Mexican sun. Without food, water, and shelter, the two critically injured climbers were lost in their agonies—overwhelmed at the prospect of never being found.

But Guller, above all, is a fighter. Even though the men's precarious situation consistently worsened, he held out hope. Three hellish days dragged by before rescue teams found the injured Americans. Local climbers had brought only body bags because they didn't expect to find anyone alive. Evacuated by helicopter off the mountain, Guller was then transported to a primitive medical clinic in Puebla. Nurses cut away his filthy climbing clothes and washed away sun-seared clots of dirt, blood and skin. After stabilizing him, anxious doctors explained to Guller that something was seriously wrong with his neck and arm—requiring immediate treatment in the United States. With Cianciulli on the mend in a separate hospital, Guller was taken by ambulance to Mexico City, where he was medivacked to Charlotte, North Carolina, on a private jet organized by his stepfather, with the help of the American Embassy.

Safely aboard, Guller felt a range of emotions: utter relief, gratitude to the rescuers, profound grief and guilt over the loss of his best friend. Returning home, he was quickly transported to Presbyterian Hospital. After a battery of X-rays and CAT scans, doctors concluded that, in addition to a few frostbitten fingers and toes and a broken ankle, Guller's neck was crushed and the nerve roots going to his left arm were pulled out of the spinal cord, resulting in paralysis of the arm and shoulder. Their grim prognosis: the young American's climbing days were over.

In the two years following the accident, Guller experienced his darkest hours. Crippled by chronic pain and treated with heavy medication, he underwent high-risk surgery to repair his broken neck and alleviate nerve damage—both successful. He then had more experimental surgery at Duke Medical Center to regain partial movement of his left arm. The procedure was performed by Dr. Allan Friedman, the same physician who treated Coach Joanne Boyle. Unfortunately, this operation was not successful, and Guller made the difficult decision to have the arm amputated. "I said, 'this will drive me crazy having this arm on my body, useless. It's like carrying around a fifteen-pound dumbbell.'"

Guller's brush with death is just one of many survival stories of other high-profile amputees who have come back from the brink. Among them:

—Aron Ralston of *Between a Rock and a Hard Place* fame. The twenty-four-year-old climber sliced off his lower right arm with a dull pocketknife to free himself from an 800-pound boulder in Utah's Canyonlands National Park. "I'm climbing as well, if not better, than ever," he now says. His prosthetic arm is a kind of Ronco five-in-one miracle tool, which he uses to climb grade-five ice pitches and rappel down rock walls on some of the continent's most challenging mountains.

—Similarly, South Carolina farmer Sampson Parker cut off his right arm after it got stuck in a corn harvester. After being trapped for an hour, with no responses to his calls for help, his arm became numb. Worse yet, a fire broke out, and his skin began to melt. Faced with the prospect of being burned alive, he chopped off his arm—also with a pocketknife. Parker has put the ordeal behind him. Using a prosthetic arm, he's back at work full-time. "I wake up every day and thank God that I'm alive," he says.

—Hawai'i surfer Bethany Hamilton was a shy thirteen-year-old in 2003 when a tiger shark attack took off her left arm. Six years later, she's a professional surfer, motivational speaker, product endorser, and best-selling author. "I'd never take my arm back for anything," she told the *Honolulu Advertiser*. "So much good has come out of it."

—Scott Rigsby, thirty-eight, of Atlanta became the first below-the-knee double amputee to complete a full 26.2-mile marathon on prostheses. Rigsby, who was injured in a 1986 auto accident, finished the 2007 ING Georgia Marathon in five hours, four minutes.

—Lindsay Thomas, another car-wreck victim, found herself, at age eighteen, trapped five days in calf-deep water before being rescued and airlifted to University Hospital in Iowa City. Although her lower legs were amputated, she is an active cyclist and cross-country runner—and also designs prostheses.

These recoveries didn't come easily. In every instance, there were dark clouds. So, too, for Guller. With his arm gone (he doesn't use a prosthesis), Guller could move freely again, but the emotional adjustment took much more time. The near-death ordeal left him feeling as though he was a physical and psychological cripple. For several years, he was at loose ends, grappling with post-traumatic stress. There were prolonged dark periods of heavy drinking and drug use, when, he admits, he "was definitely not at my best." A road trip through the Eastern States and Canada, however, began to recharge his passion for the outdoors and climbing.

"Cycling and hiking through the mountains really reminded me of why I started climbing to begin with," he says. "The feeling you get when you're in the mountains. It's as though all the barriers are down—and people tend to be at their best."

During this period of struggling, Guller went to stay with his grandfather in England. The visit proved transformative, as he soon began to trek the Scottish Highlands and North Wales. "Even in the summer, the weather was absolutely brutal," he says. "The extreme conditions helped explain why so many great mountaineers come from the United Kingdom."

Reinvigorated, Guller resumed high-altitude climbing. He traveled throughout Europe and South America testing his abilities. In 1997, he attempted Nepal's Lhotse, the fourth-highest mountain in the world. For the next few years, he spent the majority of his time in Nepal and Tibet, trekking the high Himalayas.

In 2001, Guller made his first stab at the big prize—Everest. Critics said the one-armed climber had no business combating the mythical mountain—that he was a huge liability. Ignoring the naysayers, Guller wanted to prove that people with disabilities could reach the top of the world. Unfortunately, he failed—turning back at 24,000 feet, just 5,000 feet shy of the summit, because of bad weather.

"It wasn't the right time for me, probably more mentally than physically," he told me over dinner in Los Angeles. "I just wasn't ready. In my heart, I didn't really think I could make it to the top." The thirty-six-year-old adventurer returned home to Austin, feeling the mysterious draw to Everest undiminished. He immediately launched a lecture tour and began planning his next attack on the world's highest peak.

Invited to speak at a convention of the Coalition of Texans with Disabilities (CTD) two days after 9/11, Guller was asked by some audience members if he would take them to Everest. Describing the session as a "turning point," he realized that "I no longer had to go it alone, because I was accepted for who I was before anything else. I finally came to terms with my own disability."

Team Everest '03 was born. Its goal: raise awareness for people with disabilities. Timing the event with the much-anticipated fiftieth anniversary of the first summit climb of Everest, Guller would lead the first team of people with diverse disabilities on a three-week trek to the base camp at 17,500 feet. The groundbreaking expedition piqued interest immediately. People with disabilities across the country inquired about the trip, and several dozen applied. "It was so motivating," Guller says. "Their support gave me the power to keep pushing on."

Raising funds, however, proved more difficult. Initially, organizers hoped to secure $1 million to finance the trip and provide endowment funds for the CTD. Guller generated the lion's share of support through his lecture fees and speaking appearances. Sponsors, although encouraging, reduced their earlier pledges—pruning the expedition's budget to $270,000. Those selected for the trek had to fork out the $6,100-per-person fee.

While financial cheerleading, Guller began to recruit the kind of bravehearts who wouldn't let their disabilities stand in the way. He reminded potential prospects that only one in ten climbers reaches Everest's base camp. The treacherous thirty-mile trek would take them over dangerous, unforgiving terrain. They would have to battle extreme temperatures, thin air, and emotional and physical discomfort.

"The thing that you don't realize at base-camp altitude, you burn more calories than you can possibly consume in a day, so you lose weight regardless of your level of activity," according to team physician Janis Tupesis, who had accompanied Guller on his first Everest expedition. "You wind up looking like a skeleton."

At base camp, the air pressure is half of that at sea level—making even slow movement feel like running a marathon. The trip is so arduous, Dr. Tupesis warned them, that more than half of all trekkers have headaches and other altitude-induced symptoms of acute mountain sickness. "The secret is to allow your body time to acclimatize and to eat, drink—and then eat and drink some more," Guller says. "The very last thing you want to be doing is rushing at altitude in Nepal or anywhere else. If you feel even slightly sick, descend."

That's one reason Guller recommended a good eight- to twelve-week period of intensive training. For the more able-bodied: longer days of six- to ten-mile runs, carrying a ten- to fifteen-pound pack.

Over the next several months, Guller assembled an eclectic team of twenty-six climbers: eleven with disabilities, including five men in wheelchairs—two with quadriplegia and three with paraplegia. They were joined by others with varying disabilities, from limb amputations to hearing loss to chronic pain.

Riley Woods, twenty-eight, who was paralyzed from the chest down in a 1997 skiing accident, recalls the preparation: "I didn't know what to anticipate. There was definitely going to have to be a lot of teamwork, especially with five of us in wheelchairs. It was probably going to be a whole lot tougher than we thought it would be. We would be doing everything from pushing ourselves to riding in baskets to riding yaks."

Another team member, Matt Standridge, a spunky twenty-four-year-old paraplegic, had hoped that the climb would serve a greater purpose—noting that he had never gotten over the way people looked at him and saw only his wheelchair, not the person sitting in it. "I hate the way that feels," he told the *Austin American-Statesman*. "I want to show them, look, I'm in the chair, I'm disabled, but my life hasn't ended because of it. I can still get out and do a lot." He believed the trip to Nepal would prove that disabilities don't hold people back.

"For me 'disabled' is a label, not a lifestyle, and it's a label that other people place on me," adds Renata Domatti, twenty-nine, who lost her left leg above the knee when she was five. "I never see myself as different or unable to do things. When other people see me that way, it's shocking."

Gene Rodgers, too, knew all about labels. "Why do we need labels, period?" he asked. "For me, this isn't a disability issue. I'm here to enjoy the camaraderie of other people whether they're labeled disabled or not." Fond of one-liners, the forty-seven-year-old quadriplegic sometimes tells people that he's in a wheelchair because it beats lying on the floor. He joked with Guller that he'd be fine on the trip as long as he didn't get cold, because, if he did, it would take days to defrost him.

Among those assisting the American team was Christine Kane, a speech pathologist and special-education instructor, whom Guller would marry four years later. His colleagues in Nepal also recruited two men with disabilities—one with one arm, the other with one leg. They were from the Sherpa tribes whose members had made careers of helping Westerners scale Everest.

By March 2003, Guller had assembled his band of brothers, experienced alpinists, doctors, film crews, Sherpa porters and guides—and shipped almost five tons of food and gear for the unprecedented expedition. Before shoving off, he gathered his trekkers, stressing the importance of teamwork. "It would be difficult for any of us to do this on our own," he told them. "Together, as a team working for the same goal and being wise, we can make Team Everest a success."

On March 15, the adventurers flew 7,500 miles from the United States to Kathmandu, the capital of the Himalayan kingdom of Nepal and gateway to the mountains. Upon arriving, they found world attention turned to the fiftieth anniversary of Everest's historic first summit climb by Sir Edmund Hillary and Sherpa Tenzing Norgay. Navigating the city's busy streets, they experienced the ancient appeal of this poor, but picturesque country of 28 million people. From trekking agencies to curry houses, the travelers met sari-clad women and Hindu holy men for the first time—and were greeted by a cacophony of motorcycle engines, truck horns, rooster calls, police whistles, and fruit hawkers. While Kathmandu might not be the mythical Shangri-la—crumbling buildings, rusted-out vehicles, emaciated dogs, and impoverished families fill the poorly drained streets—the proximity to the snowcapped Himalayas make it one of the planet's most powerful magnets for adventure seekers.

From Kathmandu, at 4,200 feet, the team took a hopper flight to Lukla, 5,000 feet higher, the preferred starting point to the great mountain. There, they began the long, deliberate process of acclimatization critical to survival. Their course would cut across the Himalayan watershed, surmounting passes higher than the Rockies, plunging into steep valleys, and carrying the trekkers over foaming torrents and swift-flowing rivers, up steep hillsides. It is a path that had been used for more than 100 years as a trading route.

The trail is sometimes smooth and wide, sometimes rocky and narrow, often treacherous as it weaves its way upward in Everest's shadow.

"Just take care on the trail," Guller warned the team. "There are some points where it's going to go up and down, very, very steeply. And there are other places where there's been a history of landslides. Just take care and go slowly."

Sherpas would do the heavy lifting. Their legendary strength and cheerful smiles have been an integral part of Everest climbing from the very beginning. In fact, very few significant successes have been achieved without them. Although many human footprints have been left on Everest, the Sherpas still regard the mountain as a holy place. Consequently, the expedition began in traditional fashion with a *puja* ceremony, with Sherpas and other team members leaving offerings and paying homage to the gods of the mountain.

"Goodness in, badness out!" Guller exhorted his troops, as they began their march. At first, the going was painfully slow, as Sherpas carried the most immobile members in wicker baskets, or *dokos*, over difficult to nearly impossible terrain. As the days passed, "we finally got the hang of it—pushing, pulling, carrying folks," Guller recalls. Along the way, the iron-willed climbers ate with redoubled appetite and catnapped at every opportunity.

Commencing every day at 6 A.M., the caravan pushed steadily upward. Villagers along the route greeted the team with barrels of *chang*, a rice-brewed beer, and gaily decorated pots of Sherpa tea, an astringent brew made with salt and melted yak butter. Pressing on, they passed Nepalese girls a-jingle with earrings, glass bangles, and necklaces of crimson beads. The wide-grinning Nepalese men had close-cropped hair and were scantily attired.

Several days out of Kathmandu, the team climbed the last ridge overlooking the village of Namache Bazaar, at 11,300 feet. There, ahead of them, overwhelming the horizon, loomed the solid mass of Mount Everest, its peak swept almost bare of snow. The wind-whipped monolith was a daunting sight.

From there, they climbed with ever-increasing exhilaration to the monastery of Thyangboche—perhaps the most magnificent grandstand ever provided for viewing mountain scenery. Although cold and exhausted, the sojourners were transfixed by the icy splendor of the peaks that rose around them, the Everest group: Ama Dablam, whose cruel summit makes the Matterhorn look tame; the twin spires of Kangetga and Thamserku; Kwangde's long and lofty barrier. Here, the Sherpas lit candles for a safe expedition, while the local abbot served buttered Tibetan tea to the climbers and warned them of Yeti, the Abominable Snowman.

Continuing up steep, rocky paths broken by swinging bridges, the caravan trudged on. With the higher altitudes, they began to see the tombs of Sherpas who had fallen prey to the mountain (an estimated one-third of all the deaths on Everest have been Sherpas). These visible reminders of the increasing risks awaiting them caused all the trekkers to take added precautions.

Beyond two other camps came Pheriche, at 13,900 feet, where the team rested for two days to further acclimatize. Breathing was taking much more effort, and the climbers were reminded that acute mountain sickness could lead to pulmonary or cerebral edema, with fatal consequences. Already, many of them were experiencing varying degrees of nausea, fatigue, and irritability.

At Gorak Shep, the penultimate stop on the route, the expedition experienced its first serious casualty. Just a day away from their final destination, Gene Rodgers, the feisty quadriplegic, developed a potentially life-threatening bowel obstruction that required him to be evacuated by helicopter to Kathmandu. Although disappointed with not completing the climb, Rodgers proudly pointed out: "The important thing is making the effort. This has definitely been the most exciting time of my life."

On April 6, Team Everest reached base camp, after twenty-two days on the march. While several members, including Rodgers, had to turn back because of physical ailments, eight of the disabled climbers beat the odds to ascend 17,500 feet. The proud survivors "radiated energy," Guller recalls. "All the heartache and injuries were forgotten, as we celebrated the success that only comes when people work together."

That evening, the Sherpas performed another *puja* ceremony, giving thanks to the sacred mountain for the expedition's bright triumph. Several Sherpas then approached Guller and suggested one last group climb: the famous Khumbu Ice Fall, a treacherous passage likened to an outsized Scotch glass full of frozen waterfalls.

The next day, the emboldened team took on the challenge. Some members stayed in their wheelchairs and pulled themselves up with rope. Others performed in their own unique way. "But everybody stood or sat at the top of the ice wall," Guller says. "It was the most incredible thing I've ever seen in my life."

Two days later, the group returned to Pheriche, where they were flown by helicopter off the mountain, en route home. For Guller, however, the final battle remained. After several days of training and acclimatization, he and four Sherpas continued their quest to scale the highest place in the world. Timing was critical, and the clock was ticking.

For only a few weeks each year is Everest ascendable at all. In May, the darkness and the hurricane-force winds fade and create the most favorable weather. During this peak climbing season, growing numbers of tenacious men and women pay between $35,000 and $80,000 to test mind and body. Most guide companies take their clients up the South Col route, the way Hillary and Tenzing first made the summit in 1953, and the way Guller and more than 2,400 climbers have followed.

Given the Herculean task, summit-seekers still struggle to answer the basic question: Why do they pit their frail resources against such a difficult citadel? To what end? Ed Viesturs, America's premier high-altitude climber and conqueror of the world's fourteen highest peaks, says: "It's a very internal thing. A great climb is a wonderful mix of difficulty and intimacy. The challenge is both physical and mental. If your body is willing, your mind can push it to do amazing things."

"It's definitely a head game," Guller agrees. Under the glare of national and international media, he knew that his second attempt at the summit would be no cakewalk. What makes Everest so murderous is that its cold, its gale-force wind, and its climbing difficulties converge upon mountaineers at altitudes that have already robbed them of strength. The air at 28,000 feet contains only one-third as much oxygen as at sea level. On the ground, even when exercising strenuously, our lungs need fifty liters of air per minute. Near Everest's upper reaches, a climber struggles to suck in as much as 200 liters.

"Run in place for a few minutes, then try to breathe through a straw," Guller explains. "That's how it feels at Everest's base camp. Now, run in place and do the same thing with a skinny coffee stirrer. That's what it'll be like at the summit."

The stress on parched lungs and respiratory passages also becomes appalling, as climbers inhale cold, dry air and exhale it warm and moist. The effect can sap the body of vital fluids at an alarming rate—sometimes almost a cup per hour.

Like men in a nightmare of slow motion, Guller and his team of four Sherpas struggled up the steep, icy mountain, gasping for air. Upward. Always upward. Foot by painful foot. Braving the elements, the exhausted, half-frozen alpinists were pinned down by bad weather for three nights at the mountain's Camp 4 at 26,000 feet—a height so forbidding that it is known as the "Death Zone"—because, Guller explains, "your body is basically dying at these altitudes." With more foul weather approaching, other mountaineers warned them to go down. But the tenacious team stuck to its plan, pressing onward at a monotonous, dreary pace to the top of the world.

Dangers lurk in the mountain's epic shadow, especially during the most ambitious leg of the climb: the final ascent. "I've always found that the summit day is five to ten times harder than any of the load-carrying days during the expedition," mountaineer Viesturs wrote in his 2006 biography, *No Shortcuts to the Top*. "After weeks of hard work on the mountain, you're physically drained and emotionally tattered. You need tremendous focus and desire to keep it all together on the final push to the top."

Of course, good weather helps. The omens were as favorable as they could be for Guller, who remembers: "We were blessed. We had no wind. We had blue sky. The day was picture perfect."

On May 23, after a torturous seventeen-hour climb—and 47 days after leading his disabled team on its trek to the base camp—Guller and his mates stood atop Everest. "When we got to the top, we had the summit to ourselves," he says. "I could see across Nepal and Tibet, and what seemed like the whole world." He and Sherpas Nima Dawa, Da Nima, Pem Tenji, and Namgya fell to their knees, put their heads together, cried and prayed. According to local Buddhist beliefs, if you reach the summit and come back alive, you'll enjoy a longer life.

The team's bright triumph came just six days before the anniversary of Hillary and Tenzing's original ascent on May 29, 1953. Back then, upon returning to base camp, Hillary, the thirty-three-year-old New Zealand beekeeper, irreverently remarked, "We knocked the bastard off!"

Reeling from the brain-altering effects of oxygen depletion, Guller was slightly more circumspect. "Goddammit, I did it!," he shouted. "Ever since I could remember, I'd dreamed of climbing Everest. But I truly thought that it would be just another dream that wouldn't come true— especially after my accident." Against all odds, he became the first one-armed person and the third disabled climber to summit the menacing mountain. (Earlier, a leg amputee and a blind man had also succeeded.)

After only twenty minutes on the peak, the team made the difficult and always dangerous descent. The route was perilous, with steep, two-mile drop-offs into Nepal and Tibet. Balance, made more difficult for Guller with just one arm, was especially worrisome. Weary and dulled, the climbers continued their careful plod downward. "It's scary as hell," Guller says. "You're facing all the things you don't want to face descending. One step in the wrong direction, and you're dead."

That evening back in Camp 4, Guller awoke to excruciating snow blindness that caused the entire team to hunker down for another day until he recovered. Coming down the mountain, one Sherpa broke his leg; another, who had become like a brother to Guller, died from what was believed to be septic shock from an abdominal infection.

On May 26, Guller returned to base camp. Two weeks later, he attended celebrations in Kathmandu marking the anniversary of Hillary and Norgay's first summit. Then it was back home to Austin in a blaze of glory.

Team Everest had captured the public's attention. The climbers' unprecedented accomplishments were featured in countless newspaper and magazine articles and numerous national and international television reports. They had achieved a goal many considered unthinkable: In the face of adversity, they had overcome the odds. "The freedom to explore is a freedom that everyone should have, regardless of their abilities or disabilities," Guller told his admirers.

Fresh off the Everest ascent, the celebrity amputee returned to serious climbing. In 2004, he conquered Kilimanjaro (19,344 feet), Africa's highest mountain, as well as the more challenging Cho Oyu (26,900 feet) and Shishapangma (26,290 feet) in the Himalayas. But increasingly, he came to realize that mountains are never really conquered—and should be treated with respect and humility.

"Mountains are the means, man is the end," Italian alpinist Walter Bonatti once observed. "The goal is not to reach the top of mountains, but to improve man." Slowly, Guller eased away from the highest peaks. Instead, he shifted his focus to educating people to accomplish their dreams and reach their potential.

Now an accomplished motivational speaker, Guller still tackles the occasional peak for rejuvenation from his current lair in Taos, New Mexico. The forty-two-year-old, high-altitude hero encourages others to look deeply into themselves, inspiring them to maximize their talents—placing fear and doubts aside to succeed in business and life. "If I can get in front of 50, 100, or 500 people and make them feel differently about their careers and lives, that's a very special gift. So that's where I'm devoting my current energies," he told me, before departing for India to enlighten an audience of IBMers.

Vintage Gary Guller. When he finishes one challenge, he's on to the next. "Use the mountain in a positive way, and new opportunities will open up," Sherpa Nima Dawa advised him at Everest's summit.

With full-time climbing behind him, Guller's second life as a motivational speaker inspires audiences around the world to believe that anything is possible. His determination in the face of adversity helped him scale the world's highest peak and shatter stereotypes. Now, he is on a mission to impart those lessons to others. "Don't give up on your goals," he tells them. "Never give up on what you believe in—and what you want to accomplish."

6

THE FROZEN CHOSIN

The safest place in Korea was right behind
a platoon of Marines. Lord, how they could fight.

—MAJ. GEN. FRANK E. LOWE, *U.S. Army*

At the Chosin Reservoir on the frozen Korean peninsula, the U.S.
Marines escaped the deadly fog of war to fight another day.

SEMPER FI. The few, the proud. From the Halls of Montezuma to the Shores of Tripoli. Once a Marine, always a Marine. The United States Marine Corps, with its 233-year tradition of excellence in combat, its hallowed rituals and its unbending code of honor, represents what is arguably America's most revered fighting force. From once-obscure places such as Belleau Wood, Guadalcanal, Iwo Jima, Hue, and Fallujah, Leathernecks have proven their mettle time and time again.

Inspired by the likes of Lewis B. "Chesty" Puller, long considered the greatest of them all, Marines would triumph even in retreat—"an attack in a different direction," the command later called it. And they were right. Against overwhelming hordes of Red Chinese regulars, Puller helped to lead 8,000 Marines, along with their dead and wounded, through blinding snow and subzero temperatures, on a harrowing seventy-six-mile withdrawal from Korea's Chosin Reservoir down a tortuous two-lane road to the port of Hungnam, where they were evacuated in the winter of 1950.

"This was no retreat," Puller bellowed. "All that happened was we found more Chinese behind us than in front of us. So we about-faced and attacked." No matter how one labels it, the Marines' perilous two-week retrograde highlights the merits of how and why to overcome the darkest hours to fight another day.

A tortuous series of miscalculations had brought Puller and his courageous combatants to the frozen Korean peninsula in what military historian S.L.A. Marshall would call "the twentieth century's nastiest little war." A conflict that would claim the lives of 33,000 Americans, 415,000 Koreans, and roughly 1.5 million North Korean and Chinese troops. On

June 25, 1950, nearly seven divisions of the elite North Korean People's Army (NKPA)—many of them bloodied in the great Russo-German battles of World War II, including Stalingrad, and the Chinese Civil War—invaded South Korea, with the intention of conquering the entire southern half of the 575-mile peninsula in three weeks. Supporting the 120,000-man force was a mass of Soviet muscle: 122mm howitzers, 76mm self-propelled guns, 100 Yak and Stormovick fighter planes, 150T-34 tanks, and a host of well-seasoned advisers. The NKPA, said Marine Col. Robert D. Heinl Jr., an expert in military history, "was, among the armed forces of the Far East, probably better trained and equipped for its intended work than any army but Russia's."

The roots of the Korean War were planted in an earlier agreement between the United States and the Soviet Union to partition the country, with the Soviets north of the 38th parallel and the U.S. taking the south. Supposedly, once the war-torn country recuperated, Koreans would establish their own governments through United Nations–supervised elections. In 1948, however, the Soviets recanted, installing Kim Il Sung as leader of the communist Democratic People's Republic of Korea in Pyongyang. Shortly thereafter, the United States endorsed the election of Syngman Rhee, a Korea-born resident of the U.S., as the president of the Republic of Korea (ROK) in Seoul. However, the Truman administration had been reluctant to provide the fledgling Rhee regime with tanks and heavy artillery for fear it would mount an invasion of North Korea.

The North Korean blitzkrieg quickly overwhelmed ROK army units. With rapidly advancing armored columns moving almost at will, Seoul fell in less than four days. Roughly half of the republic's forces were missing. It was clear to U.S. military intelligence and to Gen. Douglas MacArthur, commander of all U.S. forces in the Far East, in Tokyo, that without immediate American assistance, the NKPA would seize the entire peninsula in weeks, not months.

On June 27, the United Nations Security Council authorized member nations to help repel the invasion. President Harry S. Truman immediately ordered American forces under MacArthur to come to the rescue of the besieged ROK troops. The arrival of the U.S. Army units in Korea, however, failed to turn the tide. The first Americans thrown into battle

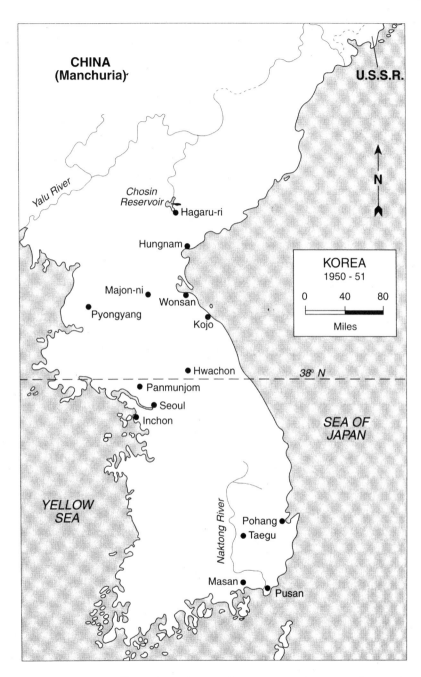

CHINA
(Manchuria)

U.S.S.R.

Yalu River

Chosin
Reservoir

Hagaru-ri

Hungnam

Majon-ni

Wonsan

Pyongyang

Kojo

N

KOREA
1950 - 51

0   40   80

Miles

Hwachon

38° N

Panmunjom

Seoul

Inchon

SEA OF
JAPAN

YELLOW
SEA

Naktong River

Pohang
Taegu

Masan

Pusan

MAP 1 Source: Jon T. Hoffman, Chesty: The Story of Lieutenant General Lewis B. Puller, USMC
(New York: Random House, 2001), p. 325

were poorly armed, in terrible physical shape and were, more often than not, poorly led. Most of the U.S. soldiers came from Japan, where they had become, according to Gen. William F. Dean, a flabby force accustomed to "Japanese girlfriends, plenty of beer, and servants to shine their boots." After their easy life of occupation duty, they were woefully unprepared for combat. In addition, their World War II–era bazookas and 75mm recoilless rifles were completely ineffective against NKPA T-34 tanks. "The mighty army that stood victorious in two great theaters of war, Europe and Asia, just five years earlier, was a mere shell of itself," wrote Pulitzer Prize–winning author David Halberstam in *The Coldest Winter.*

The first weeks of the war were a disaster. Undermanned and poorly trained American and South Korean troops failed to slow the enemy's ferocious drive south. In one early engagement, Army First Lt. Philip Day Jr. recalled: "This was a terrible time. All around I saw enemy fire kicking up spurts of water. Guys stopped and removed their boots, threw their helmets away, stripped themselves of everything that slowed them down. Everything had broken down and it was every man for himself." Many American soldiers cut and ran soon after making contact with the advancing North Koreans, leading military experts to call the early days of the war among the darkest hours in the history of the U.S. Army.

By the end of July, Lt. Gen. Walton H. Walker, commander of the Eighth Army (composed of all American and ROK ground forces in Korea), issued a dramatic edict to fight to the death. By that time, the joint forces found themselves backed up into the southeastern corner of the Korean peninsula, soon to be known as the Pusan Perimeter. With NKPA units on the verge of driving his forces into the Sea of Japan, MacArthur had to do something—and fast.

On July 10, when Lt. Gen. Lemuel Shepherd, the Marine commander in the Pacific, visited Tokyo, MacArthur told him he wished he had a Marine division on hand, and, if he did, he'd land them behind North Korean lines. Pointing at the map of Korea, he said: "I'd land them here at Inchon . . . and cut the North Korean armies attacking the Pusan Perimeter from their logistical support and cause their withdrawal and annihilation." He then asked Shepherd if he could mobilize the vaunted First Marine Division by September 1. Although the Truman administration's budget cuts had left the Marine Corps vulnerable (it had less than 80,000 men), Shepherd promised MacArthur he could field a combat-ready division on time.

If the Marines were going to make it, they would have to call up the reserves—many of them combat veterans of World War II. Moving at record speed, Shepherd sorted through a myriad of administrative and logistical challenges to deploy the war-strength First Marine Division and First Marine Aircraft Wing in just sixty-seven days.

Advanced Marine units were already engaged on the Pusan Perimeter and began to turn the tide against the enemy. For the first time, the NKPA found itself up against Americans who were well trained, well equipped, and stonewalling their advance. "Never again would the North Koreans mount a serious assault on the Pusan Perimeter," wrote James A. Warren, author of *American Spartans*.

In the meantime, MacArthur was preparing the most brilliant maneuver of his career. Against all advice, he was organizing a bold, amphibious landing at Inchon, 150 miles northwest of Pusan and some 20 miles from Seoul. Such a landing was fraught with danger. Inchon had no beaches, only seawalls and piers; its currents were fast and its tides notoriously tricky. "It was not so much a beach as it was a potential killing field," according to military historian Heinl.

Then there was the command structure. Most senior officers in Washington and some in Tokyo expected the leadership role to go to Shepherd, the experienced Marine commander who was a veteran of amphibious landings. Instead, MacArthur turned to his chief of staff, Maj. Gen. Ned Almond, without even conferring with the Joint Chiefs of Staff. The Marines viewed the appointment as a disaster. The fifty-eight-year-old Almond, known as Ned the Dread, was considered to be MacArthur's martinet—an officer called "arrogant, ignorant of amphibious subtleties, erratic in his judgment, and overly emotional in front of the troops." In addition, they were dismayed that Almond, as the commander of X Corps—the invasion force of 70,000 Marines and soldiers—had shabbily treated Maj. Gen. Oliver P. Smith, leader of the First Marine Division, referring to his fifty-seven-year-old counterpart as "son." During the campaigns that followed, the tensions between the egocentric, mercurial Almond and the low-key, professorial Smith would extract a heavy price.

On September 15, D-Day, waves of small boats darted for shore bearing the First Marine Division, followed by the Army's Seventh Infantry Division. It took the Marines exactly forty minutes to seize Wohli Island, the key to Inchon's defense. Racing down a thousand-foot causeway, they then headed for Seoul; as MacArthur announced to the world: "The Marines have never shone more brightly."

It would take the Marines just five days to push into the outskirts of Seoul. On September 27, the Stars and Stripes replaced the North Korean flag in the capital city. The Inchon landing enhanced the Leathernecks' long-standing reputation as the "first to fight"—a formidable band of brothers who would not quit until the job was done. For its efforts, the First Marine Division suffered 415 deaths, 2,029 wounded, and six men missing in action. Estimated enemy deaths: 14,000.

Only weeks earlier, Truman, an Army veteran and no fan of the Marine Corps, had accused the Marines of having "a propaganda machine almost the equal of Stalin's." The next day, the president recanted, offering a public apology. Nevertheless, his ill-advised comment aroused a great outpouring of public support for the Corps.

By October 1, the North Korean army was all but defeated. Half of its men were prisoners of war; the rest were attempting to escape in small units to the north. The United Nations forces held everything south of the 38th parallel.

Feeling invincible, MacArthur argued that now was the time to deliver the decisive blow to communism and unite all Korea. Truman and the Joint Chiefs of Staff, however, were deeply concerned that an invasion into North Korea would result in the direct intervention of Chinese and even Soviet forces into the conflict. They ordered that any incursions north of the 38th parallel be conducted exclusively by ROK units. Furthermore, American troops were to be withheld if and when any major Chinese or Soviet combatants appeared on the scene. Nor were MacArthur's soldiers to go anywhere near the Korean provinces that abutted China or Russia.

However, America's old and stubborn proconsul for Asia refused to accept any defensive role that inhibited his defeat of the Red Menace.

His earlier stroke of genius, the surprise attack at Inchon, proved costly "because it led to the complete deification of MacArthur and the terrible, terrible defeats that happened next," according to a *Time* magazine correspondent.

When U.S. intelligence sources reported Chinese divisions massing in Manchuria, just across the Yalu River from Korea, Truman summoned his most colorful general for a face to face meeting on lonely Wake Island. The commander in chief asked the critical question—what were the chances of Chinese or Soviet intervention? "Very little," MacArthur answered. "Had they intervened in the first or second month, it would have been decisive. We are no longer fearful of their intervention. We no longer stand hat in hand. . . . If the Chinese tried to get down to Pyongyang, there would be the greatest slaughter."

The aging general, promising that American boys would be "home by Christmas," had tragically misread the enemy. China's leader, Mao Tse-tung, had always supported the liberation of Korea. He knew that he could not beat American military forces on sea or in the air, but the strikingly harsh terrain of North Korea seemed an ideal venue. U.S. troops pushing north would be strung out, extremely difficult to resupply and vulnerable because of the hostile nature of the topography and freezing weather. The Chinese would also have a vast advantage in manpower— with an army four times larger than the American forces. Finally, Chairman Mao believed that the political purity and revolutionary spirit of his battle-hardened men greatly outweighed America's superior weaponry.

Eager to bog down U.S. interests in Asian quicksand, Mao had assembled 850,000 soldiers in Manchuria. Already, 120,000 well-disciplined fighters, the vanguard of his veteran Fourth Field Army, were south of the Yalu River. They had been slipping over every night, bringing their armor and heavy guns with them and hiding before daybreak in the rugged hills of North Korea. Exploiting MacArthur's bellicosity, Mao waited patiently for the enemy to proceed north into one of the greatest natural traps in the history of warfare.

Although technically MacArthur needed no authorization to cross the 38th parallel, he relied on an earlier United Nations mandate encouraging "the establishment of a unified, independent, and democratic

Korea" to launch his northern assault. He ordered the swift conquest of all North Korea, confident that the Chinese would not dare challenge him. "The bet had been called," Halberstam wrote, "and other men would now have to pay for that terrible arrogance and vainglory."

The disastrous path that led to the massive entry of Chinese forces began with MacArthur's aggressive push to the Chinese border. The delusional general was so sure of a quick victory that most troops were issued summer uniforms. In a highly controversial move, he also opted to split his attacking forces in two commands: X Corps, including the First Marine Division, under Gen. Almond, would drive northwest of the Tae-baek Mountains, and the Eighth Army, under Gen. Walker, would push up the western side of the peninsula. The high ground—approximately eighty miles of rugged mountains—separating the two commands would be held by ROK units. Intoxicated by his earlier victories, MacArthur's violation of a basic military axiom—dividing forces—would contribute heavily to the carnage that followed.

On October 1, Walker's Eighth Army drove into North Korea and, after some initial difficulties, encountered only scattered resistance. Three weeks later, they secured the North Korean capital, Pyongyang. MacArthur himself showed up for the victory ceremonies. "Any celebrities here to meet me?" he asked. "Where's Kim Buck Tooth?" he joked, referring to Kim Il Sung, the seemingly defeated North Korean leader. He then got back on his plane to his Tokyo command post. MacArthur, who hadn't set foot on the Asian mainland since 1905, never spent a single night in Korea during the entire conflict.

As the Supreme Commander returned to his comfy confines in Japan, he remained steadfastly convinced that the North Koreans had lost heart and that the Chinese would not enter the war. His last great offensive would proceed as planned. U.S. intelligence officers, however, continued to receive more and more information that blue-uniformed Chinese soldiers had already entered North Korea—in strength. In late October, Chinese forces struck both ROK and Eighth Army units. On November 1, a group of Soviet MiG-15 jets challenged U.S. fighters, briefly scrimmaged with them and then returned to the Chinese side of the Yalu River. A few days later, the First Marine Division identified three

Chinese divisions in its sector; the Army's First Cavalry had found five. Yet, again and again, MacArthur and his subordinates downplayed this intelligence. The general told the Pentagon that while Chinese Communist intervention was "a distinct possibility," he did not have "sufficient evidence at hand to warrant immediate acceptance."

As the Eighth Army, under Gen. Walker, advanced up the west coast of the Korean peninsula, the First Marine Division landed at Wonsan, on the east coast, 150 miles north of the 38th parallel. Once again, the Army's Seventh Infantry Division, along with one ROK division, were in the rear. The North Koreans had fled. In fact, comedian Bob Hope, who often entertained troops in combat areas, had beaten the Marines ashore. "It was wonderful seeing you all," he told an audience of South Koreans and U.S. military brass.

On October 25, Almond defined the Marines' new theater of operation: fifty miles, east to west, running from Wonsan in the south to Majon-dong in the west—and 300 miles, south to north, from Koto-ri to the Chinese border. Because of its wide scope, Gen. Smith organized his command into three regimental combat teams. The 1st Marine Regiment, under the legendary Col. Chesty Puller, would remain temporarily in the vicinity of Wonsan, fighting the remnants of broken North Korean divisions struggling to get north. The 7th Marines, under Col. Homer Litzenberg, another highly decorated World War II vet, was in the vanguard, with Col. Raymond Murray, also battle-tested in the earlier war, following with the 5th Marine Regiment.

With the Eighth Army encountering limited resistance in the west, an emboldened Almond ordered the Marines to "advance rapidly in zone to the Korean northern border." In their motorized march, only the Taebaek Mountains covered the division's left flank; eighty miles separated them from the Eighth Army's right flank. On the Marines' right were other elements of X Corps, including the 7th Army Infantry Division and several ROK units. The main supply route (MSR) up to the Chosin Reservoir was a tortuous two-lane, dirt-and-gravel road that stretched from Hamhung to Yudam-ni.

The first combat of the new campaign fell on Puller's Marines in the Majon area near Wonsan. In a series of ferocious ambushes, the Marines

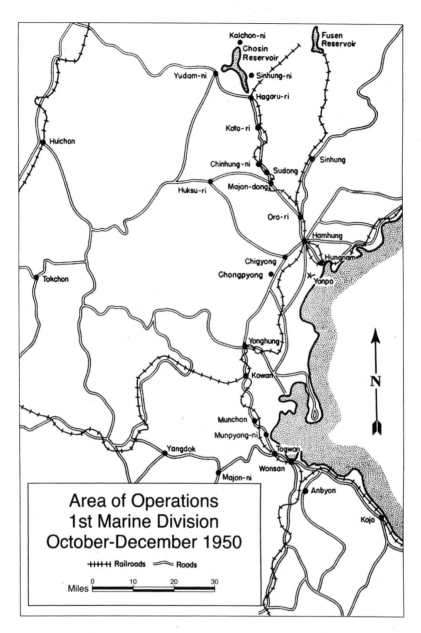

MAP 2 Source: Edwin H. Simmons, *Frozen Chosin: U.S. Marines at the Changjin Reservoir* (Washington, D.C.: U.S. Marine Corps Historical Center, 2002), p. 5.

lost twenty men, with another forty-five wounded; NKPA casualties approached 2,000. The fighting took place along this very tough stretch of the MSR that became known as Ambush Alley.

While the 1st Marines were busy in the south, Litzenberg's 7th Marines, followed by the 5th Regiment, led the seventy-six-mile trek north to the Chosin Reservoir. Informed by intelligence that Chinese were in the area, Litz the Blitz, as he was known to his troops, told his men that they might soon be fighting the first battle of World War III. "We can expect to meet Chinese Communist troops," he said. "And it is important that we win the first battle. The results will reverberate around the world."

What Litzenberg didn't know was that his 7th Marines were almost completely surrounded by a Chinese People's Liberation Army (PLA) division. On November 2, just before midnight, Chinese flares and bugle calls signaled the attack. Scurrying forward in small, uncoordinated skirmishes, Mao's screaming volunteers broke through gaps in Marine-held hills and inflicted heavy casualties. The clashes continued the next day. Eventually, Marine firepower, reinforced by close air support of World War II–vintage Corsairs, melted down PLA resistance. Total Marine casualties were 49 killed, 163 wounded, and one missing. More than 600 Chinese corpses were uncovered in just one zone of action.

The initial skirmish left the Marines impressed with their new adversaries. Taller than Koreans, Chinese troops were dressed in padded, two-piece uniforms with caps to match, but with little protection for their hands or feet. They all had American or Soviet weapons and were much less encumbered by heavy equipment, ammunition, and food than the Americans. That lightness made ambushes a favorite tactic. Assaulting at night, PLA soldiers could minimize U.N. forces' superior artillery and air support. By day, they would disappear in the formidable Taebaek Mountains. The Marines knew they were now fighting a highly disciplined, professional opponent.

For the next two weeks, the 7th Marines proceeded carefully north on the serpentine MSR from Chinhung-ni to Koto-ri to wind-blown Hagaru-ri, elevation 4,000 feet, just below the Chosin Reservoir, where they established their forward base. The advance was virtually unmolested, causing the relentlessly aggressive Gen. Almond to order Smith to pick up the pace. With the temperature dropping alarmingly and the terrain becoming more forbidding, the cautious Marine general was not about to string out his division along a single mountain road for 120 miles, from the Hamhung to the Chinese border.

O. P. Smith, if anything, was more careful than the average Marine officer. Earlier in his career, he had landed on the island of Peleliu, one of the cruelest and costliest battles of the war in the Pacific. It was the kind of experience that tempered a man forever. The Professor, as he was known to his men, systematically undermined Almond's orders. Instead of chasing wildly north, Smith focused the division's energies on buttressing the supply dumps at Hagaru-ri and Koto-ri, building short airstrips and fortifying the forward perimeter. "Because he was so careful and obstinate, he not only saved the First Marines from total destruction, but saved Almond's command as well," wrote Halberstam.

As U.N. forces readied themselves for the push north, the Korean front fell silent. The Chinese had disappeared almost as mysteriously as they had appeared. Patrols couldn't flesh out a single PLA soldier. Apparently, they had all vanished. To MacArthur and the optimists in Tokyo, the war was over.

But most ground commanders, including Gen. Smith, disagreed. They believed the Chinese were regrouping for a full-scale attack. It came on the night of November 25, when the PLA struck with thirty-three divisions—300,000 men. In short order, they ruptured the entire U.N. front. The center, held by ROK divisions, quickly cracked. South Korean troops, terrified of fighting the Chinese, broke and disappeared. The Army's First Cavalry—along with British and Turkish units—rushed to replace them. They, too, were driven back. In the west, the Eighth Army, in particular its Second Division, was badly mauled by an estimated 200,000 Chinese. Gen. Walker immediately chose retreat over annihilation.

To the east, Army and ROK elements of Almond's X Corps were also taking appalling casualties. In their haste to retreat, many soldiers left their heavy weapons, their dead and wounded. More than a thousand disorganized men stumbled into the Marine perimeter, with horrific tales of entire units being swallowed up by hordes of Chinese infantry. It was one of the most disastrous days in U.S. Army history—likened by Secretary of State Dean Acheson to the Battle of Bull Run in the Civil War.

The situation had deteriorated so quickly that, in just four days, MacArthur abandoned his great dream of pushing north and ordered both the Eighth Army and the X Corps to pull back to a more defensible line to the south. The shocking reversal of fortune represented "the worst defeat the United States has ever suffered," according to *Time* magazine. The *New York Herald Tribune* described the rout as a "colossal military blunder, which demonstrated that MacArthur can no longer be accepted as the final authority on military matters."

Although the central command's leadership had been terrible, the Marines—under O. P. Smith—were in much better shape. As usual, the Leathernecks had been out in front of every U.N. unit—in this case, forty miles ahead. They were at the Chosin Reservoir when the first Chinese bugles blew. Being alert, they had been buttoned up at night in perfect defensive positions on the high ground. Mobilizing every available Marine—cooks, clerks, truck drivers—along the perimeter, Smith consolidated his forces, already dangerously close to being entrapped, for what he knew would be the inevitable move eastward through thousands of enemy troops.

Despite its preparations, the First Marine Division found itself surrounded by six Chinese divisions, roughly 60,000 soldiers. In Washington, Gen. Omar Bradley, chairman of the Joint Chiefs of Staff, feared that the entire division might be slaughtered. Marines on the ground also knew the odds were stacked against them. "I really thought we'd had it," said Col. Alpha Bowser, the division operations officer. "We knew the size of the Chinese against us. I wouldn't have given a nickel for our chances of making it."

In the darkest hours of the Korean War, the Marines would redefine retreat as "an attack in a different direction." Cut off and surrounded, Puller confidently exhorted his troops: "The enemy is in front of us, behind us, to the left of us, and to the right of us. They won't escape *this* time."

With only three days of fuel, food, and ammunition, Smith called upon Puller's 1st Marines, deployed at Koto-ri, eleven miles south of the forward command, to provide reinforcements and knock out PLA roadblocks along the way. U.S. Army forces augmented the 1st regiment's thin lines. But when their commander asked the pugnacious Puller about his line of retreat, the Marine officer called up his artillery officer and told him to fire on any American soldiers who abandoned their position. Puller then turned to the Army lieutenant colonel and said: "That answer your question? There will be no withdrawal." In the bitter fighting that followed, 300 of Puller's men, including some highly regarded Royal Marines, came to the rescue of the Marines at Hagaru-ri.

Meanwhile, Litzenberg and Murray would lead the withdrawal of their regiments from the ridges of Yudam-ni, as elements of at least three Chinese divisions nipped at their heels. With units leapfrogging one another, 8,000 Marines—exhausted from the bone-numbing cold and brutal combat—slowly progressed down the narrow MSR. Only the dead and seriously wounded rode in vehicles; everyone else marched alongside the column, fending off periodic attacks.

Day after day, for two weeks of subzero cold, the Leathernecks moved eastward on a corkscrew trail of icy dirt, through snowy blizzards and thousand-foot chasms. In the eerie darkness, exhausted men stumbled into one another, fell on slick, packed snow, and rolled off the windswept road. "Officers and noncoms had to prod and kick those who fell, urging them to get up quickly, to resist the natural temptation to rest—or even worse—to fall asleep and risk dying of hypothermia," reported *American Spartans'* author Warren.

Onward they marched, faces lashed by wind and blowing snow. Temperatures dropped almost by the hour, every day bitterly cold, except that the next day was even colder. Each Marine carried what he needed to live and fight: a forty-pound load of weapons, ammunition, rations, and sleeping bag. Some officers and NCOs carried whiskey in one of their canteens—doled out on a most-needed basis. On the march, it was impossible to heat up daily C-rations, which had to be carried under armpits to avoid freezing. Navy corpsmen carried morphine syrettes in their mouths to keep them from freezing, and lifesaving plasma needed warmth in order to flow. In makeshift operating tents, hastily set up alongside the MSR, Navy surgeons operated while wearing woolen gloves. Small arms fired sluggishly or not at all, fuel lines froze up, batteries had a much shorter life and mortar and artillery rounds fired erratically.

At one point, the battle-weary troops almost gave up hope that they might escape. A few miles south of Koto-ri, the PLA had blasted a twenty-four-foot gap in the single-lane road, near Funchilin Pass. Under the direction of Lt. Col. Jim Partridge, pilots of the Combat Cargo Command arrived overhead with a huge suspension bridge dangling from their flying boxcars and parked it perfectly in the canyon. On December 11, the First Marine Division marched across the repaired treadway to Chinhung-ni, with only sporadic resistance. Three days later, they departed from Hungnam, but only after memorial services honored the dead; volleys were fired and taps sounded.

During these dark hours, the courageous combatants had fought their way out of the Frozen Chosin, bringing out not only their guns, but also the vast majority of their vehicles and all but 117 dead. Those men were buried in a frozen grave at Koto-ri. Amid talks of annihilation, a division of Leathernecks had punched its way through what the day's media called the "unconquerable Chinese horde." In the agonizing two-week battle, an estimated 40,000 Chinese were killed and perhaps another 20,000 wounded. Total Marine casualties: 561 dead, 182 missing, 2,894 wounded, and another 3,600 suffered from frostbite. The Marines' breakout from the Chosin Reservoir remains one of the classic moments in their exceptional history—a testament to the leadership and valor of extraordinary men, fighting a vastly larger force in the worst kind of mountain terrain and weather conditions. "Of all the battles of the Korean War," wrote Halberstam, "it is probably the most celebrated—deservedly so."

The courage displayed was emblematic of Marine esprit: the self-confidence that, being Marines, they would find a way out—no matter the odds. "Quitting was no more an option than leaving behind the dead or heavy weapons," wrote historian Warren. The Corps' time-honored creed—Semper Fidelis, always faithful—would not be forsaken.

Forty-two Medals of Honor were awarded to Marines in the Korean War. Of that number, fourteen went for action during the Chosin campaign, seven of them posthumously. The First Division's three regimental commanders—Puller, Litzenberg, and Murray—received the Navy Cross, the nation's second-highest award. But all the valor of individuals and units could not obscure the central fact: It was a retreat imposed by a once-beloved five-star general's foolhardy action to invite the Chinese to enter the war. Later, *Time* magazine asked the fire-eating Puller what was the greatest lesson of the Korean War. "Never serve under X Corps," he immediately answered.

Shortly after leaving Hungnam, the First Marine Division returned to combat. There would be new battles to be fought. U.N. forces, using air-power and ever increasing quantities of artillery, eventually checked the communist advance. For the next two-and-a-half years, the combatants reached a stalemate, as each side neutralized the other in endless skir-mishes over anonymous hills and villages. On July 27, 1953, the Korean War came to a long-overdue conclusion, with the signing of a truce. That evening, a cease-fire commenced that remains in effect today.

Driving down Interstate 95, thirty-six miles south of the nation's capitol, one sees the gleaming 210-foot central mast, surrounded by a cone of glass, that anchors the National Museum of the Marine Corps in Triangle, Virginia. The stark silhouette represents the flagpole at the famous flag-raising on Iwo Jima. Dedicated on November 10, 2006, on the 231st birthday of the Corps, the museum invites visitors to walk in the footsteps of Marines: from the Halls of Montezuma to the sands of Iwo Jima to the streets of Fallujah. Perhaps the most impressive exhibit fea-tures the Korean War. A climate-controlled room, chilled to 30 degrees Fahrenheit, recreates the snowy landscape in which Marines fought at the Chosin Reservoir. While it was about sixty degrees colder in those Korean mountains in 1950, visitors come away with a small sense of what it was like for the Leathernecks as they battled an overwhelming Chinese foe amid the harshest conditions.

This sobering look at the Frozen Chosin, fought by 8,000 Marines more than fifty years ago, defines the bright triumphs that have shaped the Corps. It serves as a constant reminder of a band of brothers whose courage, resourcefulness, and fortitude rescued them from their darkest hours.

7

SACAGAWEA:
The Legendary Bird Woman

*Madonna of her race, she had led the
way to a new time. To the hands of this
girl, not yet eighteen, had been entrusted
the key that unlocked the road to Asia.*

—EVA EMERY DYE

One of America's most idealized figures, Sacagawea was the lone Indian, the lone mother, the lone female, and the lone teenager on the perilous Lewis and Clark expedition.

CALLED THE MADONNA OF HER RACE, Sacagawea was the lone Indian, the lone mother, the lone female, and the lone teenager on the Lewis and Clark expedition, one of the most foreboding journeys ever conceived. For a year-and-a-half, she endured many dark hours to help unlock the spirit of the New West. Because of her courage and that of her cohorts, many changes would come: the covered wagon, the stagecoach, railroads, and highways. Future generations of Americans would populate the plains, the high country, and the coast of what once was virgin territory. Against all odds, Sacagawea—along with Lewis and Clark—had been there first. And the West would never again be the same.

Fall 1800. The attack came at midday. The Indian girl, then perhaps eleven or twelve years old, was camped at the Three Forks of the Missouri River with others from her band. As members of the northern Shoshone, who lived in the Rocky Mountain foothills of eastern Idaho, venturing out on the Montana plains to hunt buffalo was a way of life. Food had been scarce for the nomadic tribe, with roots and berries the typical bill of fare. A successful buffalo hunt promised a winter's supply of meat, as well as valuable hides for clothing.

The peace-loving Shoshone had horses, coveted dearly by marauding bands of Indians. Raiders from the hostile Hidatsa tribe descended on them from the dense woods. As soon as the attack began, the overmatched Shoshone mounted their horses and attempted to flee. In the onslaught, several braves were killed. Women and children dispersed in every direction. The young girl headed for a nearby river and began to swim downstream with the swift current. The next instant, she felt a heavy blow to the head. Consciousness faded.

When she came to, the maiden found herself and several other Sho-shone bound with leather thongs. The Hidatsa then herded their for-lorn victims on the long trek eastward to the North Dakota flatlands. Back home, the victors gave the captive girl a new life and a new name: Sacagawea—Bird Woman.

Traded from one warrior to another, Sacagawea eventually was bought—or won in a gambling game, as one story goes—by a French Canadian fur trader, Toussaint Charbonneau. In his forties, Charbonneau had once worked for the North West Co., but was now living among the Hidatsa. Short and swarthy, he was high-strung and quick-tempered. The Indians regarded him with amusement, derisively nicknaming him Chief of the Little Village and Great Horse from Afar.

A constant pursuer of native women, Charbonneau frequently took multiple wives. At the time of his "marriage" to Bird Woman, he had at least one other Shoshone squaw. "It was the pinnacle of many Indian girls' ambitions to marry a fur trader," explains historian Harold P. Howard. "It was customary to think of girls as chattel. Charbonneau had the typical fur trader's careless attitude toward Indian womanhood." In no time, the slight, now sixteen-year-old girl with black hair and copper skin became pregnant. As Sacagawea prepared for the responsibilities of childbearing, the Great White Father in Washington was finalizing a plan that would profoundly affect her life and the course of American history.

For a long time, President Thomas Jefferson, a man of restless intelli-gence, had wanted an expedition launched to explore the West in hopes, among other things, of shortening the treacherous and time-consuming voyage around South America. In 1792, he first proposed such a venture while serving in George Washington's cabinet (although he had promot-ed transcontinental discovery as early as 1783). Not until assuming the presidency in 1801, however, was he in a position to have his plan prop-erly implemented.

On January 18, 1803, Jefferson persuaded Congress to approve $2,500 to mount a military campaign to explore the Missouri River to its source in the Rocky Mountains, then down the nearest westward-flowing stream to the Pacific. The notion of a Northwest Passage was prevalent at the time, and many—Jefferson included—thought there was an all-water route from the Atlantic to the Pacific through the continental United States.

The trek had two objectives: to prepare the way for the extension of the American fur trade to the West and to advance geographical knowledge of the North American continent. When the president sent his message to Congress, none of the territory he wanted explored lay within the United States. By a stroke of fate, the young nation purchased the Louisiana Territory from France for $15 million a few months later. Thus, in ascending the Missouri, the mission would be charting American lands; by completing the journey to the Pacific, it would be strengthening the U.S. claim on the Pacific Northwest, then shared with England, Spain, and Russia.

To command the first overland expedition to the West Coast and back, Jefferson selected his private secretary and fellow Virginian, Capt. Meriwether Lewis of the First United States Infantry Regiment. A frontiersman of Welsh stock, Lewis was a lover of nature, an amateur doctor, and a dreamer. In preparation for the trek, he was dispatched to the University of Pennsylvania for a crash course in science and medicine. With the president's concurrence, Lewis chose an army friend, William Clark, to be co-leader of "this darling project of mine." Clark was managing his family's plantation near Louisville, Kentucky, when he received his appointment. Although commissioned only a second lieutenant, on the journey Clark was treated as a captain, equal in every respect to Lewis.

The gregarious, good-natured Clark was the perfect complement to the moody, introverted Lewis. Nicknamed The Red-Headed Chief by the Indians, the Virginia-born Kentuckian was an experienced geographer, surveyor, mapmaker, and artist. He was charged with leading the water-bound segments of the pilgrimage and with portraying, in meticulous detail, animal life observed on the journey. The better-educated and scientifically trained Lewis was to bring back observations and samples of the indigenous flora and fauna; he also served as the team's principal journalist. With a fondness for whiskey, Lewis tended to be sullen and withdrawn. The outgoing Clark, on the other hand, was a born diplomat, known especially for his effective dealings with Native Americans.

Believing that America's destiny lay in the West, Jefferson instructed the men to win over the Indians. "In all your intercourse with the natives," he insisted, "treat them in the most friendly and conciliatory manner which their own conduct will permit." The president also demanded that Lewis and Clark proclaim U.S. sovereignty over all native inhabitants of the uncharted areas—while identifying potential trading posts and preparing tribal delegations to visit Washington. America's "diplomats in buckskin," as William Goetzmann called them, would discover that harnessing the continent's first denizens meant overcoming a series of seemingly insurmountable obstacles.

The captains, both in their early thirties, began assembling a team of thirty-five adventurers, made up of Americans, French Canadians, and Indians—and Clark's slave, York. Members of the all-male crew were in top physical condition and variously skilled in botany, meteorology, zoology, celestial navigation, and Indian sign language, as well as carpentry, gun repair, and seamanship. On July 5, 1803, Lewis departed Washington for Pittsburgh, traveled down the Ohio River, where he picked up Clark at Louisville and then moved on to St. Louis. There, the company camped for the next five months, training and gathering supplies and equipment.

On May 14, 1804, the Corps of Discovery officially made its way up the Missouri River—the untamed emblem of the New World—in a fifty-five-foot-long keelboat and two canoes. Averaging about fifteen miles a day, the voyagers made the difficult ascent upstream, reaching the mouth of the Knife River in what later became North Dakota, in late October.

Fifty years earlier, as many as 9,000 Mandan Indians had populated the region. A combination of smallpox and belligerent Sioux, however, had decimated the peaceful tribe to approximately 1,200. That fall, the Mandan warmly welcomed the troop to their village. The wayfarers then spent a long and chilly winter at nearby Fort Mandan where Lewis and Clark made copious notes in their journals, drew maps of their route, and counseled various frontiersmen. To help communicate with the Indians, the captains hired Toussaint Charbonneau and his Shoshone squaw, Sacagawea, as interpreters and guides. The lazy, complaining Frenchman was to prove more troublesome than useful, but his spunky wife would be of inestimable value.

On April 7, 1805, the expedition broke camp, resuming its westward journey on two large pirogues and six dugout canoes. The party, described by Lewis as "zealously attached to the enterprise," now numbered thirty-three, including Charbonneau, Sacagawea, and her two-month-old son Jean Baptiste, nicknamed Pomp, Shoshone for "first-born."

On May 14, a near-tragic incident occurred, which Lewis recalled with "utmost trepidation and horror." Both captains had left their boats to walk along the riverbank, something they rarely did together. A fierce squall suddenly struck one of the pirogues commanded by Charbonneau, a nonswimmer and the man least qualified to cope with the situation. The vessel contained the Corps of Discovery's vital papers, books, instruments, medicines, and "almost every article indispensably necessary to insure the success of the enterprise," Lewis wrote.

Charbonneau panicked. Instead of cutting the halyards and hauling in the sail, he "lifted her into [the wind]." The boat turned on its side, taking in large quantities of chilly water before one of the crew finally pulled in the sail. Even as the boat righted, Charbonneau cried out hysterically, dropping the tiller and begging God for mercy.

Sacagawea alone remained level-headed. Up to her waist in choppy water and cradling her papoose in one arm, she calmly retrieved various pieces of scientific equipment, medicines, clothing and, most important, the Corps' precious journals. Lewis, who was particularly impressed with the Shoshone squaw, wrote of her glowingly the following day: "The Indian woman to whom I ascribe equal fortitude and resolution with any person on board at the time of the accident caught and preserved most of the light articles which were washed overboard." That night, the captains allowed each man a ration of grog to celebrate the teenage mother's courageous rescue of their priceless supplies.

Passing through country never before visited by any paleface, the corps soon reached the Great Falls of the Missouri, beyond which lay eighteen miles of raging whitewater rapids. To bypass this obstacle, the men were forced on a twenty-five-day portage over difficult trails, often in gale winds or under the burning summer sun. By mid-August, the adventurers had reached the navigable limits of the Missouri River. From there, they had to get over the harrowing Rockies.

Once again, the Bird Woman proved invaluable. She was near her home country and pointed out important landmarks and often acted as the lead guide. Lewis, heading an advance party, struck out overland, following an Indian trail through the treacherous Beaverhead Range. He then crossed the Continental Divide at Lemhi Pass, where he made initial contact with a large Shoshone hunting party. The overwhelmingly superior braves were at first edgy and ready to attack, but after the main party of explorers appeared, suspicious grumbles suddenly turned to shouts of joy. Incredibly, the Shoshone chief, Cameahwait, was Sacagawea's brother, and, by this most fortuitous circumstance, the Indians were won over. "We were all caressed and besmeared with their grease and paint until I was heartily tired of the national hug," Lewis recounted in his journal. Because of Sacagawea, "the stars had danced for Lewis and Clark," wrote historian James Ronda, author of *Lewis and Clark Among the Indians.*

A few days later, the captains called upon the Bird Woman to negotiate with the Shoshone council for badly needed horses. The Indians had about 700 ponies at the time, but bartering was precarious because the items they wanted most—guns and ammunition—were also in short supply for the explorers. Despite her negotiating skill, the Indians extracted a stiff price: one pistol, one knife, and 100 rounds of ammunition for each nag. Eventually, the adventurers bought twenty-nine horses and a mule, but as one observer put it: "The Shoshone had proven to be better Yankee traders than the Americans."

More worrisome, the Indians warned Lewis and Clark that the mountains ahead were impassable and food scarce. Nevertheless, the captains could not be dissuaded from pressing on, even when they later learned that the broad river they had hoped to find, which would send them floating swiftly downstream to the Pacific, was nowhere nearby. Instead, the venture westward meant menacing mountain travel before navigable waters could be reached.

On September 1, 1805, the Corps of Discovery proceeded cross-country over steep, rugged hills to today's North Fork of the Salmon River, using packhorses obtained from the Shoshone. Trudging tediously along the Lemhi and Salmon rivers, the explorers axed their own trail through the thick brush of the ominous Bitterroot Range. Their course took them through narrow, rocky hillsides, where horses and men had to struggle constantly to keep their footing. Creeping along 7,500-foot-high granite ridges, the adventurers were assailed by snow, hail, sleet, and rain. "I have been wet and as cold in every part as I ever was in my life," Clark penned on September16. Sgt. Patrick Gass described the snow-covered peaks as "the most terrible mountains I ever beheld."

Hunger was their steady companion. Thanks to Sacagawea's clever foraging, a supply of camus roots provided some nourishment. On several occasions, however, the half-starved crew had to kill their horses for meat and even eat candles. Completing the treacherous mountain passage on September 22, the troopers descended into a gentle valley, the home of the Nez Percé nation. "Stout likely men, handsome women," Lewis wrote of the tribe.

Like the Shoshone, the Nez Percé had little contact with white men and, according to oral history, considered killing the explorers for their weapons. But the sight of the Bird Woman and her infant child turned potential foes into friends. Once welcomed, the travelers gorged themselves on buffalo meat, dried salmon, and roots. "The pleasure I now felt in having triumphed over the Rocky Mountains and descending once more to a level and fertile country where there was every rational hope of finding a comfortable subsistence for myself and [the] party can be more readily conceived than expressed," exulted Lewis. "Nor was the flattering prospect of the final success of the expedition less pleasing."

The Corps of Discovery took to the water on October 7, after pausing to build five dugout canoes. Descending the swift-flowing Clearwater, Snake, and Columbia rivers, the voyagers ran a series of dangerous rapids. It took all their effort and skill to avoid countless boulders toward which the rushing whitewater propelled their canoes. Yet compared to the alternative of mountain climbing in the winter, the adventurers reckoned the perils of river travel were far preferable.

With mounting hope, the men steered their boats down the raging torrents of the Columbia—the Great River to the West that would lead them to the sea. The country "rises here about 200 feet above the water and is bordered with black rigid rocks," Clark observed, as the little fleet sped toward a succession of falls that still barred the way to the Pacific. After more days of running the rapids, the party mounted a final portage around the upper and lower cascades of the Columbia. Then, it was more bouts of motion sickness on the river, as choppy wavelets buffeted their canoes.

In early November, Clark spied "a high mountain of eminent height covered with snow." The 12,000-foot peak, now called Mount Adams, loomed far to the east. This sighting of the Cascades represented the first connection, the first transcontinental linking, of what would become the United States.

Increasing numbers of Indians gathered along shore to watch the strangers. Characteristically nervous about palefaces, they deduced that "we came from the clouds and were not men," Clark reported, after the natives had seen a bird felled from the sky by an explorer's bullet. Not until the braves spotted the Bird Woman was their anxiety relieved. "They immediately all came out and appeared to assume new life," he wrote. "The sight of this Indian woman confirmed our friendly intentions, as no woman ever accompanies a war party of Indians in this quarter."

Further down the Columbia, the discoverers began to see the first signs of white men. Some of the Indians, apparently from bartering with trading ships along the coast, wore Army blankets and blue cloth and cooked with Western utensils. On November 7, 1805, Clark spotted the Pacific. "Great joy in camp, we are in view of the ocean, this great Pacific Ocean which we [have] been so long anxious to see," he wrote. But the explorer was mistaken, for they were still deep within the Columbia River's broad estuary.

Pressing on, Lewis and Clark next encountered the Chinooks. Lewis desperately wanted to trade with them for a beautiful sea otter robe—"the finest fur I ever saw," one trooper declared. No price was too high. The skipper offered blankets, red and white beads, a handkerchief, a silver dollar, even a watch. However, the Indians only wanted blue beads, which had long since been traded away.

Sacagawea again saved the day. She gave the captains her belt of blue beads, an earlier gift from Clark, and the much treasured robe was theirs. In compensation, the Bird Woman received a coat of blue cloth.

On November 18, 1805, the crusade reached the Pacific Ocean. "Men appear much satisfied with their trip beholding with astonishment this immense Ocean," Clark noted in his journal. Having decided to winter near the coast, the Corps erected and occupied a fortified post on the south side of the Columbia River. Lewis and Clark named it Fort Clatsop, after a nearby Indian tribe. They built a fifty-by-fifty-foot stockade and two log buildings inside it as shelter and protection from attack. The wayfarers spent the winter gathering and researching information about the surrounding country and its native inhabitants. Living conditions were dreadful—aggravated by boredom, constant rain, thieving Indians, and scarcity of edible game. The close confines of the camp were a source of constant anxiety for both Lewis and Clark.

As winter turned into spring, the explorers eagerly prepared to leave Fort Clatsop. On March 23, 1806, they headed home along much the same route they had blazed. In early July, on the Lolo Creek, the party split into two groups. Lewis, with nine men, went directly across country, exploring the Marias River and northern Montana as they headed to the Falls of the Missouri. With Sacagawea's guidance, Clark and the rest of the party, returned to the Three Forks of the Missouri and crossed over to the Yellowstone River, which they descended. During the trek, the red-headed captain's detachment came upon a large sandstone formation rising high above the flat Montana plains. Named after Sacagawea's infant son, Pompey's Pillar, as it is known today, is a bold landmark of the trail west.

On August 12, the two groups joined forces near the union of the Yellowstone and Missouri rivers. The Corps traveled down the Missouri until it reached the original Mandan villages, two days later. "Those people were extremely pleased to see us," Clark wrote. The news from the chiefs, however, was bad. The mission's earlier efforts to forge a peace treaty with the warring tribes had failed. Most of the upper Midwest was under siege. Even the docile Mandan were divided by internal squabbles. After considerable arm-twisting, one of the chiefs, Big White, agreed to accompany the expedition to St. Louis and on to Washington to accept the Great White Father's promise of protection and trading posts.

On August 17, Lewis and Clark settled with Charbonneau. For his services, the French Canadian received $500.33 and 320 acres of land. Sacagawea got nothing. Clark later recognized the inequity in a letter to Charbonneau: "Your woman who accompanied you on that long, dangerous and fatiguing route to the Pacific Ocean and back deserved a greater reward for her attention than we had in our power to give." Perhaps to make amends, Clark offered to take her son to St. Louis and raise him in civilization. But Sacagawea, citing Pomp's tender age, declined. In a year, perhaps, "the boy will be sufficiently old to leave his mother," Clark hoped, "and [she] will then take him to me."

Leaving the Charbonneaus at the Mandan village, Lewis and Clark began the final leg of their journey. They covered fifty to sixty miles a day, propelled by the Missouri's swift currents. On September 23, 1806, the voyagers arrived triumphantly in St. Louis, then a tiny frontier outpost of 1,000 people. The entire town turned out to greet the heroes, cheering and toasting them. One resident reported: "They really have the appearance of Robinson Crusoes—dressed entirely in buckskins."

Lewis quickly dispatched a letter to President Jefferson, one of the few Americans confident that the explorers were still alive. "In obedience to your orders," he wrote, "we have penetrated the continent of North America to the Pacific Ocean, and sufficiently explored the interior of the country to affirm with confidence that we have discovered the most practicable route which does exist across the continent." While dispelling the myth of an easy water crossing of the continent, the Corps of Discovery proved that, by water and land, it was possible to reach the Pacific.

The epic voyage was over. Against all odds, Lewis and Clark had forged a bright triumph. During their absence of nearly two-and-a-half years, they had covered 8,000 miles—enduring months of cold, weeks of hunger and fatigue, days of backbreaking labor under the prairie's sweltering summer sun, and harassment from more than a dozen Indian tribes. The clever captains "had taken thirty-odd unruly soldiers and molded them into the Corps of Discovery, an elite platoon of tough, hardy, resourceful, well-disciplined men," wrote Stephen E. Ambrose, author of the best-selling *Undaunted Courage*. "They had earned the men's absolute trust."

Amazingly, on the entire 8,000-mile journey, only one man, Sgt. Charles Floyd, lost his life, probably due to a ruptured appendix. After encountering thousands of Indians, the adventurers had only one violent incident, resulting in two native deaths. Following Jefferson's instructions, the resourceful co-leaders brought back with them a vast array of invaluable information on the flora, fauna, geography, and human inhabitants of the strange new world to the west. Lewis and Clark were, as one historian put it, "the writingest explorers of their time." Their copious notes and comprehensive journals and maps left a rich legacy for scholars and adventurers alike. Of strategic importance, the captains also established the American claim to the lands now known as Oregon, Washington, and Idaho.

The total cost of the extraordinary undertaking was less than $40,000. For this piddling sum, Lewis and Clark had opened up the West to the United States. After Discovery, waves of trappers and fur traders would begin to work in the Rocky Mountains and the Pacific Northwest, providing the first permanent American presence in the region.

On the other hand, the crusade's efforts at Indian diplomacy were disappointing. While Lewis and Clark did forge warm and trusting personal relations with Native Americans—"Children of the Great Spirit," one tribe called them, citing the explorers' generous habit of gift-giving—Discovery's attempts to assert American rule over a powerful and independent people fizzled out. The majority of Indian nations rejected American status. In fact, the Sioux and the Blackfeet, the strongest and most warlike tribes, vowed to remain enemies of the United States.

Despite these setbacks, Jefferson and the country feted Lewis and Clark royally. The heroes were each given 1,600 acres of public land, plus $1,228 in double pay. With his "darling project" ended, Meriwether Lewis resigned from the Army to accept a presidential appointment as governor of the Upper Louisiana Territory. Unsuited by temperament and experience for public office, he failed miserably and became unpopular with many of his constituents. His discontent was compounded by his inability to find a wife and finish his written account of the journey. At the age of thirty-five, just three years after the epic trek, he either killed himself or was murdered at a dingy roadside tavern in southwestern Tennessee. At the time of his death, Capt. Lewis was on his way to explain his problems as territorial governor to Jefferson.

William Clark was appointed brigadier general of the militia for the Louisiana Territory, as well as superintendent of Indian Affairs. He settled in St. Louis, where he would marry and raise a family. After Lewis died,

Clark was offered the position of governor of the Louisiana Territory but declined, though he later served as governor of the Missouri Territory and as surveyor-general for Illinois, Missouri, and Arkansas. Throughout his career, the Red-Headed Chief displayed an intense concern for Native Americans and appealed frequently to the federal government to demonstrate justice and humanity to the country's first inhabitants. By the standards of the time, Clark treated the Indians with fairness, understanding, and compassion. In return, he enjoyed their respect and confidence. He died in 1838, at age sixty-eight.

After almost a year with the Mandan in upper Missouri, Charbonneau took Sacagawea and Pomp to St. Louis, where they hoped to make a new life for themselves. There, the youngster received a first-rate education, thanks to Clark's generosity. Later, Pomp traveled extensively in Europe and became fluent in French, German, and Spanish. When he returned to the United States in 1829, he opted to lead his life as a pioneer on the western frontier. He died in Oregon in 1866.

Toussaint Charbonneau also concluded that contemporary civilization was not for him. After failing as a farmer on land purchased from Clark, the dispirited French-Canadian decided to return to hunting and trapping. In 1811, he and Sacagawea relocated to Fort Manuel, a rough-and-tumble trading post located just below the North Dakota border, on the banks of the Missouri. Charbonneau survived well into his eighties, sadly estranged from his children.

The ever-devoted Sacagawea attempted to placate her loutish husband in their new environment. While giving birth to a daughter, Lisette, she contracted putrid fever and later died on December 20, 1812. According to one area resident: "She was a good [woman] . . . the best woman in the fort, aged about 25 [when] she left a fine infant girl."

Since the founding of the Republic, the American West has symbolized the geography of promise. No other exploring party so fully captured the hopes and dreams of ordinary Americans as the Lewis and Clark expedition. It was an integral and symbolic part of what historian James Axtell has called "the American encounter."

The Corps of Discovery aroused the country's imagination in ways that defy explanation, particularly in gauging Sacagawea's proper place in history. Few personalities in the past two centuries have been more idealized than the Shoshone maiden. "More memorials honor Sacagawea than any other American woman," writes historian Harold P. Howard. "Monuments, markers, schools and statues have been erected in her honor, and dozens of mountains, lakes and rivers have been named for her." Invariably, she is depicted as a young Indian girl bearing a baby on her back, pointing an extended finger westward—directing a pack of confused white adventurers to the Pacific.

Although Sacagawea was not the primary guide, "the young woman did make significant contributions to the exploration's success," argues Professor Ronda, author of one of the most balanced accounts of the transcontinental mission. Indeed, Lewis told Clark, in a rare unguarded moment: "She is the only necessity. I—we—need her."

Consider Sacagawea's place in Discovery. For a year-and-a-half, she endured discomfort and starvation and survived tortuous travel, much of it on foot, while accepting her share of difficult tasks. The Bird Woman helped nurse the sick and injured, mended clothes and moccasins, fetched firewood and water, and scraped and tanned hides—all while caring for her infant son. Alert and industrious, she prepared many of the meals, showing the men Indian ways of cooking and how to eke out a scanty meal. Whether it was gathering precious roots and berries or converting elk-bone marrow into grease and tallow, she won the respect of every trooper. Indeed, her biggest challenge may have been in appeasing her loathsome and abusive husband, who frequently quarreled with her and mistreated her. On at least one recorded instance, Charbonneau, whom Lewis called "a disease in boots," hit her until Clark intervened.

Sacagawea shone especially well as an ambassador to Indian nations along the way. With her son, she represented a visible sign that Lewis and Clark were not members of a hostile war party. Their presence assured various tribes of Discovery's friendly intentions. "A woman with a party of men is a token of peace," Clark wrote. "She was a living, breathing flag of peace."

As the expedition's principal interpreter, Sacagawea's role carried added meaning. Translating was tedious at best. The captains' short, uncomplicated remarks often took half a day to decipher to patient Indian chiefs. Typically, the men gave their message, one sentence at a time, to an English-speaking Frenchman in their party, who repeated it in French to Charbonneau. The fur trader, who spoke only broken English, relayed the point in Hidatsa to Sacagawea, who then translated it into Shoshone or via sign language to the anxious Indians. Yet the cumbersome process worked surprisingly well.

Finally, there is Sacagawea the pathfinder. While Lewis and Clark never expected the teenage girl to direct their campaign, they did hope she would recognize some parts of the country, particularly the Shoshone hunting grounds. On this score, she performed admirably.

In the summer of 1805, the Bird Woman spotted a hill that she thought resembled the head of a beaver. Just across the mountains to the west, she told the captains, lay the summer retreat of her people. "This piece of information has cheered the spirits of the party who now [have] begun to console themselves with the anticipation of shortly seeing the head of the Missouri," Lewis wrote. Conceding Sacagawea's importance after she became ill at the Three Forks of the Missouri, he added: "Her being [represented] our only hope for a friendly negotiation with the Snake [Shoshone] Indians on whom we depended for horses to assist us in our portage from the Missouri to the Columbia River."

On the return leg in 1806, the Shoshone squaw once again came to the rescue. In some of its darkest hours, Clark's detachment floundered through frustrating detours around the marshes of the West Gallatin River. As Clark looked eastward, he saw the Bridger Range and, southward, the Gallatin Range. The East Gallatin River emerged between the ranges. But the gap to the south, Sacagawea advised, was the most direct route through the lofty mountains to the Yellowstone River. That path, now called the Bozeman Pass, saved the trekkers many miles. "The Indian woman has been of great service to me as a pilot through this county," Clark noted at the time.

Taken together, Sacagawea's deeds, shaped under the most adverse circumstances, are worthy of a legend. Against all odds, the young Shoshone woman helped to unlock the spirit of the New West. Because of her grit and that of her cohorts, America would never again be the same.

part three

COMEBACK KIDS

8

SCOTT WADDLE:

Lost at Sea

*Man cannot discover new oceans unless
he has courage to lose sight of the shore.*

—ANDRÉ GIDE

Navy Cmdr. Scott Waddle, shown with wife Jill, heads for military court in the aftermath of the Ehime Maru disaster.

ON THE FATEFUL DAY—February 9, 2001—Navy Cmdr. Scott Waddle's life changed forever. He gave the order to perform an emergency maneuver that inadvertently caused the 360-foot nuclear submarine USS *Greeneville* to collide with the 196-foot *Ehime Maru*, a Japanese fishing boat, off the coast of Hawai'i, killing nine people on board the smaller vessel. The story made international headlines, inflamed U.S.–Japan relations and ended the veteran's 20-year naval career.

Unlike many other leaders in the public eye who have denied or made excuses for their behavior, Waddle assumed responsibility for his actions. His resilience from this tragic collision helped him emerge as a published author and inspirational speaker. Against all odds, his comeback from his split-second mistake offers an important lesson to anyone facing life's darkest hours.

The *Greeneville* disaster was a sad ending to a naval career that appeared destined for flag rank. With twenty years' experience in the construction, maintenance, and operation of nuclear-powered vessels, Cmdr. Waddle was touted as a rising star, clearly on the fast track to higher command. As protégé of the chief of the Pacific fleet submarine force, Vice Adm. Albert H. Konetzni Jr., he had been recommended for promotion to captain and was hand-picked from a highly competitive field of 250 naval officers to lead the *Greeneville*.

That Waddle's star would rise in the military service seemed evident. The son of an Air Force pilot, he was born in Mizawa, Japan, where—ironically—his first spoken words were in Japanese. As a military brat, he spent much of his childhood on other Air Force bases in the United States and overseas. In high school in Naples, Italy, he was elected class president, played football and learned basic Italian. Later, at the United States Naval Academy, he graduated in the top third of his class.

At Annapolis, the young midshipman met a former submarine commander who piqued his interest in the submersibles. "Not many people knew much about submarining," Waddle recalls. "And the Navy liked it that way, since many of the sub force's activities were classified or covert." Although he admits to having had no great love for the ocean, Waddle was fascinated by the high-tech wizardry that could take 140 men hundreds of feet below the surface, perform difficult maneuvers and keep them alive to tell about it. In 1978, he took his first cruise on the USS *Skipjack* and was hooked. "I looked at the sub's skipper and thought, now that's power!" he says. "I wanted that guy's job."

Pigboats. Iron coffins. Death traps. For hundreds of years, Davy Jones welcomed submariners who, in the cold and dark, faced underwater hazards far worse than those confronted by traditional seafaring men. In the early sixteenth century, Leonardo da Vinci sketched designs for a prototype submarine, but feared "the evil nature" of undersea conflict. Recognizing its potential for devastation, the U.S. Navy launched its first submersible, the fifty-four-foot *Holland*, in 1900; it ran on electric batteries when underwater, a gas engine on the surface. Submarine technology progressed rapidly in the years that followed, with diesel-powered subs wreaking havoc in the two world wars. Beginning in the '50s, Adm. Hyman G. Rickover created vessels with nearly endless power and unlimited stealth—boats powered by nuclear reactors that could remain submerged for months at a time. With them, the U.S. Navy would gain a definite edge in the Cold War under the seas.

A master of power politics, the prickly Polish immigrant used his family's congressional influence to get into the Naval Academy. When he first began working on early experiments with nuclear power, Rickover pushed the Navy to begin building nuclear subs by first getting himself appointed to a top staff job at the Atomic Energy Commission. After the first nuclear submarine, the USS *Nautilus*, snuck under the Arctic ice to reach the North Pole in 1958, Rickover's personal fleet began to move to center stage. "Now he was employing nuclear subs as public relations stars," according to Sherry Sontag and Christopher Drew in *Blind Man's*

Bluff. "The Navy budget seemed to get another boost every time another congressman got a nuclear-propelled ride."

To become an officer in Rickover's all-volunteer force, a young man had to pass a series of interviews with the Old Man himself to confirm his technical knowledge, as well as his ability to handle stress in cramped steel cylinders under the sea. Typically, Rickover's questions were extremely personal, outlandish, even bizarre. "The guy's Looney Tunes," Waddle reported, after his unpleasant grilling. "He may be father of the modern nuclear submarine age, but the guy is certifiably nuts!" A short time later, though, the eager middy received a letter from the abrasive admiral inviting him into the elite corps.

After graduating from the Naval Academy, Waddle would spend the next two decades learning his craft, watching a generation of commanders as a junior officer, listening carefully at the frequent round-table discussions that make submarining a very human profession. Time on shore was spent training in a variety of computerized simulators, attending seminars, comparing ideas with his peers.

Following several years of intense schooling, Waddle and his wife Jill were sent to Italy where he served as a staff watch officer with the submarine group stationed off the coast of Naples. But his performance was lackluster, and the junior officer left the country with less-than-glowing marks that nearly destroyed his prospects for promotion.

In early 1989, a transfer to Groton, Connecticut, "the submarine capital of the world," resuscitated his career. Working as an engineer, he helped build a new submarine, the USS *Kentucky*. For two years, Lt. Cmdr. Waddle labored in constructing, testing, and assisting in sea trials to make the boat seaworthy. Exhibiting superior engineering skills and hard work, the thirty-three-year-old officer was able to expunge the negative comments from his Naples fitness report. He describes his stint on the *Kentucky* as transformational. "That's where I found my niche," he says. "I discovered that what I really enjoyed was motivating men, bringing out the best in them, training them, instilling in them standards of excellence and then turning out an exceptional product for the Navy."

In 1992, the reinvigorated submariner moved to Hawai'i, where he spent two years inspecting the safety of nuclear reactors on subs. From there, he served as the executive officer, or second-in-command, on the USS *San Francisco*, where he received the highest marks in the submarine squadron. Then, it was off to the National Defense University in Washington for a master's degree. On March 19, 1999, after eighteen years in the Navy, Cmdr. Waddle was given command of the USS *Greeneville*, an improved *Los Angeles*–class attack submarine. The ship was named after the town in Tennessee where Davy Crockett was born, and was christened in 1996 by Tipper Gore, a native of Tennessee and wife of Vice President Al Gore.

Since his early years at Annapolis, all Waddle ever wanted was command of his own attack boat. Now he had it. "The pinnacle," he called it. "The best job an officer in the Navy can have."

The change of command ceremony took place onboard the *Greeneville* as it was moored in Pearl Harbor. The gaily dressed crowd included Waddle's family and a bevy of visiting dignitaries. In a rousing speech, Admiral Konetzni, commander of sub forces in the Pacific, stressed the importance of people. "The tribe is important," Big Al, the Sailor's Pal—as the demanding, but gregarious, admiral was known—reminded his charges. "You gotta take care of your men!" That admonition would remain deeply entrenched in Waddle's psyche—becoming "a cornerstone in my methods of command."

Following the festivities, the 7,000-ton submarine prepared to get under way with its new skipper in charge. With his father watching from the pier, Waddle commanded the power-packed vessel as it cautiously exited the Pearl Harbor channel. "I was trying to take in all the sights and sounds from the top of the bridge," Waddle says. "But it really hadn't sunk in yet that I was in charge of the nearly billion-dollar machine. It was the beginning of a new era."

When he took over command of this ship armed with every cutting-edge system available, it was like a business that had all the latest technology but only some of the productivity. Knowing that responsibility for improving performance rested with him, Waddle began to instill three basic tenets in his crew: safety, efficiency, and backup. "Be safe in all that you do," he insisted. "Be efficient; don't waste time. And we all need backup. If one person misses something, another man is there to catch it.

And if you see something wrong, potentially damaging or something that could compromise the ship's safety, speak up!"

Waddle also attempted to foster a more relaxed atmosphere on the *Greeneville*. Although this went against Rickover's methods of using fear and intimidation to insure crew performance, the commander followed Konetzni's brief to forge a more open culture on his subs. "He empowered us to lead our men, to take care of them, to improve the quality of life," Waddle says. "And we did just that."

Seeing the ship through the eyes of his men, listening carefully and communicating effectively quickly paid off. Within months, the unconventional skipper created a crew of confident and inspired problem-solvers eager to take the initiative and assume responsibility for their actions. Soon, the *Greeneville* was recognized far and wide as a model of naval professionalism, surpassing sister subs in operational and combat-readiness inspections.

"It was a sharply run and professional ship," according to Capt. Robert Snead, Waddle's immediate superior. Similarly, another submariner, Rear Adm. Charles H. Griffiths Jr., reported that the gung-ho leader "had an excellent reputation and was considered one of the stronger commanders in the force."

Active-duty and retired submariners and Cmdr. Waddle's friends also portrayed the *Greeneville*'s CEO as the perennial optimist—an uncomplicated shipmate whose idea of a good time was sitting on the lawn of his house on the base, drinking a beer, smoking a cigar, and looking out over the entry channel to Pearl Harbor. The consummate family man, Waddle was devoted to Jill, his wife of sixteen years, and their teenage daughter, Ashley. "In a world where officers put the boat first and family second, with him it's a tie," the wife of a retired Navy captain told *The New York Times*.

But it was his efforts at creating a special family-like bond on the five-year-old ship that produced one of the highest retention and promotion rates and morale levels in the Pacific submarine fleet. With 140 men at sea in a confined living area, nerves are often frayed. "The chemistry on a submarine is usually not very good," one Navy officer explains, "but people-wise, the *Greeneville* was one of the top ships."

All this was not lost on Big Al, the Sailor's Pal. "Keep doing what you're doing, Scott," Konetzni advised him, suggesting the likelihood of future advancement. Indeed, it was Waddle's golden reputation that caused his ship to be frequently chosen to carry civilians in the distinguished visitors program—an accolade that would come back to haunt the hard-charging captain.

Were it not for a disparate group of sixteen civilians, the *Greeneville* never would have left its Pearl Harbor berth on that fateful February day. "We had no other reason for going to sea that day," Waddle admits. Only days earlier, he had canceled a long-standing training exercise as unnecessary. Some suggest that Waddle's ambition to impress the visitors made this assignment appealing. "In retrospect," Adm. Konetzni, now retired, told me in a phone interview from Buffalo, "I should have spotted Scott's one blind side—his desire to impress bigwigs. And I should have brought it to his attention sooner."

Indeed, the admiral told his chief of staff, Capt. Robert L. Brandhuber, "Don't break the china!"—meaning don't authorize the excursion unless it has military purpose. While Konetzni traveled to Korea and Japan, however, others in his command saw the cruise as a chance to give potentially influential civilians a once-in-a-lifetime ride aboard a nuclear-powered sub and were loath to let them down. "They had a commitment to these folks," one officer said of the civilians, some of whom had traveled from Texas and Massachusetts.

For some time, the Navy and the other branches of the U.S. armed forces have attempted to build public support by routinely inviting visitors to tour bases and, in rarer cases, ride along in ships, aircraft, and helicopters. "It's for people who have visibility, people whose opinions will be heard, or people who have an impact on their local communities," according to one military spokesperson. With the submarine fleet declining and budgets tightening after the end of the Cold War, the Navy's top brass have used the distinguished visitor program to make a case for rebuilding the fleet. In 2000, 1,287 people were treated to submarine rides on fifty occasions—averaging seventeen civilians each trip.

The *Greeneville* was a favorite participant. Given Waddle's high marks, Adm. Konetzni often turned to him to host important guests.

Waddle, for his part, shared the admiral's enthusiasm. "Because our future is somewhat questionable with respect to the number of submarines we want to build or need to build," he claimed, "it's important to get civilians onboard to educate them and inform them of what the submarine does."

At around 5:30 A.M. on February 9, Waddle rolled out of bed for what appeared to be a routine mission. "This was going to be a short, out-and-back trip, planned carefully as a five- or six-hour event, after which I'd return home from work like a normal family man," he recalls. That evening, he and his wife planned to have a quiet, romantic dinner.

The confident captain was prepared to go to sea shorthanded. About thirty percent of his 140 shipmates were in training, including some of the ship's most experienced sonar men. Unknown to him, nine of thirteen positions on the watch list were filled by crewmen different from those who customarily handled those assignments. "It never crossed my mind that anyone on the *Greeneville* might not be competent to perform," Waddle later wrote. Shortly after boarding the ship, he also was informed that the analog-video signal display unit (AVSDU) was inoperative. This equipment serves as a backup display, separate from the three sonar stacks and screens forward of the control room. A properly functioning monitor means the officer of the deck doesn't have to check as often with the sailors responsible for tracking other ships in the ocean. When it's not functioning, it places pressure on using more care in securing information on surface contacts and, as important, communicating effectively.

"It was not a crucial piece of equipment," Waddle contends. "Or so I thought. Looking back, I wish we'd have taken the time to repair the AVSDU before embarking. It might have helped us avoid the nightmare that was coming."

With everything else functioning properly, he greeted his sixteen guests, who were accompanied by Capt. Robert L. Brandhuber, Adm. Konetzni's chief of staff, who later described the vessel as "one of the most meticulously maintained subs I have ever seen." Running slightly late, the *Greeneville* slipped out of Pearl Harbor around 9 A.M. Shortly thereafter, the submerged vessel began a variety of challenging high-speed maneuvers, which the crew performed with precision. The sailors then treated their visitors to a good Navy chow. "Everyone was enjoying the ride and having fun," Waddle recalls. "I could barely suppress a smile as I watched their joy and amazement. Even Captain Brandhuber seemed to be impressed." The program, designed to get the civilians back to shore by 2:30 P.M., however, was behind schedule.

At about 12:45 P.M., the ship's executive officer, Lt. Cmdr. Gerald K. Pfeifer, informed the skipper, "We're running a little late. We need to get this thing moving." Waddle, convinced that he could get back on schedule, told his second-in-command, "I know what I'm doing. We'll deal with it [the delay]."

Before initiating underwater maneuvers, procedures called for a three- to five-minute periscope scan of the surface. Earlier, Lt. (jg) Michael J. Coen, officer of the deck and a notoriously deliberate watch stander, had reported no contacts within reasonable distance. Neither had Patrick Seacrest, the ship's experienced fire-control technician. Petty Officer David Carter, the electronic-surveillance measure watch overseeing radar signals, also reported "no threat contacts"—confirmed by Petty Officer Edward McGiboney, the sonar room supervisor.

Because he was tight on time, Waddle picked up the pace. In preparation for rising to periscope depth, the submarine conducted two turns intended to provide accurate sonar data. The procedure, called target motion analysis, typically requires ten minutes; the *Greeneville* shortened the maneuver to six minutes. The skipper also sidestepped the usual conference with his subordinates before surfacing. The sub then rose to a periscope depth of about sixty feet. Waddle took the periscope himself and scanned the surface for about eighty seconds, a 360-degreee sweep that is supposed to take about three minutes.

"I saw nothing but blue water," he says. "The coast was clear. There were no objects within miles of us." The skipper then announced to his crew: "I hold no visual contacts."

Little did the forty-one-year-old captain know that a 400-ton Japanese fishing boat, the *Ehime Maru*, was bearing down on them at a rate of eleven knots. According to most naval experts, Waddle was let down by fire-control technician Seacrest, who was responsible for plotting the positions of surface vessels in the area, and hadn't informed the bridge that sonar readings indicated that a ship was closing within 2,500 yards. Just minutes earlier, he assumed that the *Greeneville*'s computers were wrong, because Waddle had told the crew that all was clear. Inexplicably, the seaman reprogrammed the computer to show the *Ehime Maru* out of range because of the reported lack of sighting. Also puzzling, Seacrest failed to manually plot the coordinates of nearby vessels on the paper wall chart—a required protocol designed to keep the command informed of all possible contacts. When later asked to explain his actions, the confused sailor simply said he got "a lit bit lazy."

Had Cmdr. Waddle, in fact, received or solicited more accurate information, it could have prompted him to conduct extra periscope searches or more thorough ones before concluding that there was no vessel in the area. This, however, was not the case. "Nobody challenged me," Waddle says. "Besides, we were running short of time, and I was eager to further impress our guests."

To highlight their visit, the skipper ordered an emergency main ballast blow, a rapid-surfacing drill that would catapult the 7,000-ton sub from a depth of about 400 feet to the surface in a matter of seconds. But what, under normal conditions, would have been, in Waddle's words, "the ultimate roller coaster ride," turned out to be a major catastrophe.

At precisely 1:43 P.M., the *Greeneville*'s steel rudder, designed to break through Arctic ice floes, sliced into the Japanese vessel's hull, sinking it within minutes, about nine miles south of Diamond Head, the iconic Waikiki landmark. Nine of the thirty-five Japanese aboard the ship—four teenage fisheries students, two teachers, and three crew members—drowned. "Part of me died as I watched the ship sink," Waddle later wrote in his autobiography, *The Right Thing*.

Onboard, all hell broke loose. The *Greeneville* sent an emergency distress call, while the crew raced into action to assess any damages to the sub. With the aquamarine seas heaving six- to eight-foot swells, Waddle decided that any efforts to raise the sub would capsize the *Ehime Maru* survivors who were now in life rafts. He, therefore, ordered the *Greeneville* to abandon any rescue efforts and move away from those in life rafts in the water, a decision that later would be roundly criticized in Japan as "fleeing the scene of an accident." Fortunately, Coast Guard helicopters appeared on the scene within fifteen minutes of the distress call. About thirty minutes later, a Coast Guard vessel plucked twenty-six passengers and crew members from the drink.

The search-and-rescue operation continued into the night and ran a full three weeks. Meanwhile, the *Greeneville*—with its crew and sixteen traumatized visitors—was ordered to remain at sea all night, using its image-intensifier equipment to try to locate any other possible survivors. As the submarine pulled into Pearl Harbor the next morning, Waddle and his shipmates encountered a swarm of television cameramen, journalists, and somber onlookers. "We were not coming home as heroes," Waddle wrote. "We were coming in as a 'killer sub'. Everyone knew what this meant. The gravity of the situation weighed heavily on me—an American submarine ramming a Japanese vessel near Pearl Harbor, of all places!"

Shortly after disembarking, Waddle received the bad news from his mentor, Adm. Konetzni: "Effective immediately, you are hereby detached for cause as commanding officer of the USS *Greeneville*." The message was undeniable: Waddle's once-bright naval career was over. Thirty minutes later, he removed his personal effects from the ship and returned home, in his words, "dog-tired and emotionally exhausted."

In his darkest hours, that evening the distraught commander contemplated suicide. "Evil seemed to flood my soul," he wrote, "as my mind entered one of the darkest caverns I'd ever known. But a voice in my head kept recalling the times I would sit down and counsel young sailors: 'You can get through the stressful time in your life. Put it behind you.'"

Searching for inner peace, Waddle walked outside his home into a cool Hawai'i evening. He sat down, staring out at Pearl Harbor's tranquil waters and reflected on the accident and his future prospects. Eventually, he gathered himself, returned inside, crawled back into bed, and waited for the dawn of a new day.

That same day, the Navy had already launched a full-fledged internal investigation into the incident—debriefing the crew and reviewing logs from the *Greeneville*. It paralleled a similar inquiry conducted by the National Transportation Safety Board, called in because the disaster had involved a civilian vessel in American waters.

In a sign of anger, Japanese Prime Minister Yoshiri Mori registered an official protest with the U.S. Ambassador in Tokyo, Thomas S. Foley. In addition, Japan's foreign minister, Yoshei Kono, demanded more information about what civilians were doing on board the submarine at the time of the accident. Secretary of State Colin L. Powell, in return, reported that Washington had apologized to Japan "every way we know how." He added, "We're doing everything we can to express our regret and also to make sure this doesn't affect the very strong [positive] relationship that we have with Japan."

The Navy concluded its preliminary report in just a week and presented it to Adm. Thomas B. Fargo, commander of the Pacific Fleet. On February 17, Fargo announced that the Navy would convene a rarely used court of inquiry to investigate the collision, setting the stage for a public trial of Waddle and his crew. The hearing, to be led by three admirals, with a Japanese flag officer as a nonvoting member, involved sworn testimony and cross-examination in an open court. "Parties to the inquiry," or defendants, included Waddle, the executive officer Pfeifer, and the officer of the deck Coen. The court would seek to determine whether the officers should be charged with three major crimes: dereliction of duty, improper hazarding of a vessel and, most serious, negligent homicide, a felony that could result in ten years in prison. Separately, Petty Officer Seacrest was ordered to a captain's mast, a similar administrative proceeding.

"The seriousness in which I view this tragic accident is reflected in the level of investigation and the seniority of the court members," Adm. Fargo told a news conference in Honolulu. "It will provide a full and open accounting for the American and Japanese people."

Eugene R. Fidell, a military lawyer and president of the National Institute of Military Justice, agreed that the decision to seek a court of inquiry reflected the gravity of the case, but did not necessarily predict a criminal prosecution. If the court recommended criminal charges against any crew member, a court-martial would then be convened. Fidell also believed the process could help to assuage some of the public anger in Japan over the incident. "It's a way of telegraphing to the Japanese that we're going to get to the bottom of this," he told the *New York Times*.

Waddle's friends and colleagues quickly rallied around him, setting up a fund for his legal defense. "If I were in his shoes right now, I'd be looking for three things," advised one fellow officer. "How can I get out with the benefits of twenty years of service to my country, how can I be exonerated, and how can I avoid going to jail?"

Consumed by the pending probe, just two weeks away, the sorrowful submariner engaged a civilian lawyer, Charles W. Gittins, to complement his court-appointed military counsels. Gittins, a Naval Academy graduate and reserve Marine Corps lieutenant colonel, was known for his tenacious defenses in several prominent military trials, including the Navy's *Tailhook* scandal. At Waddle's insistence, Gittens helped draft a letter of regret, which a tearful Waddle delivered to the Japanese consulate in Honolulu for the grieving families in Japan. The letter, though, stopped short of an apology, since an apology, Waddle's lawyers warned, could be viewed as an admission of guilt and seriously damage the defense.

On March 1, Adm. William J. Fallon, vice chief of naval operations, offered a formal apology, at the U.S. ambassador's residence in Tokyo, to relatives of the missing victims. The admiral also pledged that the Navy's court of inquiry would "provide a full and open accounting." One distraught family member thanked Fallon and said that "it was the most satisfying meeting we have had yet."

Four days later, the admirals convened their investigation in a small, utilitarian courtroom under heavy security and the glare of an international media corps numbering more than 400 journalists. Guards at Pearl Harbor's main gates conducted extensive security checks. For twelve days, starting at 8 A.M., Cmdr. Waddle, accompanied by his wife and his defense team, engaged in the emotionally charged proceedings. Inside the courtroom, the audience was undeniably divided. On one side were relatives of the *Greeneville* officers under scrutiny. On the other side were the Japanese, including government officials and bereaved family members flown in at the Navy's expense.

Outside the cramped courtroom, there were also stark differences. In Japan, a major brouhaha raged over the titanic mishap. People literally marched in the streets, carrying placards denouncing the United States, the U.S. Navy and, especially, Cmdr. Waddle. Back home, opinions were mixed. Many in the local media blasted the former skipper on a daily basis, labeling him a cold-hearted killer. Others were equally outraged that a dedicated naval officer was being raked over the coals to pacify the Japanese.

The court would call thirty-three witnesses, each of whom recounted the horrible accident from his own perspective. Ironically, none of the distinguished visitors was asked to provide testimony—a tactic one legal expert criticized as "a gaping hole in the investigation." The inquiry's most dramatic moments came when Waddle overrode his lawyer's concerns and testified how the submarine he commanded accidentally sank the fishing trawler. Earlier, Adm. Fargo had denied the defendant's repeated requests for immunity, which would have meant that Waddle's testimony could not be used against him later in a military court.

Waddle began his remarks apologizing to the families of the Japanese who were lost, acknowledging his sole responsibility as the sub's captain and saying he wanted to testify because it was "the right thing to do." In the combative and often emotional exchange that followed, he conceded that he had cut short or omitted several safety precautions. Although the control room's video monitor that normally displayed the position of nearby ships was out of order, he had neglected to discuss this with his senior officers, or order extra attention to readings in the sonar room to make up for the missing display.

He agreed that he had failed to compensate for the absence of a third of his normal crew, while also being unaware that a majority of sailors manning watch status had switched positions without letting him know. He also admitted deviating from his own standing orders, in order to save time, speeding through at least four procedures that might have prevented the disaster. And he was at a loss to explain why he didn't see the *Ehime Maru* through the periscope. "I just know that I didn't," he said.

In tense debate, the embattled commander insisted that he did not run a lax ship. "I was not informal," he argued. "Nor did I micromanage my crew. I empowered them to do their job." Waddle, however, refused to criticize his shipmates for their reluctance to speak their minds. "This is not a ship where you would be shot for talking to the commanding officer," Rear Adm. Griffiths had testified earlier. Waddle "was a very

nurturing commanding officer who was universally revered by his crew."
In addition, the defendant also refused to extend any blame for the collision directly on his crew.

Nevertheless, some critics believed that, indirectly, Waddle passed
some of the responsibility on to his officers for failing to follow established procedures—in effect, making himself the victim. In his autobiography, published in 2002, he wrote: "Somebody had to take the fall
for it and as the court of inquiry progressed, it became more and more
obvious that the court had already decided that the sacrificial lamb
would be me."

As for the presence of the sixteen visitors on board, Waddle refuted
the admirals' contention that they may have created a "passive" barrier to
clear, effective communications. Later, however, he recanted, saying that
"the civilians, although not directly a hindrance, were a distraction. And,
no," he added "they were not properly managed."

After Waddle had gone toe-to-toe with the three admirals in a day of
heated exchanges, defense counsel Gittins gave an impassioned closing
argument. "Cmdr. Waddle," he declared, "exercised his judgment, and he
did his level best. He may have fallen short on that day, but his actions
were not criminal."

On April 10, the panel delivered a 2,000-page report to Adm. Fargo,
who subsequently found that there was insufficient evidence of negligent
homicide to warrant a court-martial, the military equivalent of a criminal
trial. Instead, Fargo ordered an admiral's mast, a nonjudicial proceeding
that would end Waddle's naval career.

Two weeks later, the admiral conducted an hour-long private session in his conference room. He concluded that Waddle had "created
an artificial sense of urgency in preparation for surfacing on February 9
when prudent seamanship, the safety of his submarine and good judgment dictated otherwise." He also concurred with the court's opinion
that the civilians "did prove to be a distraction" and that it was "Cmdr.
Waddle's responsibility to prevent this from occurring." Fargo added that
"this tragic accident could and should have been avoided by simply following existing Navy standards and procedures in bringing submarines
to the surface." Therefore, he found Waddle guilty of dereliction of duty

and subjecting a vessel to hazard; however, he rejected the more serious charge of negligent homicide.

Cmdr. Waddle was also reprimanded and, as expected, agreed to resign. In addition, he was fined half-pay for two months—to be suspended unless he committed some other violation within the subsequent six months. He was, however, allowed to retire at full rank and full pension upon his completion of twenty years' service.

Asked if the punishment amounted to a mere slap on the wrist, Adm. Fargo vehemently defended his decision. "Cmdr. Waddle has been stripped of his command, and his career effectively terminated," he said. "For a naval officer who served twenty years for his country, I would tell you that this is absolutely devastating. He has paid dearly."

The admiral also admonished the other crew members: the ship's executive officer, the chief of staff of the submarine fleet, the chief of boat—the ranking enlisted man—and the sonar supervisor. But when the *Greeneville* returned to sea, after $2 million in repairs, the executive officer, Pfeifer, and the deck officer, Coen, were aboard. Subsequently, Petty Officer Seacrest also returned to the ship.

The Japanese, for the most part, were outraged at the commander's fate. Officially, the government seemed satisfied, noting that the verdict meant the United States had accepted full responsibility for the collision. But in the town of Uwajima, where most of the victims were from, emotions ran high. "The punishment is absolutely not one the families can accept," said Moriuki Kato, governor of the prefecture. "I had hoped they would give him the utmost, strictest reprimand." Mitsunori Nomoto, father of a seventeen-year-old boy who died in the collision, voiced similar sentiments and could not understand the logic of U.S. military justice. "If that is their system, what can we do?," he asked. "If it were not the military, there would be harsher punishment."

Over the next several months, the United States government would go to great lengths to make amends to the Japanese for the tragic incident. Washington spent $60 million to recover the *Ehime Maru* from 2,003 feet underwater, hauling it to much shallower water, where divers could recover the remains of the dead. Eventually, eight of the nine victims were returned home. In addition, the United States provided an estimated $13.9 million to compensate all family members of those thirty-five on the boat. Perhaps because of these goodwill gestures, as well as the passage of time, the pain seems to be diminishing.

On December 13, 2002, Waddle, as a civilian, made his pilgrimage to Uwajima to offer a formal apology. Although he claims that the Navy had promised to finance the trip, he traveled at his own expense. Adm. Fargo, though, later told me that a government-sponsored trip would have been authorized if it had been made sooner, not a full year after the incident. Most observers, in fact, blame Waddle's delayed return on advice he received from attorney Gittins not to visit Japan because it might lead to his arrest. In any case, Waddle simply wanted to meet with the victims' families and to place flowers at a memorial at the local high school honoring the dead. Nevertheless, he was disappointed to discover that the parents of only one crew member would talk to him. In addition, school officials rejected his offer to visit the campus, after finding that many of the affected families didn't welcome his arrival.

In January 2008, seven years after Waddle's journey, I sought to reassess the sentiments of the local citizenry. Traveling south by rail ten hours from Tokyo, one encounters the coastal fishing town of 90,000, identified as the place "where the mountain meets the sea." Famous for its yellowtail *ahi* tuna, Mikan oranges, and pearls, Uwajima remains under the radar of most Japanese. Before the well-publicized catastrophe, this sleepy seaside community was known for its bullfights, held five times a year, where the bulls do battle in a ring twenty meters in diameter— without a matador. The first bull to flee is branded the loser.

A short ride from the train station sits Uwajima Fisheries High School, where an impressive memorial and replica of the *Ehime Maru* are on display. "We won't ever forget," says assistant principal Hitomichi Hiraoka, "but we are not really angry." As for Waddle's earlier attempt to offer an apology, he and most of his contemporaries felt that "it was too late." At a nearby seafood restaurant, Asano-san of the Japanese newspaper *Yomiuri Shimbun* reiterated his country's long-standing disdain of the U.S. military justice system: "There was nothing we could do, since it was the U.S. Navy." But like the majority of his neighbors, he also believed that "most of us have gotten over the incident."

About the only words of encouragement Cmdr. Waddle received in the immediate aftermath of this very public drama came from then President George W. Bush. Asked by NBC's *Today* show to comment on Waddle's dismissal, the president remarked: "This fine American patriot is taking the heat. This is an officer who bears all the responsibility and, to me, that says something about his character."

Reflecting on this "ugly event," Waddle now says: "I took actions that at the time I thought were prudent, but in hindsight, were not. I failed."

Failure is one of the most paralyzing forces that can seize the human spirit. It constricts people's visions of futures that are theirs for the taking. But failure, when confronted directly, also provides opportunities to rebound. "I knew I could endure the crisis," the retired submariner says today of those dark days. "But it wasn't easy." After he left the Navy, he remained haunted by memories of the fatal collision. "It was the first thing I thought about in the morning, and the last thing I thought about at night," he recalls. "But, eventually, it no longer consumed me."

"All men are liable to error," philosopher John Locke once wrote. Slowly, Waddle began to realize that he was not alone, refusing to equate his split-second mistakes with defeat. Because of the *Greeneville* incident, some doors closed to him. But, eventually, others opened.

With the help of his family and friends and faith in God, the retired commander began to reinvent himself—forging a new life outside his beloved Navy. With the same grit and determination that he displayed in uniform, Waddle became a popular motivational speaker and published author. Today, the forty-nine-year-old North Carolinian reportedly reaches more than 100 audiences a year, many at $10,000 to $15,000 a pop. His message: "Failure Need Not Be Final." Complementing his inspirational talks are copies of his book, *The Right Thing*, a tearful mea culpa about the *Greeneville* collision and the lessons that followed. (Part of the book's proceeds goes to Saint Louis High School's *Ehime Maru* memorial in Honolulu.)

Looking back, Waddle remains a staunch supporter of the U.S. Navy, noting that his daughter is a cadet and track standout at his alma mater, the Naval Academy. As for Admiral Fargo, who delivered the fatal blow to his military career, the former officer describes him as "a good man, a fair man," adding that "the Navy got [the verdict] right."

Sadly, things were not as shipshape on the *Greeneville*. Less than a year after the *Ehime Maru* disaster, the ill-fated boat encountered one problem followed by another. On August 27, 2001, the vessel ran aground while trying to enter a harbor in Saipan, prompting the removal of its captain from command. On January 27, 2002, it smacked into the amphibious transport USS *Ogden* in the Arabian Sea. A court of inquiry found the commander guilty of negligently hazarding a vessel, but allowed him to remain in charge of the sub.

By all accounts, ex-skipper Waddle has fared better in weathering the storm. In the aftermath of this life-altering tragedy, he denied letting guilt or remorse steal his dreams. "From all accounts, he seems to have picked up the pieces as well as anyone could," says Adm. Konetzni. "He's a helluva young man!"

Denied a naval career, Waddle offers important lessons for anyone facing life's most difficult challenges. However, this is not meant to portray the former sailor in heroic terms. "If there was any hero in the *Ehime Maru* disaster, it was Admiral Fargo," says Jay Fidell, a former judge in the Coast Guard and now a civilian lawyer who followed the legal proceedings closely. "He saved the United States from what could have been permanently damaged relations with Japan." Fargo, for his part, describes the incident today as "a case of bad judgment—far more tragic than heroic."

Perhaps Shakespeare's words in *Julius Caesar* best describe the *Greeneville* tragedy—and its aftermath:

> *There is a tide in the affairs of men,*
> *which taken as the flood leads to fortune;*
> *omitted, all the voyage of life is bound in*
> *shallows and in misery.*
> *On such a full sea are we now afloat:*
> *We must take the current when it serves or*
> *lose our ventures.*

9
PATTIE DUNN:
Boardroom Brouhaha

*A happy life consists not in the absence
but the mastery of hardships.*

—HELEN KELLER

Former Hewlett-Packard chair and cancer patient Pattie Dunn beat
the odds to restore her reputation and her health.

IN CORPORATE AMERICA, boardroom battles can be a blood sport. In 2006, the directors of Hewlett-Packard, one of Silicon Valley's original technology giants, were engaged in open warfare that dominated the business news. For years, HP's board had been a leaky ship, as secret deliberations often ended up in the national press. Chairman Pattie Dunn, then fifty-three, would have none of it—launching what arguably became the most famous investigation since Watergate. The probe gained considerable notoriety when it was learned that the methods used included snooping into the private phone records of HP directors, employees, and journalists. Suddenly, "pretexting" became part of the American lexicon, and once-vaunted Hewlett-Packard became likened to the Enrons, Tycos, and WorldComs of the world.

The humiliating episode cost Dunn her job and her reputation. In September 2006, she agreed to resign, in one of the most widely chronicled departures in corporate history. Several weeks later, she was subpoenaed by the California Attorney General for her role in "leading" HP's surveillance. Her temporary fall from grace underscored the dramatic change in fortunes of one of America's most prominent and respected women. During the height of the spying fiasco, she was inducted into the Bay Area Council's Business Hall of Fame. Earlier, *Forbes* magazine had ranked her seventeenth on its "100 Most Powerful Women."

"Calamity is man's true touchstone," it's been said. For Dunn, the severest jolt was yet to come. The day before her subpoena, Dunn found out she had a recurrence of stage four ovarian cancer and needed immediate chemotherapy. A few years earlier, she had survived breast and skin cancer. But Dunn is no garden-variety gal. This courageous woman, who had climbed to the top of corporate America, was determined to launch a comeback, winning the two toughest battles: her life and her reputation.

Pattie Dunn knows what it feels like to get socked. She had survived hard times before, starting with her childhood in the rough-and-tumble world of Las Vegas, where her mother Ruth had been a model and show-girl and her father Henry toiled as a performer and, later, entertainment director at the Dunes and Tropicana hotels. When she was twelve, her father died of a massive heart attack, and Ruth—recognizing that glitzy Vegas wasn't the best environment for a single mother to raise her chil-dren: Pattie, her older sister Debbie, age thirteen, and her two-year-old brother Paul—moved the family to the San Francisco Bay area. That left the threesome and their bereaved mother isolated from family support.

In their new digs, the Dunns' situation rapidly deteriorated. Ruth fell into a deep depression—exacerbated by her second marriage to, in Pattie's words, a "flim-flam man," who left the family destitute. Although Pattie managed to excel in high school, winning a National Merit Scholarship and a spot on the student council, her mother's emotional and financial problems took their toll. In 1972, Pattie was forced to drop out of the University of Oregon and return home, where she and Debbie "reversed roles and effectively became parents" to their ailing mother and younger brother. Pattie worked as a leasing agent at San Francisco's Golden Gate-way Center (among her clients: Alex Haley, who wrote *Roots* there) and lived with a family in nearby Terra Linda in exchange for housekeeping and cooking. With scholarship help, she finished her degree in journal-ism in 1975, commuting on three separate buses to the University of California at Berkeley.

Two weeks after graduation, Dunn took a job as a temporary sec-retary at Wells Fargo Investment Advisors—abandoning her lifetime dream of becoming, of all things, an investigative reporter. In 1978, she accepted a full-time position with the firm. Although she had no for-mal training in finance, her flair for writing soon paid off. She quick-ly captured the attention of her seniors by helping translate complex financial products into concise language. Later, she managed important clients and was given greater responsibilities. Following the exodus of three top-ranking executives, Dunn was elevated to co-CEO. There, she met and married William W. Jahnke, a banker, whom she calls "the best husband in the world," and helped raise his four children from a previous marriage.

In 1996, England-based Barclays PLC acquired the business. Impressed by Dunn's skills in building strong client relationships, the board made her the top banana two years later. "Pattie was literally swept into the top job," husband Bill told me. "She would have been perfectly content to stay put. But the Brits really believed in her." As chairman and CEO of Barclays Global Investors, Dunn oversaw more than $1.6 trillion in global assets, more than that held by any other institution in the world, and "became deeply interested in corporate governance to support the firm's role as fiduciary on behalf of its clients." In no time, she developed something of a Midas touch when it came to governance issues. It was her expertise in managing matters of fairness, transparency, and accountability that captured Hewlett-Packard CEO Lewis Platt's attention when he invited Dunn to join the board in 1998. "Lew wanted to add new independent voices and further diversity to the board," she recalls.

Although Dunn had risen to the rarified upper ranks of the male-dominated finance world, California's Silicon Valley presented new challenges—and problems. One of America's technology behemoths, Hewlett-Packard was the by-product of the creative genius of its legendary pioneers, William Hewlett and David Packard. As in most high-tech companies, the Palo Alto-based enterprise had developed very specific business models that required highly specialized knowledge. Relying on their technical talents, the co-founders successfully led the firm through the era of mainframe computers, calculators, and oscilloscopes. Their acumen, longevity, and integrity stood in sharp rebuke to the competition.

But a ship in the technology world eventually encounters rough seas. In the age of laptops, wi-fi, and the World Wide Web, tricky currents need to be navigated, and industry experience and technical know-how are even more highly valued.

Besides the techies, Northern California's other undisputed kings are the master dealmakers. "The miracle of Silicon Valley is that it is a system finely calibrated to spit out new companies—some of which have come to be worth hundreds of millions, if not billions, and within a few years' time," explains Gary Rivlin, who covers high-tech for *The New York Times* and authored *The Plot to Get Bill Gates*. "Other locales have elite universities on a par with Stanford and Berkeley. The entrepreneurially inclined and brilliantly visionary can be found all around the world. But what distinguishes Silicon Valley from everywhere else is that it alone has Sand Hill Road, the Wall Street of Venture Capital."

Little did Dunn know that her lack of technical expertise and access to the Medici of the Valley would eventually contribute to her undoing. For years, the Hewlett-Packard board had relied heavily on the outsized egos and industry knowledge of its longest-serving members, George A. (Jay) Keyworth and Thomas J. Perkins. Both men had been close to the founders and were deeply entrenched in "the HP way." Keyworth, a nuclear physicist, had run the physics division at the Los Alamos National Laboratory and, as the President's Science Adviser in the Reagan Administration, was a principal architect of Reagan's "Star Wars" nuclear-missile-defense-shield program. His ally Perkins co-founded the famed venture capital firm Kleiner Perkins Caufield & Byers—funding such nascent companies as Genentech, Amazon, Netscape, and Google. His high-tech home runs made him a prince of Silicon Valley and a millionaire roughly 500 times over. Among his rich-guy goodies: a Norman-style mansion in Belvedere in the Bay Area, a medieval castle in England, and the world's largest private yacht, the 289-foot, $150 million *Maltese Falcon*.

The foxhole camaraderie of these heavy-hitters was most visibly on display in HP's Technology Committee, which evaluated new product development, competitive strategies and corporate priorities—as well as the strengths and weaknesses of top management. Although other board members were invited to attend these sessions, which typically took place the day before formal board meetings, nontechies frequently found themselves overwhelmed with the intricacies of the rapidly changing high-tech world. As a result, the committee effectively acted as a "board-within-the-board" and "held extraordinary power within the company," the *New Yorker's* James Stewart reported.

Enter Pattie Dunn. She was an outsider in every imaginable way— a successful female in a male-dominated culture; a financial expert in a company that worshiped engineers; a San Franciscan isolated from

Silicon Valley lifers. She soon discovered that HP, the one-time bastion of high technology, was deeply flawed. Besides a fractious board, the company lacked a comprehensive strategy and had a stultifying culture that was embalmed in tradition.

Seeking a transformational leader, the Hewlett-Packard board recruited Carly Fiorina, an executive at Lucent Technologies and AT&T, as president and CEO in 1999—only a year before the technology industry began its collapse. Fiorina, the first CEO not promoted from within, quickly sensed the need to change the culture—"the principal reason for its underperformance. Time had stood still for the people of HP," she claimed. "They did not know how to move forward without their founders. They were afraid of change."

With her doggedness and exceptional public relations skills, Fiorina began to stem the losses of HP's personal computer business, while aggressively cutting costs. In her boldest move, she convinced the board to acquire rival Compaq Computer in 2001. Although the $19 billion acquisition proved successful, the next few years saw a precipitous drop in Hewlett-Packard's shares—calling into question Fiorina's ability to run the sprawling enterprise.

In January 2005, Dunn and Keyworth had become concerned that Fiorina's strengths were not in sync with the company's needs. Three days before a scheduled board retreat, they voiced their dissatisfaction with HP's performance, share price, and organizational structure. Keyworth, in particular, "seemed more and more impatient with me as I rejected many of his suggestions," Fiorina later wrote. At the top of his list was the need to invite the return of the entrepreneurial Perkins, who had retired from the board at age seventy.

Although Fiorina informed Perkins that under S.E.C. guidelines, his nomination could not be considered until later in the year, she invited him to the strategic retreat. "Perkins immediately began to play an active role in the special session," Fiorina wrote in *Tough Choices*, her autobiography. "This was a man who had very strong opinions about everything from personnel to acquisitions [despite having been off the board for almost three years]." As for Keyworth, he "concurred vigorously with each of Tom's suggestions."

A few days after the retreat, Fiorina learned that the *Wall Street Journal* was going to report a detailed story about the sessions, including Perkins' return to the board and the alleged dissatisfaction with her leadership. "It is hard to convey how violated I felt," the shell-shocked CEO wrote of the leaks. "Until a board makes a decision, its deliberations are confidential. Whoever had done this had broken a bond of trust with me and every other board member. Trust is a business imperative. No board or management team can operate effectively without it."

Furious, Fiorina laid down the law to board members: The leaks had to stop. In addition, she asked the firm's outside counsel, Lawrence Sonsini, to conduct an investigation to identify the leaker and also to evaluate the board. After considerable sleuthing, Sonsini, one of the most sought-after lawyers in Silicon Valley, found no direct evidence that any board member had been the source of the leak. As for the directors' performance, Sonsini identified numerous weaknesses—describing the HP board as "dysfunctional."

Nevertheless, Fiorina was convinced that the strong-willed Perkins and his soulmate, Keyworth, were the leakers. "Everyone knew that both Tom and Jay were the sources," Fiorina told the *New Yorker*. "They were allies. They were the ones pushing for the reorganization described in the article. It was clear and unequivocal that this was unacceptable behavior. They didn't like that."

During the following months, Perkins's and Keyworth's styles and priorities continued to clash with the high-profile Fiorina. Whether it was over potential board members or more stringent boardroom protocols (since the 2002 passage of the Sarbanes-Oxley bill, also known as the Public Company Accounting Reform and Investor Protection Act), managing emotions became increasingly difficult. Everything was rotten in Palo Alto, as backbiting, mistrust, and loathing began to distance Fiorina from her directors. Unbeknownst to her, a behind-the-scenes power play was in progress that called into question who was really running the company.

At the same time, Hewlett-Packard was experiencing slowing sales, shrinking market share, a painful exodus of top employees, and doses of bad financial news. Despite their differences, most directors agreed that the company needed a more risk-averse leader to focus on cost controls, investment returns, and improved stock performance. They then asked Dunn to deliver the coup de grâce.

On February 7, 2005, she and fellow director Robert Knowling ousted Fiorina in a meeting that reportedly lasted less than three minutes. Although Dunn offered her the option of saying that "it was time to move on," Fiorina refused to sugarcoat the announcement, saying, "We should tell the truth: The Board has fired me."

To manage the transition, the board appointed Dunn non-executive chairman, with Robert Wayman, HP's long-serving chief financial officer, as interim CEO. As non-executive chair, Pattie had overriding responsibility for the company's activities, but with extremely limited authority. She had no direct reports, no budget, and no access to company resources without the approval of the appropriate parties. Any initiatives had to be implemented by management. This seemingly powerless role—although prevalent in many European companies—is rare in corporate America. Its duties primarily involve presiding over board meetings, recommending board committees, and consulting with the chief executive (who reports to the entire board, not the non-executive chair).

Dunn's appointment would lead to one of the bloodiest, most cutthroat board clashes in history. In the post-Enron, post-WorldCom environment, being a director had become increasingly hazardous. However, being a non-executive chairman (I've been one)—with its murky responsibilities and limited authorities—carried even higher risks. And greater risks were not something Dunn needed.

In September 2001, she had been diagnosed with bilateral breast cancer, followed by melanoma the next year. Her medical treatments forced her resignation from Barclays Global Investors in 2002, while she kept her seat on the Hewlett-Packard board. In 2004, she was further diagnosed with stage four ovarian cancer—requiring major surgery and eighteen months of chemotherapy. The threat of death seemed only to reinvigorate the ever-resilient Dunn. From her humble beginnings, she had always weathered very difficult periods. But little did she know that her new duties at HP would unleash a personal nightmare and leave her in near disgrace.

Back in 2005, Chairman Dunn's brief seemed straightforward: Identify a new chief executive and halt the board leaks. After a tumultuous period, the board seemed to be settling down. The affable Dunn was able to co-exist with the idiosyncratic Perkins and Keyworth—teaming up with them to lure Mark V. Hurd, a twenty-five-year veteran of another old-line technology firm, NCR, to HP. She considers her close involvement in hiring him one of her proudest accomplishments at the computer-maker. "Dunn, Perkins, and Keyworth were pleased that they had worked together so effectively," wrote James Stewart. "But any expectations that the Hewlett-Packard board had started on a new era of goodwill were premature."

In many respects, it was a crisis that never should have happened. But as a governance perfectionist, Chairman Dunn knew that boardroom protocols were critical for directors in the new Sarbanes-Oxley world. Among other things, she suggested that they take training courses and engage in self-evaluations—recommendations the Perkins-Keyworth duo felt were unnecessary. Besides rejecting her efforts to modernize the workings of the board, the high-tech heavyweights particularly pooh-poohed her zeal in halting future leaks.

Confronting corporate devils is not without risks. But, with the support of most HP directors, Dunn turned to identifying the sources of earlier leaks. This required tricky navigating. For counsel, she turned to acting CEO and HP CFO Wayman, who referred her, in turn, to security manager Kevin Huska. He passed her over to Ronald Delia, whose Boston-based Security Outsourcing Solutions firm had been under contract to Hewlett-Packard for ten years. Security Outsourcing, in turn, routinely contracted out work to private investigators, who often accessed private phone records.

During the first phase of the investigation, called Project Kona for her vacation home on Hawai'i's Big Island, Dunn maintained intermittent contact with Delia, providing him background that she considered appropriate to run the probe. Delia, for his part, assured her that everything (including access to phone records) was proper, legal, and in full compliance with HP's normal practices. Dunn also advised the board at its March meeting and CEO Hurd on April 1, 2005, that, in response to the directors' concerns, a leak investigation was under way. Later that spring, Hurd told his senior managers that anyone discovered disclosing corporate information would be fired.

If anything, Dunn was even more insistent on the sanctity of board materials. In a subsequent congressional subcommittee, she testified: "The most fundamental duties of a director—the duties of deliberation and candor—rely entirely upon the absolute trust that each director must have all the others' confidentiality. This is true for trivial as well as important matters, because even trivial information that finds its way from the boardroom to the press corrodes trust among directors. It is even more critical when discussions can affect stock prices. Leaking 'good' information is as unacceptable as leaking 'bad' information—no one can foretell how such information may advantage or disadvantage one investor relative to another."

During the summer of 2005, Delia revealed to Dunn and Ann Baskins, Hewlett-Packard's general counsel, that he had obtained private phone records of not only directors but also reporters allegedly on the receiving end of inside information. Later, he contended that he also told them that he was using something called "pretexting," where phone records are retrieved by subterfuge and pretense—where someone calls the phone company and pretends to be someone else in order to obtain the records. When pressed by both women about whether this process was legal, he told them he "was aware of no laws that made pretexting illegal and no criminal prosecutions for such activities." A few days later, Delia reaffirmed to HP security officials that pretexting was not illegal.

Despite the rigorous hunt to smoke out the source of the scuttlebutt, Project Kona proved inconclusive and was dropped in August. With Hurd spending his time running the company, chairman Dunn resumed her efforts to mediate boardroom squabbles. Her primary antagonists, Perkins and Keyworth, however, continued to aggressively challenge her focus on corporate governance, labeling her a nitpicker more interested in process than big-picture issues. "It was known around the Valley that Tom and Jay wanted to get rid of Dunn," Fiorina later reported.

"Tom's view of corporate governance is that a few people—he and Jay—should make the decisions and everyone else is a spear-carrier,"

Dunn told me at her Kona retreat. "I was supposed to be his puppet." She would have none of it. In January 2006, Dunn launched into attack mode again when the online technology site CNET published an article about Hewlett-Packard's long-term strategy. Although the piece seemed relatively innocuous, it quoted an anonymous source and contained materials that could have come only from a director. Dunn immediately authorized Kona II, a full-scale investigation to determine the leaker's identity.

With no authority to direct or fund the investigation, the non-executive chair turned again to HP counsel Baskins, suggesting that Kroll, a leading corporate intelligence agency, be retained. Baskins, however, opted to conduct the probe internally and assigned the task to her direct report, Kevin Hunsaker, an employment lawyer at the firm. Under Hunsaker's direction, established company protocols similar to Kona I were used: heavy reliance on contracted security experts who recruited private investigators, who again employed the questionable tactic of spying on the phone records of all the directors, including Dunn, as well as employees and journalists.

As the cloak-and-dagger operation pressed on, two HP security officials questioned the legality of the process with Hunsaker, who agreed to seek the opinion of outside counsel. That report, relayed to Baskins, concluded that the practice of pretexting was "not unlawful." It remains unclear exactly how much Dunn knew of these tactics, but, acting on the advice of company attorneys, she remained "fully convinced that HP would never engage in anything illegal." On March 11, 2005, Hunsaker issued his first draft report of Kona II to Dunn, Hurd, and Baskins. The report re-emphasized the lawful nature of the investigations and, based on phone records, concluded that Keyworth, HP's longest-serving director, was the culprit. Separately, Hurd met with the sixty-six-year-old physicist in an attempt to get him to admit to his culpability—with no luck.

Next, Dunn approached Keyworth's foxhole-mate, Perkins, who had fully supported the board's earlier efforts to ferret out the leaker. "Tom was the most hawkish of the board for plugging the leaks," she says. "He thought they were coming from management." But when informed of Keyworth's role, Perkins backpedaled big-time, urging Dunn not to reveal the identity of the informant. Instead, he argued that he and Dunn should seek a confession—with the assurance that there would be no further leaks—and inform the board that the matter was closed.

Uncomfortable with this approach, Dunn sought the advice of outside counsel Sonsini, as well as Hurd, Baskins, and Audit Committee Chair Robert Ryan. At this meeting, both Baskins and Sonsini concluded that any "behind the scenes" process was improper and that the matter should receive full board attention. Dunn agreed to so advise Perkins just before the regular May board meeting. Concurrently, Ryan would meet with Keyworth to inform him of the investigation's results.

When Ryan sat down with Keyworth, the evening before the May 18 board meeting, he produced a summary of Hunsaker's findings. The bewildered director admitted his contact with the reporters and then said: "Why didn't you just ask me?" When informed of this, Dunn said: "All of us were flummoxed by his response, as it was clear to us all that—for the prior fifteen months—Keyworth could have come forward at any time to acknowledge his culpability."

The following day, Dunn broke the bad news to Perkins. "I'm sorry that it's come to this," he said, according to Dunn. "It's very unfortunate. . . . Pattie, you had no choice but to do this investigation. It's too bad Jay has created this problem."

However, the upcoming board meeting started a mini-Armageddon between Perkins and the resolute chairman, in which Dunn would be the victim. Item one on the agenda was the Hunsaker report, with Keyworth identified as the source of the leaks. The deflated director acknowledged his involvement, but refused to resign. Threatened by the loss of his crony, Perkins railed at Dunn: "You and I had an agreement," he shouted, "that if we found out who did this, we would handle it offline without disclosing the name of the leaker."

Dunn emphatically denies any such arrangement. A secret written vote was conducted—and passed, calling for Keyworth's resignation. At that point Perkins said: "I'm resigning. I'll not be party to this." He stalked out of the room. The board then voted to accept Perkins' resignation, and Dunn proceeded to ask Keyworth to step down. Once again, he refused, arguing that the board had overreacted to a relatively minor offense.

After the tempestuous sessions in Palo Alto, Perkins received a call from Sonsini, the most powerful lawyer in Silicon Valley, asking him for the reasons for his resignation. Under S.E.C. guidelines, a company must disclose director resignations and, if material, any disagreements with the company or the board. Perkins responded that his issues were not with HP, but with Dunn because she "betrayed" him. The investigation, he charged, was "a Pattie Dunn program, 100 percent." Consequently, the company announced Perkins' departure in a perfunctory press release, with no hint of boardroom turmoil.

Meanwhile, the feisty venture capitalist stewed. That weekend, he was off to the Romantic Times Book Lovers annual convention in south Florida to launch his novel, *Sex and the Single Zillionaire*, with several ladies getting a chance to have dinner with the über-rich bachelor. From Daytona Beach, he flew to Istanbul, where his superyacht, after five years of construction, was ready for sea trials. Despite these diversions, he continued to fume about his resignation and fired off a stream of e-mails to Dunn, other HP board members, CEO Hurd, and attorney Sonsini—demanding that the company's initial S.E.C. filing, which included the minutes of the May board meeting, be amended to reflect his contention that pretexting was not only inappropriate, but illegal.

Sonsini responded, saying that "pretext calls" were "a common investigatory method" and "that the process was well done and within legal limits." He was the third attorney representing Hewlett-Packard who, when asked about the legality of surreptitiously obtaining private phone records, opined that it was legal. Nonetheless, in an abundance of caution, the company later amended its earlier S.E.C. filing—laying out the use of pretexting for public consumption, but refusing to alter the May board minutes as Perkins had requested.

Dunn's chief antagonist was far from satisfied: He wanted her scalp. In rapid fashion, Perkins blew the whistle to anyone prepared to listen, including a phalanx of federal and state officials. "It was part of the take-no-prisoners attitude he had used in venture capital and in his personal affairs," wrote David A. Kaplan, author of *Mine's Bigger*, a description of Perkins' mega-yacht. By September 2006, the seventy-four-year-old entrepreneur, often described as confident to the edge of arrogant, had ignited a firestorm of media attention, placing Dunn at the center of the spying scandal. From various press reports, she was the mastermind of a nefarious witch-hunt. *Newsweek*, in fact, put her on the cover as "The Boss Who Spied on Her Board."

"I was outraged," Dunn told me. "The idea that I supervised, orchestrated, approved all the ways in which this investigation occurred is just a complete myth. It's a falsehood—a damaging lie." Perkins, she alleges, had portrayed her as a vicious spymonger. "It was a classic disinformation campaign. If you have enough money and you're willing to spend enough, you can buy and sell somebody's reputation."

Maybe Dunn could have handled the situation better. But if she expected support from her board, she was mistaken. Pattie Dunn had emerged at the center of a national debate over privacy. "It sounds like Watergate," said Charles Wolf, a financial analyst at Needham & Co. "It's HP gate." As a leading vendor of personal computers in the United States, Hewlett-Packard couldn't afford to suffer from the perception that it didn't put the highest priority on protecting personal information; nor could it afford to lose CEO Hurd, who was almost derailed by disclosures to *Business Week.*

To restore customer confidence, employee morale, and managerial continuity, HP directors began to distance themselves from Dunn—and, on September 22, accepted her resignation. Hurd, however, embraced her as did every other board member, murmuring, "This is so unfair. We're sorry. Thank you." The outgoing chairman recalls: "I left the board with good feelings, embraces and clear messages from each director that they regretted that this happened to me."

What was especially humiliating, though, was the velvet-glove treatment the company extended to Keyworth and Perkins. In a news release, Hurd applauded Keyworth, "who leaves the board with our best wishes and gratitude." Noting that Perkins had been with HP for fifty years, the CEO apologized "for the intrusion into his privacy" and thanked him "for his service and dedication to our company." The computer-maker also agreed to reimburse the twosome's legal fees and not disparage them. "I was horrified," Dunn said, when informed of the company's action.

Her storybook career would take a further hit on October 4, when she was charged by the California Attorney General with four felonies: fraudulent wire communications, wrongful use of computer data, identity theft, and conspiracy. As she and her legal team mounted an aggressive counterpunch, Dunn had begun chemotherapy for advanced ovarian cancer. One of corporate America's most prominent women was not just fighting for her reputation, she was now also fighting for her life.

"Fall seven times, stand up eight," goes a Japanese proverb. The resilient fighter would win Round One. On March 15, 2007, a California judge dismissed all charges "in the interest of justice." "She received the benefit of advice that what was being done was perfectly legal," explained her attorney, James J. Brosnahan. "She never had the slightest criminal intent." Noting that pretexting laws were in flux at the time of the alleged offense, he added, "The law was shifting and changing. This resolution recognizes they may have gotten caught up in a changing legal landscape."

In a prepared statement, the fifty-six-year-old former chairman said, "I am pleased that this matter has been resolved fairly, and want to express my gratitude to my husband and family, who never lost faith in me throughout this ordeal." Yet, she was not totally out of the woods. In August, a group of reporters who were pretexted and their family members filed civil charges against her and the company. In addition, federal investigators were looking into the spying incidents.

The news of the dismissed charges came hours before Hewlett-Packard convened its annual shareholder meeting in Santa Clara, California. It was the first time that CEO Hurd had faced investors since being named chairman, after Dunn's departure from the board. Besides acknowledging that he "should have been able to catch [the problem]," he admitted, "I didn't. The buck stops with me. Let me assure you that no one is proud of what happened last year. We need to transform our board the same way we transformed the company."

By most measures, Hewlett-Packard has been performing well under Hurd. Today, the company is the biggest tech company on earth, with more than $100 billion in sales. Hurd has injected a simple formula for success: squeeze costs and improve efficiency while delivering innovation that customers want. He and the new board seem galvanized to guide the company into the future.

In Silicon Valley, as in life, there are rarely second acts. Keyworth, for his part, left HP under a cloud—an ignominious way to end a thirty-year run. He feels that the allegations that he leaked confidential company information have caused him irreversible harm. By contrast, Perkins seemed bathed in schadenfreude, delighted with Dunn's misfortune. He wanted her scalp—and he got it. "Yet even with his evident triumph," writes Kaplan, "Perkins came to wonder if he had overreacted in the HP matter. . . . Had he sacrificed his position in favor of principle or had he indulged in a fit of pique? . . . In the end, did he conclude he'd made the right call in going to war with Dunn? It was impossible to tell. Depending on his mood, he might answer either way."

The year off gave Pattie Dunn time to restore her reputation and her health. She had plenty of time to ponder that mistakes were made—mistakes clearly shared by others, for which she alone accepted responsibility "for the good of the company." Understandably, she has no desire to rehash history other than to reassert her regret that "inappropriate techniques" were used in the investigation, adding: "I could have done things better." Yet, at every step of the way, she acted on behalf of the board, heeding the advice of three different legal teams and supposed experts in these matters. Chairman Hurd and her fellow board members, she points out, "got the same legal advice I did."

None of this, of course, excuses Dunn—nor the HP board or management—for failing to heed red flags that the investigation was moving into unethical and potentially illegal territory. Nonetheless, most legal and ethical experts who examined the case against her seriously questioned its merits. Dunn's partisans, of which there were many, argued that, while she may have displayed poor judgment in handling the inquiry, she did not act to enrich herself or defraud investors.

"I think this is small potatoes compared to the substantial frauds at Enron, WorldCom, Tyco, and others," said Kirk Hanson, executive director of the Markkula Center for Applied Ethics at Santa Clara University. "This is a case of an overreaction to an ethics problem and, in that reaction, both the investigators and the HP officials failed to ask critical questions about the investigative techniques." What is more, subsequent straw polls of CEOs and public-company directors indicated that roughly 90 percent of them would have pursued a similar strategy in uncovering a potential leaker.

Dunn, for her part, acknowledges two fundamental missteps. First, she badly underestimated the onslaught of bad press and the toll it would take on her and the company. "The media's rush to judgment always carried a negative or hostile slant," she says. "I had no idea the impact would be so fast and so damaging." Second, and more important, she also underestimated the collective clout of Keyworth and, especially, Perkins. "I was naïve," she concedes. "I should have known better. Perkins wasn't going to cede or share power with me. He wanted me off the board. But I don't know if he ever thought through the consequences that would go beyond getting me off the board."

Looking back, Dunn believes the HP soap opera was a "'one-off' [incident], certainly not emblematic of corporate governance in our country." To avoid similar missteps, she has encouraged Congress to provide a "bright line" in the law to give companies clearer guidance for conducting routine investigations, while protecting individual privacy.

Tooling around the island of Hawai'i's swanky Hualalai resort on a golf cart, Dunn reflected on the HP scandal and her recovery. "The old saw that a reputation made over a lifetime can be ruined in minutes has a sickening resonance for me," she said. "As a stickler for the sanctity of the boardroom, it pains me that this fiasco unfolded in an area where I dedicated my career." On the positive side, she conceded that the HP imbroglio was "a learning lesson—but definitely not one I'd ever want to have again."

"Women are like teabags," Eleanor Roosevelt once said. "We don't know our true strength until we are in hot water." Instead of wallowing in self-pity, Dunn has been turning adversity into advantage. While she may never capture her former glory, she understands that fame can be a fickle friend. She's not interested in the corporate world anymore, although she has received some boardroom overtures. "For now," she says, "my top priorities are family and health."

Only a week after our visit, Dunn learned she had a recurrence of ovarian cancer. In August 2007, she underwent a seven-hour surgery, followed by more chemotherapy and radiation. Yet, she remained amazingly upbeat. "I'm almost fully recovered and I feel really good," she told me. "Even more exciting, I'm helping to organize and will be participating in a dendritic vaccine trial at the University of Pennsylvania that holds great promise in immunotherapy for cancer treatment." Subsequently, former colleagues at Barclays Global Investors raised $500,000 to support this research (as well as Dunn's other causes). Last year, Dunn completed her treatments "with some encouraging results."

"Anything's possible," wrote Lance Armstrong, another cancer survivor and high-profile crusader to raise cancer awareness. "You have to be told you have a ninety percent chance or a fifty percent chance or a one percent chance, but you have to believe, and you have to fight." With a disease where life expectancy is measured in months, not years, and where patients are advised to get their finances in order, the spunky Dunn hasn't lost an ounce of the drive that made her famous.

Dunn's sister, Debbie Lammers, says that grit was forged in Pattie's early years. "What we've been through since we were small children has put her in good stead to deal with the current circumstances," explains the Colorado-based Lammers, who talks to Dunn almost every day. "She is determined, she is focused, and she is steady."

The odd thing about near-death experiences is that they often offer a new lease on life, in every respect. For Dunn, that involves heavy doses of family bonding at her designer homes in northern California and Hawai'i, and at her Shiraz vineyard in Australia's Barossa Valley ("a place time forgot," she says). Last fall, she co-taught a new course on, of all things, corporate politics at the University of California's Haas School of Business. Additionally, she serves on the boards of the Haas School, UC San Francisco's Cancer Center, and the San Francisco Symphony.

Motivated no doubt by her health battles, she is also a major supporter of the Charlotte Maxwell Complementary Clinic, based in Oakland and San Francisco, which offers medical assistance to low income and indigent women with cancer. Perhaps her strongest ties, however, are with Larkin Street Youth Services in San Francisco. The twenty-four-year-old organization helps young people who, like Pattie, were dealt a bad hand. It assists 2,000 homeless kids each year through nineteen varied programs. Besides serving as a director and member of the executive committee, Dunn and her husband Bill are the organization's biggest donors and fund-raisers extraordinaire.

Fallen heroes rarely make it back to the top. Having reached the summit of corporate America a few years ago, Dunn was cast down the mountain. However, no one who relishes challenges as much as she does stays down for long. This courageous woman, who has defeated cancer four times, is engaged in yet another difficult period of rehabilitation. As she fights her way back to the top, the climb is hardly over.

"We know there are very tough times ahead," says Lammers. "Some of these problems—her health and remnants of the HP fiasco—aren't going to go away easily. But if anyone can deal with them, it's Pattie. It's Pattie being Pattie."

10

STEVE CASE:
Second Act

Far better it is to dare mighty things, to win
glorious triumphs, even though checkered by
failure, than to take rank with those poor
spirits who neither enjoy much nor suffer
much, because they live in the gray twilight
that knows not victory nor defeat.

—THEODORE ROOSEVELT

© REVOLUTION

Technology Titan Steve Case rebounded from the ill-fated AOL Time Warner merger to lead another revolution in an eclectic array of New Age ventures.

IN THE 1930s, F. Scott Fitzgerald, who knew about dark hours, said: "There are no second acts in American lives." As with many of our examples, Steve Case is another exception. Less than a decade ago, he stood at the pinnacle of America's media, entertainment, and communications world. In January 2000, the technology titan who gave millions of Americans their first taste of the Internet, had hammered out AOL's $350 billion merger with Time Warner. But, just three years later, he acknowledged the megamerger had turned disastrous, suggesting that the best option was to "liberate the disparate businesses and let them compete on their own." Shortly thereafter, he stepped down as chairman.

Rather than live in self-imposed exile, Case, who had built his career as a high-tech visionary, would start anew. Within days of his darkest hour, the self-described "serial entrepreneur" launched a comeback, throwing himself into an eclectic array of early-stage ventures. They included health and wellness companies, a car-sharing service, luxury eco-resorts in Arizona and Costa Rica, an online money exchange, and massive landholdings in his native home of Hawai'i.

The fifty-one-year-old Internet icon is well aware of the looming risks, especially as the economy continues to cool. Today, he continues to defy the odds, betting much of his personal net worth on these high-stakes ventures. "Maybe ten years from now, we'll be a horrible failure," he says. "But I'm willing to put my money where my mouth is."

Stephen McDonnell Case sharpened his skills at creating bold initiatives at an early age. Growing up in a close-knit, upper-middle-class family in Honolulu, he began his commercial career at age six, when he and his older brother Dan set up a juice stand using limes from the backyard, selling a cup for 2 cents. Not long after, they formed Case Enterprises, which sold seeds and greeting cards through the mail or door-to-door. "While other kids played tag, we played business," he says. "I was on a path to be an entrepreneur, and I think everybody in my family sensed it."

As a youngster, he attended Punahou School, a palm-lined, fifteen-acre citadel of academic excellence. Founded in 1841, it is the largest single independent school in the United States and the oldest in the country west of the Mississippi. A feeder school to the nation's leading universities, its graduates (including Barack Obama, class of '79) typically quicken the pulses of college admissions officers. Although a good student at Punahou, Case was primarily interested in "trying to figure out what businesses to start."

He took his entrepreneurial bent to prestigious Williams College in western Massachusetts. In addition to selling fruit baskets, the avid music fan wrote rock reviews for local papers to get free concert tickets and albums. He also helped book bands and served as lead singer in two new-wave rock groups, while studying political science ("the closest thing to business that Williams offered").

The 1980 college grad began a marketing career with Cincinnati-based consumer-products powerhouse Procter & Gamble, where he worked on hair care products. Two years later, he took his talents to Pizza Hut in Wichita, Kansas, developing new products for the then PepsiCo-owned subsidiary. Although both experiences taught him the importance of making the consumer the centerpiece of any successful business venture, he concluded that "managing a mature business was not my thing."

It was Dan Case who, in 1982, helped him get a job at the company that eventually became America Online. A successful investment banker at Hambrecht & Quist in San Francisco, Dan had helped finance Control Video Corp., a start-up based in northern Virginia. The company created a service that enabled consumers to download video games over phone lines—but just as it was introducing the GameLine service, the Atari market imploded and the company found itself on the brink of bankruptcy. Case, however, hung on and, in 1985, with the remnants of

Control Video, helped found Quantum Computer Services, an online services provider. That year, the new company struck a deal with Commodore, and soon thereafter with Tandy, IBM, and Apple.

"It was a very pragmatic strategy of partnering with companies that already had brand recognition, distribution, and a large customer base," Case recalls. This worked for a while, but the partnerships didn't last—by the late 1980s, companies like Apple decided instead to launch their own competing online services.

Undeterred, Case pressed on, but lessened Quantum's dependence on partnerships. "We've got to figure out a way to be successful on our own two feet," he said at the time. Although walking away from these alliances meant "taking on more risks, we felt we had to do it." In 1991, as president, he literally began moving thousands of Americans online. He renamed the firm America Online Inc. Back then, America Online (which soon became known by its members as AOL) had only 100,000 users and lagged behind competitors CompuServe and Prodigy.

Believing that the Internet would have mass appeal if it became easier to use, Case pushed for a "simpler, friendlier, more personal approach to online service." Attaching voice to AOL software, users began hearing the familiar greeting: "You've got mail." By 1992, the company had 200,000 customers. That year, AOL went public, raising $23 million. A year later, Case, as chief executive officer, launched a breakout strategy—sending millions of free AOL disks in magazines or via direct mail. Membership exploded, cracking the 1 million mark in 1994. In 1995, AOL's message was exported to Germany and, later, Canada, France, and the United Kingdom. In addition, Case inked lucrative cross-marketing deals with AT&T, Apple, Sun Microsystems, Hewlett-Packard, and Netscape Communications.

Simplicity again underscored Case's strategy of offering user-friendly, goof-free service to build scale. "If you want to reach a mainstream audience, you have to make it more plug-and-pay," he told *Forbes* in a 1996 interview. "One-stop shopping. One disk to install. One price to pay. One customer number to call."

Although AOL was now attracting millions of subscribers, critics contended that it was dumbing down technology—derisively referring to its unintimidating approach to the Internet as the "K-Mart network." However, most knowledgeable observers of Case's keep-it-simple strategy marveled at the company's ability to mass-market online services. According to Dr. Eric Schmidt, chairman and CEO of Google, "The secret of Steve Case is that he has figured out a way to make consumers like their computers."

Managing, though, had become an issue. Explosive growth—approaching 10 million users—strapped the system. AOL experienced a host of growing pains: blackouts, busy signals, costly refunds, and overly aggressive accounting practices. To sort through the day-to-day demands and keep things under control, Case enlisted a talented co-leader, Robert Pittman, as president and chief operating officer, while he remained focused on charting the firm's strategy and dealmaking.

In 1998, the company purchased longtime rival CompuServe and, the following year, bought Netscape, becoming the largest and most significant player in the industry. AOL's subscriber base now stood at 17 million. In 2000, the firm began offering online access to wireless customers, after recognizing the increasing use of broadband technology. Instead of running from the Web, AOL embraced it.

"Suddenly the pieces started falling together," Case recalls. Rapid expansion and successful acquisitions had transformed the company from a struggling start-up to the dominant force in the Internet industry. In the process, Case had gained a reputation as a breakout visionary among America's high-tech icons.

"Go out on a limb," Will Rogers once suggested. "That's where the fruit is." To cement AOL's future as the leading Internet player, Case would venture out on a limb again.

Although the company, with 20 million users, was the most potent force in cyberspace, and the market value of AOL had skyrocketed from $65 million at the time of its 1992 IPO to more than $150 billion by late 1999, Case knew that he would have to take risks to insure its viability. One of AOL's major weaknesses was the growing competition of high-speed broadband services through cable and phone companies. In Time Warner, Case spotted a potential ally that owned one of the nation's largest cable systems providing broadband connectivity to homes. It also controlled the largest portfolio of branded content and television networks—and generated more than $30 billion in revenue, six times more than AOL's $5 billion. Using AOL's valuable stock (the market value of AOL was double that of Time Warner, despite the fact that Time Warner was six times larger), Case proposed a merger that would give AOL shareholders 55 percent of the combined company—and agreed to step down as CEO to seal the deal with Time Warner CEO Jerry Levin.

When the deal was announced in January 2000, pundits went crazy considering the wonderful possibilities that the synergy would bring: AOL's online reach and Time Warner's content. "We will fundamentally change the way people get information, communicate with others, buy products, and are entertained—providing far-reaching benefits to our customers and shareholders," Case said at the time.

Then reality set in. Shortly after the merger, the Internet bubble popped, sending financial markets reeling. AOL's dial-up base quickly eroded as more and more Americans adopted high-speed broadband services through cable and phone companies. In addition, the Securities and Exchange Commission launched an investigation for alleged accounting violations that cost the parent company $360 million in fines. Worse yet, the much-anticipated synergies between the two companies failed to materialize.

Regrettably, AOL Time Warner's highly publicized nose-dive coincided with Dan Case's fatal battle with brain cancer. In 2001, the elder Case, one of the nation's driving forces behind the financing of high-tech companies, was diagnosed with the dreaded disease. Almost immediately, Dan and Steve created Accelerate Brain Cancer Cure, a nonprofit group designed to spur research on treatments for the disease. Steve hoped the entity would seek out more information "so that other families got better answers and better experiences."

Fifteen months after his diagnosis, Dan Case died, at age forty-four. His brother's death, Steve says, "was harder to deal with than any criticism of the company. It helped keep things in perspective." Since then, he has continued to press on in the battle against brain cancer. "There are many more clinical trials than there used to be, involving brain-cancer treatment," Case reported to *Barron's*. Combining funding for both biotechnology businesses and nonprofit organizations "strikes me as the best way to come up with innovative ideas and increase the odds of having a significant impact."

By the end of 2001, AOL Time Warner had evolved into a fractious, indecisive media giant, a tangled web of competing interests. Simply put, the parts failed to gel. CEO Levin was ousted in November 2001, and in January 2003 Case opted to resign as chairman. Even though he never had operating responsibility for the merged company, Case concluded it would be best for him to step aside.

"I was the architect of the merger," Case told CNN, at the time of his resignation. "The company has not done well; it certainly has not done anything that anyone would have expected when we did the merger, so it's not surprising that the disappointment would be directed at me. Now it's time for me to move on."

Although he would remain on the board for almost three more years, Case later would cite "integration issues" as being largely responsible for the firm's calamitous fall from grace. "I dramatically underestimated the complexity of bringing these different people, these different cultures, almost different tribes, together," he admitted. Subsequently, he argued that Time Warner had "weighted AOL down," adding that "it would be best to 'undo' the merger by splitting Time Warner into several independent companies and allowing AOL to set off on its own path."

"Disappointments should be cremated, not embalmed," Henry Haskins once wrote. The man who had succeeded in bringing the Internet to the masses refused to allow the dark days to sully his image. Determined and thick-skinned, the deal-hardened executive wasn't about to sulk. "I feel proud of the twenty years I spent building AOL," he said. "It became the most important company on the Internet and helped usher in an era when interconnectivity is a part of daily life."

Within weeks of his departure as chairman, he came roaring back, diving into a series of entrepreneurial projects—largely financed with the stock sales he made since 1992, when AOL first went public. Over a barbecued chicken pizza lunch with former AOL executive Donn Davis in Washington, D.C., Case mused about a better way to accommodate well-heeled vacationers. During a Web search, he came across Denver-based Exclusive Resorts, a destination club that sold memberships that allowed travelers to spend up to forty-five nights a year at a growing list of luxury properties. Founded in 2002 by brothers Brad and Brent Handler, the company seemed like an attractive springboard for the growing number of upper-income families seeking more than a high-end hotel, but not wanting to buy an upscale vacation home.

After staying with his wife at an Exclusive Resorts property in Los Cabos, Mexico, Case bought 50 percent of the company, and a year later he increased his stake to 80 percent and installed Davis as CEO. "I like to enter a new market, a new area that resonates with consumers, gives consumers more choices, that has the potential to have a disruptive, transformative effect on an industry," he told me. "This has already created ripples in the hospitality real estate market."

Several months later, he became passionate about the possibilities in the burgeoning wellness and healthy-living sector and acquired a 95 percent interest in Miraval: Life In Balance, a spa and resort north of Tucson. Believing the $400 billion wellness industry could grow to $1 trillion by 2020, Case felt that Miraval had the potential to become the "Nike of wellness."

All of these initiatives were contemplated after serious deliberation. "Steve almost never does anything on the spur of the moment," says Miles Gilburne, a former AOL executive and current co-investor. "He's very methodical." Case carefully continued to assemble a collection of early-stage, consumer-oriented businesses—all designed, in his words, "to change the world." But these initial ventures were simply the building blocks for another bright triumph: a bold, new empire designed "to achieve transformative change by shifting power to consumers."

On April 4, 2005, Case launched Revolution, a privately held holding company that has since grown to include more than a dozen companies organized into five groups: Revolution Health, Revolution Places, Revolution Living, Revolution Money, and Revolution Digital. Promising to "swing for the fences," he positioned Revolution as a magnet for entrepreneurs with breakthrough ideas focused on empowering consumers and giving them more choice, control, and convenience in important aspects of their lives.

Case, of course, knows something about revolutions. Just as he made so many Americans into Netizens, he is equally passionate about making the consumer the centerpiece of "disruptive change," whether it be health care, financial services, resorts, or transportation.

No doubt, his earlier experiences with his brother's treatment motivated him to make a series of high-profile investments in health care. "Consumerism is going to become a driver in health care, which represents $2 trillion, or one-sixth of the economy. The sector, which everybody hates, is ripe for disruption, and the key disrupting force is consumers," Case says.

Trying to improve America's health-care system presents incredible challenges—and opportunities. Doctors, hospitals, employees, and insurers all operate with different imperatives—leading to rising costs (a 23 percent hike in the last two years), uneven quality, and millions of consumers uninsured. To complicate matters, health care in the United States is typically purchased in an institutional setting—by employers—but consumed by individuals. And the industry has been less than stellar in informing us how to get access to the system.

On the positive side, the growth of so-called "defined contribution" health-care accounts—health savings accounts, health reimbursement accounts, and special savings accounts, have allowed employers to make tax-efficient, fixed-dollar contributions to an employee's care, while leaving the employee in charge of spending those dollars. Ironically, Americans on the prowl for health coverage don't act like regular consumers. Seven out of every eight dollars spent is somebody else's money—the employer's. As a result, many employees choose more coverage than they need and pay more than they have to. And others choose less coverage than they need.

"Consumers feel disenfranchised," Case explains. "They feel like somebody else is making the decision." The solution, he says, is "to move the patient back to the center of the system with more choices, more convenience, more control."

The starting point is providing much more comprehensive news and treatment information—in effect, pulling the pieces together. "The data is available," says Aetna CEO Ron Williams, another leading advocate of health-care reform, who predicts that "there's going to be a huge transformation in this area."

To lead this transformation, Revolution Health introduced its patient-friendly Web portal in April 2007. RevolutionHealth.com helps patients locate doctors, schedule appointments, learn about their illnesses, and manage health-spending accounts—all online. Users can also create their own pages within RevolutionHealth.com for collecting personal and general information, which they can keep private or share with others. Entirely free to consumers, the business model gets most of its revenue from advertising; eventually, the subsidiary plans to sell services— but to employers, not employees.

Revolution Health isn't the only dog on this trail. Its portal, for example, competes with WebMD Health Corp., the descendant of WebMD Inc., which was founded in 1998. Other players include NIH.gov, from the National Institute of Health; Yahoo Health; Mayoclinic.com; and the *New York Times*–owned About.com.

Revolution's other medical forays include a stake in the expanding RediClinic chain, which operates clinics in Wal-Mart and other retail stores around the country; Extend Health, a rapidly growing company that implements defined contribution plans for some of the world's largest employers such as Ford; CarePages, an online service that supports communications between family and friends when someone is receiving care; and SparkPeople, a web-based community that helps people achieve diet, fitness, and lifestyle goals.

At last count, Case had bankrolled Revolution Health with more than $100 million. Other high-profile investors and board members include some, like Case, with past scars: Carly Fiorina, the former CEO of Hewlett-Packard; Franklin Raines, ex-top gun at tarnished Fannie Mae; and Steve Wiggins, the ousted former No. 1 at Oxford Health Plans. To the threesome, whom Case describes as "underleveraged assets," he added former Secretary of State Colin Powell and ex-Netscape CEO Jim Barksdale. These luminaries are helping Revolution Health's careful and deliberate ramp-up. "We plan to invest significantly," Case says. "It will take time to build the brand and build trust."

Case's Revolution Places division includes Exclusive Resorts, the company Case bought control of in 2003 in his first post–Time Warner move. Since then, Exclusive Resorts has sold more than $1 billion of club memberships and acquired nearly $2 billion of resort real estate in more than thirty-five destinations. Case is also driving the expansion of Miraval; what was a single resort in Arizona when he acquired control in 2004 is now expanding globally, including a recently opened condominium project in New York City. Case's latest undertaking is a large resort development in Costa Rica that he hopes will set new, redefined standards for luxury resorts by preserving local environments and indigenous cultures in beautiful locations around the world. Planned to open in 2010, the $800 million, 650-acre eco-resort, called Cacique, will include 120 villas, 330 other residences, a Miraval Spa, a Tom Doak eighteen-hole golf course, and an Agassi-Graf Tennis and Fitness Center.

The Revolution Living division focuses on sustainable businesses that are good for the planet as well as consumers. Revolution is the largest investor in Zipcar, a car-sharing company that allows people living in cities to use cars (mostly hybrids) owned by the club whenever they need them, without having to purchase or maintain them.

The Revolution Money subsidiary was created after Case observed traditional and online pay platforms charging consumers billions of dollars in fees. In 2007, he launched two game-changing products: Revolution Card, an anonymous PIN-protected credit card that generates significant consumer and merchant savings, and Revolution Money Exchange, the first free, person-to-person, online money-exchange service.

Another recent addition is Revolution Digital, launched in 2007 to invest in Internet businesses. The companies Case is backing include Clearspring, a leading widget software and services company, and Snag-Films, which provides Internet distribution of movies that matter, such as documentaries.

Case is ready to prove to the world that Revolution is a winning proposition. Relaxed and unassuming, he maintains a passionate belief in his life-changing portfolio, a mark of his entrepreneurial zeal. The notorious hard worker, who regularly logs sixteen-hour days, says that "changing the world isn't a part-time job."

The key to Case's strategy at Revolution is insuring that its seemingly disparate parts come together—a missing dimension at AOL Time Warner. "We actively encourage and manage cooperation among companies," he says. "Synergy done right allows business relationships to happen that otherwise would not. . . . Each Revolution company will amplify the overall success of all Revolution companies."

Challenges remain, no doubt. However, Case's fresh start at Revolution has re-energized the executive, who describes himself as a better builder than a manager. "This is my thing," he explains. "This is what I do. I'm having more fun than at anytime in the past five or ten years."

As Case works his magic in the nation's capital, his presence also looms large in his native Hawai'i, where he is the second-biggest private landowner on Kauai and Maui. In 2000, he purchased Kauai's Grove Farm Co. for $26 million. His grandfather had lived on the former sugar plantation and served as its treasurer until 1959; his father grew up on the property. Earlier, Case acquired a major stake in Maui Land and Pineapple Co., a century-old outfit and Hawai'i's largest pineapple producer. Both companies are developing fresh operating models for developing sustainable communities for residents and visitors.

In the end, however, Case's legacy may involve more than just a track record in business. Doing well by doing good has long been one of his favorite mantras. To change the world, he contends, "you have to use the whole tool box [profit, nonprofit, and hybrid approaches]." And he has been in the forefront of social entrepreneurship, drawing on the best practices from every sector.

At the twelve-year-old Case Foundation in Washington, Case and his wife, Jean, have pioneered unconventional approaches to philanthropy. In 2008, working with *Parade* magazine, they launched "America's Giving Challenge," an online initiative giving the public a direct role in deciding who should receive some of its money. The foundation asked individuals and small nonprofit groups to send ideas for improving their communities. After careful screening by independent judges, winners received up to $50,000.

The idea was "a way of using technology as a force for good," Case says. Giving the public a role in giving has won the praise of many in the philanthropic community. "These are relatively radical ideas in a world that is somewhat dominated by insiders and professionals," according to veteran foundation consultant Cynthia Gibson, in describing the Case Foundation's innovative approach. "At the very least, it can spur other philanthropic institutions to consider new ways of involving 'real people' in the decisions they make."

What's particularly exciting about Steve and Jean Case's campaign for social entrepreneurship is how timely it is. "Americans, in particular, are hungry for this kind of hybrid thinking," writes Alan Webber, founding editor of *Fast Company* magazine. "Americans want a new operation for making real change, one that runs like a business and delivers real help to needy people." Whether it's funding brain-cancer research, integrating technology in schools, or putting a human face on capitalism, the Case Foundation has a new idea for creating innovative solutions to difficult problems.

"A smooth sea never made a skilled mariner," goes an old English proverb. Philosophical about his experience at Time Warner, Steve Case has come roaring back in the world he savors, building a world-changing start-up. "I focus less on looking back and more on looking forward," he told me on a recent visit to his Washington, D.C., headquarters. "Rather than celebrating the past, why not embrace the future?"

In his new skin, Case remains optimistic. "We live in extraordinary times," he says. "Anything is possible, but it starts with having a dream and sticking with it through thick and thin." Act Two: a revolution that never ends.

11

STRATEGIES FOR
A BRIGHT TRIUMPH

Life is a promise; fulfill it.

—MOTHER TERESA

AT A TIME WHEN LIVING IN AMERICA resembles a roller-coaster ride on the way down, I hope our stories are instructive in offering suggestions on how we can overcome life's darkest hours. Today, untold numbers are living Thoreau's "lives of quiet desperation," without the drive to shift gears. Yet *anyone* can overcome tough times, not just the few who seem to soar effortlessly.

No doubt, choreographing these changes takes courage—the courage to take risks. As Walt Disney once put it: "Courage is the main quality of leadership—it implies some risks." Therefore, trumping a world turned dark and dangerous requires fearless commitment, with many stops and starts along the way. What then have we learned from these relentless bravehearts? Here are six lessons, exemplified by the individuals profiled in this book.

1. Learn From Adversity

"Success is going from failure to failure with no loss of enthusiasm," said Winston Churchill, whose life was littered with disappointments. The Last Lion, as William Manchester called him, was the dominant personality of the last century. He understood that setbacks are inevitable when we pursue a bright triumph. What set him apart was his incredible grit. To Churchill, anything was possible. Victory was always at hand. Remember his words at Harrow: "Never give in!" he told students. "Never give in, never, never, never never!"

Like Churchill, the folks we have profiled refused to equate the occasional setback with defeat. They expected some dry spells along the way. Recall that Gary Guller and Joanne Boyle refused to be debilitated by their brush with death. Guller returned to high-altitude climbing, while Boyle reemerged as one of the nation's most successful coaches.

The only person who never stumbles is the person who always plays it safe. Triumphant personalities understand that not everything is going to work. Overcoming those disappointments requires "a delicate balance of remembering and forgetting," says self-help author Rabbi Harold S. Kushner.

Fessing up helps. In shaping a comeback after her dark days at Hewlett-Packard, Carly Fiorina was asked if she felt responsible for the company's stagnant stock price in the years before her ouster. "Oh yeah," she said. "In some cases, I put the wrong person in the wrong job, or I didn't assess someone's capabilities properly." As we learned, her successor, Pattie Dunn, later acknowledged her own shortcomings for the pretexting scandal, admitting: "I could have done things better."

But there's a fine line between self-criticism and self-excoriation. Rather than overstating their deficiencies, resilient men and women don't wallow in the darkness. They accept adversity and move on. Although haunted by memories of his fatal collision with the *Ehime Maru*, submariner Scott Waddle eventually got over it, forging a new life as a motivational speaker. "A high failure, a catastrophic event, doesn't define you," he tells his audiences today. "Keep your character intact. That defines you as a person."

However, even when the stakes are high, the challenge should be winnable—not impossible. There definitely are hellholes out there, situations resembling what C. S. Lewis called "shadowlands," places of disappointment and faded dreams. Far too often, headstrong personalities make a Faustian bargain trying to right what is clearly a sinking ship. In the process, they give up everything. They lose touch with their spouses. They become strangers to their children. Friends drop away. In extreme cases, parents are lost and barely mourned. At some point, their obsessive ambition costs them soul and substance.

Look at the extraordinary beating Pattie Dunn, Scott Waddle, and Steve Case took in the press a few years ago. They discovered that you may be a hero one minute and a zero the next. Savvy people know when to sidestep disaster and walk away. So don't forsake your dreams: shift to those that are more manageable. Remember, in his rational moments, even Don Quixote recognized when he was tilting at windmills.

2. Fashion a New Dream

"Not failure, but low aim, is a crime," wrote poet, critic, and diplomat James Russell Lowell. Swim in bigger ponds. Set giant goals. Construct a grand vision of where you want to go and how you'll get there. You don't have to be superhuman to achieve a bright triumph. But you do have to imagine both your goals and the pathway to success.

"Aim for the stars," Shirley Ann Jackson's father told her at an early age. The message took. Her lofty ambitions led her to excel at M.I.T., Bell Labs, the Nuclear Regulatory Commission, and, more recently, Rensselaer Polytechnic Institute, where she transformed a sputtering university into a scientific and engineering powerhouse.

"Go confidently in the direction of your dreams. Live the life you've imagined," Henry David Thoreau advised. People like Dr. Jackson link their goals to life's big picture. They aim high.

Oftentimes, though, it's necessary to recalibrate your dreams. Corporate titans, for example, inevitably make mistakes, new competitors emerge, new technologies and consumer habits disrupt established practices in unseen ways. When things begin to spiral downward, successful folks make the appropriate corrections. The alternative to grime-encrusted lenses isn't rose-tinted glasses: It's a healthy dose of reality.

Fabled Marine Chesty Puller understood the need to dramatically change course. Against overwhelming hordes of Red Chinese regulars at the Chosin Reservoir, Puller's Leathernecks would find victory in retreat—"an attack in a different direction," the commander called it. "This was no retreat," Puller bellowed. "All that happened was that we found more Chinese behind us than in front of us. So we about-faced and attacked." No matter how one labels it, the Marines' perilous reversal highlights the importance of tweaking the game plan—in effect, fashioning a new dream.

Rediscovery will expand your world. As we have seen, winners cultivate the art of making themselves up as they go along. Scott Waddle and Gary Guller discovered happiness as motivational speakers. Highly accomplished attorney and business executive Joel Klein turned educator. World-class physicist Shirley Ann Jackson stepped up to become a university president. And Steve Case shifted his technology talents to health care and philanthropy.

3. Sell Your Vision

"A leader must be a dealer in hope," Confucius wrote. Those who can illuminate the darkness are experts at restoring people's faith in the future, especially the faith of talented people who have run into brick walls.

The golden core of leadership is the ability to raise aspirations. Transition is an ideal time to do so. Upon joining the laughing-stock Kansas State Wildcats in 1988, Bill Snyder immediately began his crusade to elevate his team's expectations. "The major task was to get youngsters to expect more out of themselves than they actually expected," he explains. In short order, he had them believing there were no limits to what they could do. By breathing life into this moribund program, Snyder fashioned the greatest turnaround in football history—transforming a perennial loser into a national championship contender, with average athletes who dared to dream big.

Our intrepid adventurers have a desire to confront the impossible, taking on assignments that nobody in their right minds would want. Ignoring the enormity of obstacles, people like Joel Klein, Shirley Ann Jackson, and Steve Case are unflagging optimists. In many respects, this special species of leaders is "delusional," according to veteran executive coach Marshall Goldsmith. "They are not as good as they think they are, but they have the confidence to pursue big things."

So tune out the cynics and second-guessers who say you can't beat the odds. Don't let pouting pessimists rob you from pursuing—and capturing—your dreams.

4. Share Your Dream

"We can do as partners what we cannot do as singles," Daniel Webster observed. Therefore, build alliances. New York Mayor Michael Bloomberg's recruitment of outsider Joel Klein as the head of the city's schools succeeded where a long line of predecessors had failed. The talented twosome used their close links to affluent New Yorkers to lure much-needed funds to their reform effort. These powerful allies, in turn, have been invaluable in helping turn around the Big Apple's long-troubled school system.

Keep good company. Create a brain trust. Connections are invaluable. Develop a cadre of knowledgeable people—mentors, peers, and friends—you can consult in tackling tough times. Here, trust is the coin of the realm. "Lean on someone you trust," says management expert Stephen Covey. "Good colleagues and mentors give you honest feedback about your failings. People who don't provide unearned praise will shake you out of your comfort zone. If you don't see the big picture, they can help you frame it."

The Marine Corps' storied history reflects this commitment to the team over the individual. Witness the escape from the Frozen Chosin. However, the planting of the American flag on Iwo Jima is perhaps the most famous image of Leatherneck valor. It captures the essence of the Marines' esprit de corps in a single frame—a faceless team of men struggling to achieve a larger goal. Indeed, two of the men have their backs turned to the camera, two are seen only from the side, and the fifth is hidden except for his arms and hands, which support the flag. There are no famous generals here, just five anonymous riflemen, winning a crucial battle in modern history.

Like the Marines, other organizations are creating their own co-leadership cultures. Look at Joanne Boyle's tactics in resuscitating the University of California's long-suffering women's basketball program. The plucky new coach quickly blended what had been two different and competing cultures: upperclassmen, who were mired in mediocrity, and talented freshmen, who lacked experience and discipline. Boyle got both groups to buy into the team concept, leading them to the school's first winning season in thirteen years. Our message: Share your dreams.

5. Focus, Focus, Focus

Make life as simple as possible. Focus on what you know you can do. Know what you're capable of on any given day, what you can count on. Do the simple things well, and then use that confidence to forge your own bright triumph. Learn to differentiate between what is truly important and what can be dealt with at another time.

Every organization has a distinctive culture, a set of mutual assumptions that governs how it operates. If you don't master it, you will be stymied at every turn. For example, an organization that goes by the book will not welcome your attempt to initiate reforms, no matter how superior. The group will perceive it as an affront to tradition, a crime against institutional memory. You must first understand the entity you want to overhaul. Failure to focus on the unwritten rules of the organization leads to frustration, bad decision-making, and, all too often, the creation of dangerous and unnecessary opposition. Nontechie Pattie Dunn learned these lessons in Silicon Valley the hard way. Although she conceded that the Hewlett-Packard boardroom imbroglio was "a learning lesson," it is definitely not one she would ever want to have again.

Similarly, Revolution's Steve Case refuses to get sidetracked. He believes zeroing in on the endgame has led to his success in business and beyond. "Anything is possible," he says, "but it all starts with having a dream and sticking with it through thick and thin." People like Case possess a tenacity that eludes those who wilt in the face of adversity. They don't let a few potholes in the road erode their confidence. They share a steadfast determination to secure a bright triumph.

Sacagawea exhibited the same grit on the Lewis and Clark expedition. For a year-and-a-half, she endured starvation and discomfort to help pioneer what was then unknown territory. Against all odds, the tenacious teenage mother helped Lewis and Clark unlock the spirit of the New West.

Resilient personalities are able to smile in the face of adversity. They enjoy the exhilaration of living dangerously, of taking on Everest-size challenges. As Harvard psychologist Erik Erikson reminds us, happiness depends on equal doses of work, love, and play. But choreographing those elements takes courage—the courage to change. Technology giant Case got his second wind enjoying life in his new digs at Revolution—tackling reform of America's much-maligned health-care industry. "This is my thing," he says. "I'm having more fun than at anytime in the past five or ten years."

6. Start Now

"In any moment of decision, the best thing you can do is the right thing; the next best thing is the wrong thing; and the worst thing you can do is nothing," said Theodore Roosevelt. Far too often we are unwilling to try something new because we fear the outcome. But the more you push your comfort zone, the easier it gets.

Let new ideas take root. Explore. Rattle hidebound thinking. Chuck yesterday's assumptions. Don't rely on what made you successful, but no longer works. The worst baggage we can carry is the baggage from a successful past.

Therefore, maintain a maverick mind-set. The trick is to learn to suspend what you do know to free yourself to discover what you don't know. Pattie Dunn morphed from a temporary secretary to financial superstar to Hewlett-Packard chairperson—all while battling cancer. Unbowed, she never stopped learning or moving forward.

But pace yourself. Quick fixes tend to end in tears. Think incrementally. Running psychologist Ethan Gologor says the biggest mistake marathoners make is thinking about the last mile as they start the first. Or, as William Faulkner advised: "The man who moves a mountain begins by carrying away small stones."

Set goals that are specific and attainable, then break them down into manageable pieces—one step at a time. In the process, passing each milestone builds confidence and creates momentum. Self-confidence, in turn, develops much like a coral reef—layer on layer compresses into a solid base.

Don't lose sight of your main goal by focusing on intermediate objectives. Take a wide-angle view of the challenge. As Gary Guller slogged his way up Mount Everest one painful step at a time, he never forgot the endgame: shattering stereotypes of the disabled. Summiting the top of the world was simply part of the process.

But don't dillydally. "A degenerative disease will not be cured by procrastination," said management guru Peter Drucker. "It requires decisive action." Unlike sports, you can't call for a time-out when things get rough. You must get out of the blocks quickly.

Even by New York standards, Schools Chancellor Joel Klein began sprinting—imposing an immediate dose of culture shock on an organization that had chewed up ten of his predecessors in twenty years. With a brass-knuckles management style and political deftness, he initiated a series of rapid-fire changes in what had long been considered one of the nation's worst and most reform-proof school systems. By all accounts, his unexpectedly fast start has won the hearts and minds of cynical New Yorkers.

A three-hours' journey north of the Big Apple, straight-talking Shirley Ann Jackson also warned her constituents at Rensselaer Polytechnic Institute that there would be no foot-dragging. "If you know there needs to be change, and you know there's a lot of ground to cover," she declared, at her inauguration, "you don't waste time." Even her staunchest critics have been impressed by the speed with which the new president has reinvigorated the nation's oldest technological university.

Regardless of what steps they took, our heroes exemplify how skills to achieve the brightest triumphs often are learned during the darkest hours. As Shakespeare put it: "Sweet are the uses of adversity." Tough times remade Pattie Dunn, saved Scott Waddle, rescued Chesty Puller's Marines, prodded Bill Snyder, re-energized Joanne Boyle, carried Gary Guller to the top of the world, and repositioned Steve Case to launch a revolution in health care. Dark hours, then, are inevitable. Learn from them.

Hopefully, our lessons carry the unmistakable accent of commitment and a willingness to act. "The moment one definitely commits oneself, providence moves too," Goethe wrote. "Whatever you can do or dream you can do, begin it. Boldness has genius, power, and magic in it. Begin it now!"

NOTES

Unless otherwise indicated, quotations are from interviews with the author. The following references, in chapter sequence, complement those interviews.

INTRODUCTION

1   J. K. Rowling's quotes are reported in Sam Dillon, "Messages of Exhortation, Counsel and Congratulation," *New York Times*, June 15, 2008, p. 16.

2   Henry Ford's "Think you can . . ." quote is found in www.brainyquote.com.

4   For more on dark hours, see my "Attacking the Impossible," *New Management*, Fall 1985, pp. 22–25.

4–5   For more on Alexis de Tocqueville, see Clell Bryant, "Tocqueville's America," *Smithsonian*, July 2005, pp. 104–107. See also Hugh Brogan, *Alexis de Tocqueville: Prophet of Democracy in the Age of Revolution—A Biography* (New Haven: Yale University Press, 2006).

5   William James' quote may be found in www.whatquote.com.

5   Professor Lothar's views are from Sharon Jayson, "Gen Nexters have their hands full," *USA Today*, August 21, 2006, p. 7B.

5   President Obama's remarks are found in "Words of Wisdom for 2006 Grads," *Christian Science Monitor*, June 14, 2006, p. 14.

5   Condoleezza Rice's quote is from ibid.

5   Norman Vincent Peale is quoted in Cynthia Crossen, "Whether People Define Themselves as Happy Depends on the Era," *Wall Street Journal*, March 6, 2006, p. B1. See also Peale, *The Power of Positive Thinking* (New York: Prentice Hall, 1952).

5   The Coleridge quote may be found in www.famousquotesandauthors.com.

6–7	Churchill's quotes are from www.winstonchurchill.org. See also James C. Humes, *The Wit & Wisdom of Winston Churchill: A Treasury of More Than 1,000 Quotations and Anecdotes* (New York: HarperCollins, 1994).
7	For more on the Marshall episode, see David A. Heenan and Warren Bennis, *Co-Leaders: The Power of Great Partnerships* (New York: Wiley, 1999), Chapter 6, especially pp. 101–105.
7	Churchill's description of Marshall is from M. A. Stoler, *George C. Marshall: Soldier-Statesman of the American Century* (Boston: Twayne, 1984), p. 130.
7	André Gide's quote may be found in Douglas S. Looney, "What We Learn from Sports," *Christian Science Monitor*, November 19, 1999, p. 11.
8	Hillary's remarks are from Cord Cooper, "The Power of Preparation," *Investor's Business Daily*, October 4, 1999, p. A4.
8	Matt Grough's quote is from Robin McKie, "Taking risks: A basic human need," *San Francisco Examiner*, October 12, 1997, p. A23.
8	Robert Bailey is from ibid.
9	The Edison quote is from Sonja Carberry, "Using Failure As a Learning Opportunity," *Investor's Business Daily*, November 24, 2006, p. A5. See also Adelio Cellini Linecker, "Move On From Mistakes," *Investor's Business Daily*, February 17, 2005, p. A4.
9	See Diane L. Coutu, "How Resilence Works," *Harvard Business Review*, May 2002, p. 55. See also Christine Gorman, "The Importance of Resilence," *Time*, January 17, 2005, pp. A52–55.
9	See John O. Whitney, "Strategic Removal for Business Units," *Harvard Business Review*, July-August 1996, p. 85.
10	Professor Bandara's views on the importance of self-efficacy are reported in Melinda Beck, "If at First You Don't Succeed, You're in Excellent Company," *Wall Street Journal*, April 29, 2008, p. D1.
10	Faulkner's quote may be found in www.thinkarete.com.
10	The Fitzgerald quote is from Cord Cooper, "Persistence: The Right Approach," *Investor's Business Daily*, July 10, 2000, p. A4.
10	See Cullen Murphy, "Against All Odds," *Atlantic*, October 1995, p. 22.
11	See John W. Gardner, *No Easy Victories* (New York: Harper & Row, 1968), p. 134.

17   Gerry House is quoted in Sol Hurwitz, "The Super Bowl," *New York Times*, August 4, 2002, p. 15.

18   Michael Casserly's description is from Rebecca Winters, "A Job For A Superhero?" *Time*, February 7, 2000, p. 71. See also Harry Bruinius, "Running big-city schools: A job fewer want," *Christian Science Monitor*, January 4, 2000, pp. 2–3, and Laurel Sharper Walters, "Can White Knights Really Save America's Schools in Distress?," *Christian Science Monitor*, April 30, 1996, p. 10.

18   Paul Vallas' response is from "A job nobody can do," *Economist*, January 15, 2000, p. 27.

18–19   Klein's "Most Americans . . ." quote is from his address "Changing the Culture of Urban Education," Academy of Management, Atlanta, GA, August 13, 2006, p. 2.

19   Gerstner is quoted in his "Bad Schools + Shackled Principals = Outsourcing," *Wall Street Journal*, October 7, 2004, p. 18A, and "How to Rescue Education Reform," *New York Times*, October 10, 2004, p. 10.

20   See Tom Lowry, "The CEO Mayor," *Business Week*, June 25, 2007, p. 58.

20   Michael Kirst's quote is from Howard Blume and Joel Rubin, "Villaraigosa still isn't at head of the class," *Los Angeles Times*, May 17, 2007, pp. A1.

20   Bloomberg's quote is from his "Flabby, Inefficient, Outdated," *Wall Street Journal*, December 14, 2006, p. B10.

20–21   See Frederick Hess' remarks in Gail Russell Chaddock, "In U. S. education, the buck stops here," *Christian Science Monitor*, January 26, 1999, p. 18. See also Sara Terry, "Why he wants 'one of the toughest jobs in America,'" *Christian Science Monitor*, June 12, 2000, p. 2.

21   Bloomberg's belief in the need for an outsider is from John Heilemann, "The Chancellor's Midterm Exam," www.nymag.com, October 23, 2005. See also Anemona Hartocollis, "Schematic for a Schools Chancellor; a Hard Shell and 'Fire in the Belly,'" *New York Times*, July 14, 2002, p. 23.

21   Joel Klein's ascent is variously described. See, for example, Tony Mauro, "Cross-trained lawyer to the rescue," *USA Today*, August 8, 2002, p. 11A.

22	Bloomberg's description of Klein is reported in www.schools.nyc.900.com, March 21, 2007.
22	Klein's "not afraid of breaking glass" is from Heilemann, p. 13.
23	Klein's "That's the problem . . ." may be found in his 2006 Academy of Management address, p. 2.
24	See William G. Ouchi, with Lydia A. Segal, *Making Schools Work* (New York: Simon & Schuster, 2003).
24	The "Children First" initiative is outlined in Klein's 2006 Academy of Management Address, pp. 5–7. See also www.schools.nyc.gov/offices/childrenfirst.com, and "The great experiment," *The Economist*, November 10, 2007, pp. 35–36.
25	Klein's quotes on the changing role of school principals are from Jia Lynn Yang, "He's at the Head of the Class," *Fortune*, February 19, 2007, p. 35.
25	His comments on turnover are found in Elissa Gootman, "Heavy Turnover in New York's Principal Ranks," *New York Times*, May 22, 2006, p. A21.
25–26	Klein's quote is from ibid. See also Craig Savoye, "Bring on the 'kid principals,'" *Christian Science Monitor*, October 2, 2001, p. 16.
26	For more on Klein's fund-raising, see David M. Herszenhorn, "Mayor Made Public Schools Into a Private Philanthropy," *New York Times*, December 30, 2005, p. A23. See also "How Many Billionaires Does It Take to Fix a School System," *New York Times Magazine*, March 9, 2008, p. 50.
26	Klein's comments on "low expectations" are from his address to the Partnership for New York City, January 18, 2006, pp. 2–3.
27	"We are trying to devolve . . ." is from David M. Herszenhorn, "New York Rethinks Its Remaking of the Schools," *New York Times*, April 9, 2006, p. A14.
27	Klein's remarks on teaching quality are from his 2006 address to the Partnership of New York City, p. 9.
28	Klein's union battles are described in Heilemann, pp. 1–14. See also Elissa Gootman, "Klein Assails Job Protection For Teachers," *New York Times*, October 17, 2003, p. C14.
28	Ms. Weingarten's comments are from her "Schools Aren't Factories," *USA Today*, April 13, 2006, p. 12A. See also Heilemann, p. 8, and Jennifer Medina, "A Veteran of Education Combat in New York Ponders a Broader Battlefield," *New York Times*, April 3, 2008, p. C14. (Note: In July 2008, Randi Weingarten was elected

to the presidency of the American Federation of Teachers.) See also Stacey Childress, Richard Elmore, and Allen Grossman, "How to Manage Urban Schools," *Harvard Business Review*, November 2006, p. 64.

28   Klein's "We want to be able to measure . . . ," is from Elissa Gootman, "The New York Schools, A Plan to Grade the Schools Themselves," *New York Times*, April 12, 2006, p. A20.

28   Ms. Levy's response is from ibid. See also Heilemann, p. 6.

28–29   The most recent performance results are discussed in Jennifer Medina, "New York Students Show Sharp Gains in Reading and Math," *New York Times*, June 24, 2008, p. C13. Earlier results are reported in Medina, "New York Schools Win Award for Improvement," *New York Times*, September 19, 2007, p. A25. See also Elissa Gootman, "Debate on New York Schools Pivots on One Man at the Top," *New York Times*, March 3, 2009, p. A1.

29   Klein's response and that of Mayor Bloomberg are from p. C13, June 24, 2008.

29   The Mills quote is from ibid.

30   Jack Welsh's sentiments may be found in Heilemann, p. 13.

30   Klein's "luckiest man in the world" is from Yang, p. 35.

CHAPTER 2. **Shirley Ann Jackson: Aim for the Stars**

33   The alleged difficulties of America's universities are discussed in Peter Berkowitz, "Our Compassless Colleges," *Wall Street Journal*, September 5, 2007, p. A17; Eugene Hickok, "No Undergrad Left Behind," *New York Times*, October 11, 2006, p. A27; and Charles Murray, *Real Education: Four Simple Truths for Bringing America's Schools Back to Reality* (New York: Crown Forum, 2008).

33   The difficulty recruiting and retaining college presidents is highlighted in Paul Fain, "Crisis of Confidence," *The Chronicle of Higher Education*, June 23, 2006, pp. A28–30. See also Robert Hahn, "How Tough Is It to Be a College President?," *The Chronicle of Higher Education*, January 6, 1995, p. A64.

33   John DiBiaggio's remarks are from Fain, p. A28.

34   Wells' quote may be found in Warren Bennis, *An Invented Life: Reflections on Leadership and Change* (Reading, MA: Addison-Wesley, 1993), pp. 111–112.

34   The rise of women college presidents is discussed in Rebecca Knight, "Women crack academia's glass ceiling in the US," *Financial Times*, July 5, 2007, p. 7.

34–35	The Jackson quote and a discussion of her early years are from Diane O'Connell, *Strong Force: The Story of Physicist Shirley Ann Jackson* (Washington, D.C.: John Henry Press, 2005).
35	O'Connell, p. 23.
36	Paul Gray's assessment is from O'Connell, pp. 46–47.
37	Samuel Heffner's quote is from Audrey Williams June, "Shirley Ann Jackson Sticks to the Plan," *The Chronicle of Higher Education*, June 15, 2007, p. A26.
37	For Jackson's remarks, see her Inauguration Address, September 24, 1999, pp. 1–6. See also Nancy Connell, "Aim for the Stars," *Rensselaer Magazine*, September 1999, pp. 11–15.
39	The Rensselaer Plan is discussed in *Rensselaer Magazine*, June 2000, pp. 1–6, and "Renaissance at Rensselaer," June 2000.
41	Professor McLaughlin is cited in June, p. A26.
41–42	The Bennis quote is from his *Invented Life*, pp. 28–29.
42	Jackson's remarks are from RPI's press release dated April 28, 2006.
42	Heffner's comments may be found in an RPI press release, "Board of Trustees Enthusiastically Endorses Leadership and Presidency of Dr. Shirley Ann Jackson," May 3, 2006. See also June, p. A26.
43	The dissenting opinion is from News Blog response dated May 9, 2006 to "No-Confidence Motion Fails at Rensselaer Polytechnic," *The Chronicle of Higher Education*, April 27, 2006, p. 1.
44	For more on the "quiet crisis," see Shirley Ann Jackson, "Waking Up to the 'Quiet Crisis' in the United States," *The College Board Review*, Winter/Spring 2007, pp. 21–27.
44	See Marc Parry, "RPI engineers a way for students to span the globe," (Albany, NY) *Times Union*, April 11, 2008, p. D1.
44	Secretary of State Clinton's remarks are from June, p. A27.
45	Jackson's commencement address is cited in Alan Finder, "With Iraq War as a Backdrop, Speakers Reflect on the Future," *New York Times*, June 10, 2007, p. 20.

CHAPTER 3. **Bill Snyder: Miracle in Manhattan**

| 49 | For additional background, see Mark Janssen with Bill Snyder, *Bill Snyder: They Said It Couldn't Be Done* (Champaign, IL: KCI Sports, 2006) and Ned Seaton, *The Miracle in Manhattan* (Manhattan, KS: The Manhattan Mercury, 2005). |
| 49 | Dennis Dodd, "Kansas State's Manhattan Project," *The Washington Post*, September 19, 1998, p. E4. |

49	Rob Goode is quoted in ibid.
50	Bob Stoops is quoted in "Kansas State's Snyder Ends Building Project," *New York Times*, November 20, 2005, p. B3.
50	President Wefald's remarks and his leadership efforts are described in Tim Layden, "Miracle Worker," *Sports Illustrated*, November 9, 1998, p. 61. Also see Douglas S. Looney, "Turnaround Team," *Christian Science Monitor*, October 6, 1998, p. 1.
51	Schembechler's crusty remarks are reported in Layden, p. 61.
51	AD Miller's quote is from Janssen, pp. 50–51.
52	Snyder's "turnaround" comments are from Lars Anderson, "Kansas State," *Lindy's College Football Forecast*, 1995, p. 108. See also Sexton, p. 6.
52	For more on Snyder's early years, see Janssen and Seaton, p. 6.
52	For Snyder's quote on his mother and their living conditions, see Janssen, Chapter 1, and Layden, p. 58.
53	His Indio High School remarks are from Janssen, pp. 32–33. See also Layden, p. 61.
53	"There were no scholarships . . ." is from Janssen, p. 34.
53	Coach Fry is quoted in Janssen, p. 36.
53	"Bad husband" is from Layden, p. 63.
53	Fry's high praise of Snyder is from Janssen, p. 6.
54	See Douglas S. Looney, "Outsider claws his way into college football elite," *Christian Science Monitor*, November 20, 1998, p. 12.
54	The Neinas quote is from "Snyder admired for improbable success at K-State," www.sports.espn.go.com, November 16, 2005.
54	Switzer's assessment is from Layden, p. 60. See also Sexton, p. 8.
54	Vermeil's praise is from "Bill Snyder: Biography," unpublished document, Kansas State University, Manhattan, KS, 2007, p. 2.
55	Vince Lombardi's quote may be found in "Thoughts on the Business of Life," *Forbes*, February 12, 2007, p. 116. See also Sexton, p. 5.
55	Bill Walsh's sentiments are from Michael Mix, "Bill Walsh's Football Title Rush," *Investor's Business Daily*, February 1, 2007, p. A3.
55	Neinas is quoted in "Snyder admired for improbable success at K-State," www.sports.espn.go.com, November 16, 2005.
56	The Quentin Neujahr remarks are from Dodd, p. E4.
56	Miller's "focus" comments are cited in Layden, p. 62.
56	Epps is quoted in ibid. See also Dodd, p. E4.
57	Barrett Brooks is quoted in Layden, p. 62.

57–58	Snyder's comments on the team's improvement are from Janssen, p. 104.
59	Bob Krause is quoted in Looney, "Turnaround Team," p. B5.
59	See Sexton, p. 95. See also Joe Drape, "Football Powerhouse Grows on the Prairie," *New York Times*, November 13, 1998.
60	Josh Buhl is quoted in Sexton, p. 7.
60	Jerome Clary's quote is from Mark Janssen, "Snyder stays steady in rugged times," *The Manhattan Mercury*, November 10, 2007.
60	Snyder's respect for Geppetto is reported in Layden, p. 63.
61	"They expect me to reach . . ." is from ibid., p. 60.
62	The Bennett quote is from Sexton, p. 9.
62	Snyder's exchange with daughter Meredith is from Layden, p. 63. See also Janssen, Chapter 37.
62	The Stoops quote is from "Kansas State's Snyder Ends Building Project," p. 3.
63	James Coffman is from Looney, "Turnaround Team," p. B5.
64	The Albert Einstein quote may be found in Alice Calaprice, ed., *The Quotable Einstein* (Princeton, NJ: Princeton University Press, 1966).
64	Snyder's comments on retirement are from "Snyder steps down at Kansas State," www.allsports.com, November 16, 2005. See also "Bill Snyder's final thank you," *The Manhattan Mercury*, November 20, 2005, and "Kansas State's Snyder retiring after 17 seasons," *USA Today*, November 16, 2005, p. C1.
65	John White is quoted in Phil Taylor, "The Last Emperor," *Sports Illustrated*, April 16, 2007, p. 20.
65	Snyder's remarks are from Doug Tucker, "Bill Snyder is back as coach at Kansas State," *Associated Press*, November 24, 2008.
65	Wefald's comments are from Kirk Seminoff, "Snyder says he's ready to be K-State football coach again," *The Wichita Eagle*, November 24, 2008.

CHAPTER 4. **Joanne Boyle: Hoop Dreams**

69	Coach Boyle's description of her initial symptoms is variously reported. See, for example, Jerry Crowe, "No Fear of Failure," *Los Angeles Times*, February 22, 2007, p. D5. See also Ron Kroichick, "On A Mission To Be Her Best," *San Francisco Chronicle*, December 18, 2005, p. 4.
70	Ms. Boyle's quote is from Kroichick, p. 4. See also Debbie Rosenfeld-Caparzy, "'The Place I'm Supposed To Be," *Cal Sports Quarterly*, Winter 2005–06, pp. 1–3.

70–71	Her post-operation remarks and those of Andrew Schuler are from Joan Tupponce, "In The Moment," *Richmond*, March 2005, p. 61.
71	Dr. Friedman's comments are from Kroichick, p. 4.
71	The Goestenkors' quote is from ibid.
73	See Tupponce, p. 61.
73	Goestenkors' praise is cited in Kroichick.
74	AD Miller's remarks are from Tupponce, pp. 60 and 85.
74	Boyle's "breaking out" is found in Crowe, p. D5. See also Patrick Dillon, "Season to believe," *California Magazine*, March/April 2006, p. 2, and Michelle Smith, "Cal Women Conquer Stanford at Maples," *San Francisco Chronicle*, February 5, 2007, p. 2.
74	Coach Griffin's praise is from Tupponce, p. 88.
75	Sandy Barbour's comments are found in "Joanne Boyle Named Head Coach at California," www.collegesports.com, April 15, 2005, and University of California Press Release, April 15, 2005. See also Eric Gilmore, "Boyle Changed by Near-Death Experience," *Contra Costa Times*, March 4, 2007.
75	Goestenkors' quote is from ibid. See also Dillon, p. 1.
75–76	Pat Summit's praise is cited in Jay Heater, "Boyle reaps praise, brings lofty credentials to Bears," *Contra Costa Times*, May 1, 2005.
77	The Gottleib quote is from Crowe, p. D5.
79	Teresa Edwards' comments are reported in Richard Zoglin, "The Girls of Summer," *Time*, August 12, 1996, p. 50.
79	Vince Goo's sentiments are from Peter Boylan, "Better Than Men," *Honolulu Magazine*, August 1996, p. 122.
79	See William Rhodes, "For Rutgers Women, Wisdom Is a Victory on a Path to Maturity," *New York Times*, March 31, 2007, p. 13.
79–80	Professor Harold's views are from ibid.
80	See Candace Putnam, "Stanford Women Wrote Book About Great Expectations," *San Jose Mercury News*, March 21, 1996, p. 50.
80	AD Barbour's "huge commitment" remarks are from Kelli Anderson, "The New Pressure-Cooker Sport," *Sports Illustrated*, March 5, 2007, p. 65.
80	Coach Thorne's remarks are from Robin Wilson, "Where Have All the Women Gone?," *The Chronicle of Higher Education*, May 4, 2007, p. A40.

80	Ms. Bass' prediction may be found in Sara Lipka, "In Defense of a Practice," *The Chronicle of Higher Education*, February 23, 2007, p. A34. See also Dick Patrick, "Rising salaries increase pressure on top women's coaches," *USA Today*, March 8, 2007, p. C9.
81	AD Livengood's quote is from Wilson, p. A41.
81	The DeMoss quote is from Mechelle Voepel, "Another busy week in the coaching carousel," www.ESPN.com, April 11, 2007, p. 2.

CHAPTER 5. **Gary Guller: Shattering Stereotypes**

90–92	The Mexican disaster is described in Pamela LeBlanc, "Conquering a Mountain of Stereotypes," *Austin American-Statesman*, March 15, 2003.
92	Aron Ralston is quoted in Rick Reilly, "Second Acts In 'Life,'" *Sports Illustrated*, March 7, 2005, p. 70.
93	Sampson Parker's story is reported in "Farmer Cuts Off Arm," www.9news.com, November 27, 2007, and Christie Barlow, "Harrisburg man adjusts after severing his own arm in a fight-for-life," (Concord & Kannapolis, NC) *Independent Tribune*, January 11, 2003, p. 3.
93	See Diane Leone, "Bethany's loss has helped her gain much more," *The Honolulu Advertiser*, June 1, 2008, p. A1.
93–94	Guller's "turning points" are variously described. See www.everestnews.com and www.teameverest03.org. See also W. Scott Bailey, "Heavy hearts, high hurdles won't stand in way of hope," *San Antonio Business Journal*, April 18, 2003, pp. 1–3.
95	Dr. Tupesis' quote is from his interview in *Mason Spirit*, Fall 2003, p. 2.
96	Riley Woods is quoted in Lee Hancock, "Reaching their peak," *The Dallas Morning News*, March 9, 2003, p. 2.
96	Matt Standridge's sentiments are from LeBlanc, p. 2.
96	Ms. Domatti's remarks are from Spike Gillespie, "Trek to the Top of the World Challenges Austin Exposition," *The Good Life*, December 2002, p. 2.
96	Gene Rodgers' quote is from Gillespie, p. 2., and Hancock, p. 2.
97	For more on the great mountain, see Conrad Anker, "The Mystery of Everest," *National Geographic*, October 1999, pp. 108–113, and Gregory Crouch, "Everest: Because It Is There," *National Geographic Adventure*, August 2002, pp. 45–48.

99	Rodgers' quote is reported in the film "Team Everest Documentary," produced by Guller and Andy Cockrum, April 2008.
99	Guller's quote is from Ilena Brito, "Against All Odds," *Jobpostings*, September 1, 2004. See also Pamela LeBlanc, "Austin amputee recalls conquering Everest," *Austin American-Statesman*, June 7, 2003, p. 3.
100	For more on Everest climbs, see Sean Markey, "First Teams Summit as Everest Season Begins," *National Geographic News*, May 2003, pp. 1–2.
100	See Ed Viestus with David Roberts, *No Shortcuts to the Top* (New York: Broadway Books, 2006), pp. 302 and 314. See also Viestus' interview in "Online Extra," www.nationalgeographic.com.
101	Viestus' comments on the final ascent are from ibid., p. 130.
102	Hillary's crusty remarks may be found in his, "The Conquest of the Summit," *National Geographic*, July 1954, pp. 45–62. See also David Robert, "Sir Ed," *Adventure*, April 2008, p. 59.
103	Walter Bonatti is quoted in www.amccomb.blogspot.com.
103	Guller's "Don't give up" is from Brito, p. 2.

CHAPTER 6. **The Frozen Chosin**

107	Puller's comments are from Lt. Col. Jon T. Hoffman, *Chesty: The Story of Lieutenant General Lewis B. Puller, USMC* (New York: Random House, 2001), p. 411.
107	S. L. A. Marshall's description may be found in David Halberstam, *The Coldest Winter: America and the Korean War* (New York: Hyperion, 2007), p. 1.
108	Col. Heinl's assessment is from James A. Warren, *American Spartans* (New York: Free Press, 2005), p. 124.
108–109	For more on the Korean Conflict and the Frozen Chosin, see Brig. Gen. Edwin H. Simmons, USMC, Ret., *Frozen Chosin: U.S. Marines at the Changjin Reservoir* (Washington, D.C.: U.S. Marine Corps Historical Center, 2002); Martin Russ, *Breakout: The Chosin Reservoir Campaign, Korea 1950* (New York: Fromm International, 1999); Lynn Montoss and Nicholas A. Canzona, *U.S. Marine Operations in Korea, 1950–1953* (Washington, D.C.: U.S. Marine Corps Historical Center, 1957); Clair Blair, *The Forgotten War: America in Korea, 1950–53* (New York: Doubleday, 1987); Max Hastings, *The Korean War* (New York: Simon and Schuster, 1987); Robert Leckie, *The March to Glory* (Cleveland:

World, 1960); and Joseph Owen, *Colder Than Hell: A Marine Company at Chosin Reservoir* (New York: Ivy Books, 1996).

110	Dean's description is found in William Manchester, *The Glory and The Dream* (Boston: Little, Brown and Co., 1973), p. 650.
110	See Halberstam, p. 138.
110	Lt. Daly's quote is from Warren, p. 122.
110	MacArthur's wish is cited in Warren, p. 124, and Halberstam, p. 295.
111	See Warren, p. 129.
111	Heinl's quote is from Halberstam, p. 295.
111	The uncomplimentary description of Gen. Almond is found in Halberstam, pp. 160, 307, and 531, and in Warren, p. 134.
112	MacArthur's praise is from Manchester, p. 661.
112	Truman's ill-advised comment is reported in Warren, pp. 129–130.
113	The *Time* citation is from Halberstam, p. 607.
113	MacArthur's "greatest slaughter" prediction and subsequent quote are from Warren, p. 152. See also Manchester, pp. 663–664, and 669, and Halberstam pp. 368–369.
113–114	The U.N. mandate is reported in Manchester, pp. 661–663, and Warren, p. 149.
114	See Halberstam, p. 44.
114	MacArthur's "celebrities" remark is from Halberstam, p. 11.
115	His report to the Pentagon is found in Simmons, pp. 25, 34, and 72. See also Manchester, pp. 669–670.
115	Bob Hope's quip is reported in Warren, p. 152.
115	Almond's order is cited in Warren, p. 143, and Halberstam, pp. 309–310.
117	Litzenberg's comments are from Warren, p. 154.
118	Halberstam's description of Smith is from Halberstam, p. 307.
119	"The worst defeat" is from Manchester, p. 671.
119	*The Herald Tribune* description may be found in ibid.
119	Col. Bowser's dire assessment is reported in Warren, p. 160.
119	Puller's crusty response is from Manchester, p. 670. See also Hoffman, p. 411.
120	His "no withdrawal" order is from Hoffman, p. 400.
120	See Warren, pp. 167–168.
121	"The unconquerable Chinese horde" is found in Simmons, p. 122.
121	See Halberstam, p. 468.

121	Warren, p. 180.
122	Puller's "greatest lesson" is reported in Halberstam, p. 473, and Hoffman, p. 417.
122	For more on the National Museum of the Marine Corps, visit www.usmcmuseum.org. See also Mark Yost, "New Museum Puts Visitors in Marines' Combat Boots," *Wall Street Journal*, November 8, 2006, p. D8.

CHAPTER 7. **Sacagawea: The Legendary Bird Woman**

125	For more on Sacagawea and the Lewis and Clark Expedition, see Stephen E. Ambrose, *Undaunted Courage* (New York: Simon and Schuster, 1996); Gary Moulton, ed., *The Journals of the Lewis and Clark Expedition* (Lincoln: University of Nebraska Press, 1988); James R. Ronda, *Lewis and Clark Among the Indians* (Lincoln: University of Nebraska Press, 1984); David Lavender, *The Way to the Western Sea: Lewis and Clark Across the Continent* (New York: Harper & Row, 1988); Joseph Bruchac, *Sacagawea: The Story of Bird Woman and the Lewis and Clark Expedition* (Orlando, FL: Whistle, 2000); Landon Y. Jones, *The Essential Lewis and Clark* (New York: HarperCollins, 2000); Dayton Duncan and Ken Burns, *Lewis & Clark* (New York: Alfred A. Knopf, 1997); Eva Emery Dye, *The Conquest: The True Story of Lewis and Clark* (Chicago: A. C. McClung, 1902); Ella E. Clark and Margot Edmonds, *Sacagawea of the Lewis and Clark Expedition* (Berkeley: University of California Press, 1979); Gerald S. Snyder, *In the Footsteps of Lewis and Clark* (Washington, D.C.: National Geographic Society, 1970); and William Goetzmann, *Exploration and Empire* (New York: Alfred A. Knopf, 1966).
125–126	Her early days are best described in Howard P. Howard, *Sacajawea* (Norman: University of Oklahoma Press, 1971); Cokie Roberts, *Ladies of Liberty* (New York: William Morrow, 2008), pp. 123–134; and Marion Marsh Brown, *Sacagawea* (Chicago: Children's Press, 1998). See also www.pbs.org/lewisandclark/inside/saca.html.
126	See Howard, p. 17.
126	Jefferson's efforts to launch the Lewis and Clark expedition are described in Snyder, pp. 9–10. See also Howard, pp. 4–5 and Ronda, pp. 2–8.
127	"This darling project . . ." is from Ronda, p. xiv.

127	Jefferson's brief to Lewis, June 1805, is cited in ibid., p. 1.
128	Goetzmann's "diplomats" is cited in Ronda, p. xii.
128	The hiring of Toussaint Charbonneau and Sacagawea is discussed in Brown, Chapter 3; Clark and Edmunds, Chapter 2; and Ambrose, p. 187.
129	Lewis' description is from Ambrose, p. 224.
129	His "utmost trepidation . . ." is in ibid., p. 225.
129	Lewis' praise of Sacagawea is from Ambrose, p. 225; Howard, pp. 31–32; and Snyder, p. 116.
130	His "we were all caressed . . ." is from Moulton, p. 134, and Snyder, pp. 136–137.
130	"The stars had danced for Lewis and Clark," is from Ronda, p. 147. See also Ambrose, p. 227.
130	"The Shoshone had proven . . ." is from Ronda, pp. 152–153. See also Ambrose, p. 283.
131	Clark's "wet and as cold . . ." is from Snyder, p. 139.
131	Gass' description of "the most terrible mountain . . ." is from ibid., p. 139, and Ronda, p. 157.
131	Lewis "Stout looking men . . .," is from Snyder, p. 140.
131	His "having triumphed over the Rocky Mountains . . ." is from Ambrose, p. 253.
131	Clark's observation is from Moulton, pp. 267–268.
131	His "high mountain of eminent height . . ." is from Ambrose, p. 299.
132	His quotes on the Indian encounter are from Moulton, pp. 267–268; Snyder, p. 162; and Ambrose, p. 255.
132	Clark's joy on spotting "the ocean . . ." is from Moulton, p. 283, and Ambrose, p. 305.
132	"The finest fur . . ." is from Ambrose, p. 315.
132	Clark's astonishment upon reaching the Pacific Ocean is from Snyder, p. 167.
133	Clark's "Those people were extremely pleased . . ." is from Ambrose, p. 388.
133–134	His letter to Charbonneau is from Howard, p. 141.
134	Clark's offer to help Pomp is from Moulton, p. 441.
134	"Robinson Crusoes—dressed entirely in buckskins" is from Ambrose, p. 395.
134	Lewis' letter to Jefferson is reported in Snyder, p. 195.
134	See Ambrose, p. 394.
135	The "writingest explorers of their time . . ." is from Snyder, p. 35.

135	"Children of the Great Spirit" is from Ronda, p. 255.
135	Lewis' death is variously reported. See, for example, Michael Pritchett, *The Melancholy Fate of Capt. Lewis* (Denver: Unbridled, 2007). See also Snyder, p. 198, and Ambrose, pp. 466–469.
136	Sacagawea's death and the description of her are from Howard, pp. 157–160.
136	"The American encounter" remarks are cited in Ronda, p. xi.
137	See Howard, p. vii.
137	See Ronda, p. 257.
137	Lewis' "She is the only necessity . . ." is from Ron Charles, "Unhappy Trails," *Washington Post*, November 4, 2007, p. 8. See also Ambrose, p. 414.
137	For Lewis' description of Charbonneau, see Charles, p. 8.
137	Clark's discussion of Sacagawea as "a token of peace" is from Ronda, p. 258.
138	For Lewis's description of her contributions, see ibid., pp. 136 and 258.
138	Clark's comments on Sacagawea's "great service to me as a pilot . . ." is from Moulton, p. 427.

CHAPTER 8. **Scott Waddle: Lost At Sea**

144	Waddle's "not many people" is from his *The Right Thing* (Brentwood, TN: Integrity Publishers, 2002), p. 27.
144	His "power" comment may be found in ibid., p. 30. See also "Scott Waddle Tells His Side of the Story," transcript of CNN Larry King Live, April 26, 2001.
144–145	Rickover's nuclear-propelled rise is from Sherry Sontag and Christopher Drew, *Blind Man's Bluff* (New York: HarperCollins, 1998), p. 40.
145	Waddle's description of the Rickover interview may be found in his *The Right Thing*, p. 39.
145	His "found my niche" remarks are from ibid., p. 64.
146	His "pinnacle" comment is found in Elaine Sciolino, "*Greeneville's* Skipper Known for Devotion to His Job and Crew," *New York Times*, March 4, 2001, p. A1. See also CNN Larry King Live.
146	Adm. Konetzni's admonition and Waddle's response are reported in CNN Larry King Live. See also Waddle, pp. 82–83.
146	Waddle's discussion of leaving Pearl Harbor is from his *The Right Thing*, p. 83.

146	His three tenets are discussed in ibid., p. 84.
147	Waddle's remarks about Konetzni are from ibid, pp. 102–103.
147	Capt. Snead's assessment is from John Kifner, "Captain of Sub Is Reprimanded and Will Quit," *New York Times*, April 24, 2001, p. 2.
147	Adm. Griffiths' quote is found in Steven Lee Myers, "Defense Lawyer Challenges Idea That Sub Crew Rushed," *New York Times*, March 8, 2001, p. 2.
147	For more on "the family man," see Sciolino, pp. A1–2.
147	The discussion of *Greeneville*'s chemistry is from ibid.
148	Konetzni's encouragement is reported in Waddle, p. 101.
148	Waddle's "no other reason" remarks are from ibid., p. 115.
148	The "commitment" comment is from Steve Lee Myers with James Dao, "Sub's Only Mission on Day of Incident Was Civilian Tour," *New York Times*, March 4, 2001, p. A1. See also Waddle, p. 112.
148	The rationale for the distinguished visitor program is from Myers et al., pp. A1–4.
149	Waddle's support of the program is reported in CNN Larry King Live, and *The Right Thing*, p. 108.
149	Waddle's belief in the routine nature of the February 9th cruise is from *The Right Thing*, p. 113.
149	His later comments on the ability to perform may be found in ibid., p. 111.
149	His "not a crucial piece" quote is from ibid, p. 117.
149	Capt. Brandhuber's assessment is from Waddle, p. 208.
150	Waddle's "having fun" remarks are from *The Right Thing*, p. 121.
150	His exchange with Pfeifer may be found in Kifner, p. 3.
150	His clear sailing comments are from *The Right Thing*, p. 122.
151	Seacrest's admission of "a little bit lazy" is reported in James Sterngold, "Sailor Admits Not Reporting Japanese Boat," *New York Times*, March 20, 2001, p. 21.
151	The lack of a challenge is described in *The Right Thing*, p. 125.
151	His "roller coaster" remarks are from ibid., p. 127.
151	"Part of me died" is from ibid., p. 129. See also CNN Larry King Live.
152	Waddle's return to port is from *The Right Thing*, p. 140.
152	Konetzni's order is reported in ibid., p. 144.
152	Waddle's reactions are found in *The Right Thing*, pp. 142 and 145–148.

153	Powell's quote may be found in Douglas Jehl, "Clues Sought in Sub Accident; Some Japanese Fault Rescue," *New York Times*, November 8, 2007, p. 1.
153	Adm. Fargo's news conference is reported in Steven Lee Myers, "Navy to Conduct a Public Inquiry on Sub Accident," *New York Times*, February 18, 2001, p. A1.
153	Eugene Fidell's remarks are from ibid., p. 2.
154	The "in his shoes" comments are from Sciolino, p. 3.
154	Adm. Fallon's apology is treated in Steven Lee Myers, "Submarine Conducted Only a Brief Surface Check, Board Says," *New York Times*, March 3, 2001, p. A1, and Elaine Sciolino, "Sub Commander Apologies More Directly to Families," *New York Times*, March 1, 2001, p. A1.
155	The "gaping hole" criticism is from James Sterngold, "A Question Unasked," *New York Times*, March 22, 2001, p. A1.
155	Waddle's "right thing" remarks are from Mike Gordon, "Final report out on sub collision," *Honolulu Advertiser*, October 20, 2005, p. A1.
155	His inability to see the Japanese vessel is from James Sterngold, "Captain of Sub Accepts Blame, and Spreads It," *New York Times*, March 21, 2001, p. A2.
155	His rejecting "informality" or "micromanagement" is reported in Sterngold, p. A1.
155–156	Griffiths' remarks are reported in Steven Lee Myers, "Sub's Crew May Have Hesitated to Question a Trusted Captain," *New York Times*, March 12, 2001, p. A2.
156	The "Somebody had to . . ." quote is from Waddle, pp. 188 and 198–199.
156	Waddle's comments on managing the visitors are from Gordon, p. A1.
156	Gittins' defense is cited in Steve Lee Myers, "Navy Panel Set to Decide on Charges in Sub Case," *New York Times*, March 5, 2001, p. A1. See also Waddle, p. 204.
156–157	Adm. Fargo's conclusions are variously reported. See, for example, "From Statement by Admiral Fargo," *New York Times*, November 8, 2007, p. A1.
157	Fargo's defense of his decision may be found in Kifner, pp. A1–2, and Waddle, p. 216.
157	Kato's comments are from Kifner, p. 2.

157	Nomoto's remarks are from Waddle, p. 217. See also Calvin Sims, "Japanese Outraged at Commander's Fate," *New York Times*, April 25, 2001, p. A1, and Shin'ya Fujiwara, "In Japan, Waiting for the Captain to Appear," *New York Times*, February 17, 2001, p. A1.
159	President Bush's quote is from Waddle, p. 218.
159	Waddle's reflection on the "ugly event" is found in *The Right Thing*, p. 234. See also CNN Larry King Live.
159	Waddle's crisis management is reported in "Remembering the *Greeneville*," CBS News, February 28, 2003, p. 1. See also "Waddle hopes his lessons prevent other disasters," *Honolulu Star-Bulletin*, February 7, 2006, p. A3.
159	The John Locke quote may be found in P. Nidditch, *An Essay Concerning Human Understanding* (Oxford, UK: Clarendon Press, 1975), p. 17.
159–160	Waddle's respect for Adm. Fargo is from CNN Larry King Live.
160	Brutus' famous quote is from William Shakespeare's *Julius Caesar* (1623); see also William and Barbara Rosen, eds., *The Tragedy of Julius Caesar* (New York: Penguin Putnam, 1998), p. 84.

CHAPTER 9. **Pattie Dunn: Boardroom Brouhaha**

163	"Calamity is man's touchstone . . ." was offered by the English dramatists Francis Beaumont and John Fletcher. See Ian Fletcher, *Beaumont and Fletcher* (London: Longmans, Green, 1967) and www.quote@cosmos.com.
165	Dunn's remarks on Platt's desire for independence may be found in her unpublished statement, "Life History in Brief," September 24, 2006, p. 4.
165–166	Gary Rivlin's comments are from "If You Can Make It In Silicon Valley, You Can Make It . . . In Silicon Valley Again," *The New York Times Magazine*, June 5, 2005, p. 66.
166	See James Stewart, "The Kona Files," *New Yorker*, February 19 and 26, 2007. Refer to www.newyorker.com.
167	Carly Fiorina's remarks are from her *Tough Choices* (New York: Penguin, 2006), pp. 154 and 191. For more on the HP culture, see Michael S. Malone, *Bill and Dave: How Hewlett and Packard Built The World's Greatest Company* (Knoxville, TN: American Book Company, 2007).

167	Fiorina's discussion of Keyworth may be found in ibid., p. 281.
167	Her comments on Perkins and Keyworth are from ibid., p. 288.
168	Her "concern over the board leaks" is from ibid., p. 290. See also "Fiorina Comments on Public Firing," CBS News 60 Minutes, October 8, 2006.
168	Sonsini's description of the HP board may be found in ibid., p. 293.
168	Fiorina's sentiments are reported in ibid., p. 293. See also Stewart, p. 3.
169	Fiorina's ousting and the accompanying quotes are from her *Tough Choices*, p. 303. See also Pui-Wing Tam, "Hewlett-Packard Board Considers a Reorganization," *Wall Street Journal*, January 24, 2005, p. A1.
170	See Stewart, p. 5.
171	Dunn's remarks are from her testimony to the Sub-Committee on Investigations to the House Energy and Commerce Committee, "My Role in the Hewlett-Packard Leak Investigation," September 28, 2006, p. 5.
171	Delia's assessment is reported in ibid., pp. 12–14. See also Stewart, p. 6.
171–172	Fiorina's comments about Dunn are from Stewart, p. 8.
172	Dunn's discussion of Perkins' hawkishness is from Stewart, pp. 2 and 9.
172	Dunn and the board exchanges with Keyworth are found in Michelle Kessler, Jon Swartz, and Sue Kirchhoff, "HP execs on spying: It wasn't me," *USA Today*, September 29, 2006, p. C1. See also David A. Kaplan, "Suspicions and Spies in Silicon Valley," *Newsweek*, September 18, 2006, pp. 41–47, and Dunn's Congressional testimony, p. 23.
172	The Perkins remarks are cited in Dunn's Congressional testimony, pp. 23–24.
172	His argument with Dunn is from Stewart, p. 10. See also Dunn's Congressional testimony, p. 25.
172	His resignation is reported in Dunn's Congressional testimony, p. 26. See also "Tom Perkins Regrets Quitting HP Board," CBS News 60 Minutes, November 4, 2007.
173	His allegation of betrayal is from Yuki Noguchi, "A Lifelong Fighter's Toughest Round," *Washington Post*, October 6, 2006, p. D1.
173	Attorney Sonsini's legal analysis is found in Kaplan pp. 46–47. See also Dunn's Congressional testimony, pp. 25–27; David

Kirkpatrick, "The peculiar logic of Patricia Dunn, " www.cnn-money.com, September 15, 2005; and Stewart, p. 11.

174   See David A. Kaplan, *Mine's Bigger* (New York: HarperCollins, 2007), p. 241. For more on Perkins, see his autobiography, *Valley Boy: The Education of Tom Perkins* (New York: Penguin, 2007).

175   Charles Wolf's "HP gate" comments are from Kessler, Swartz, and Kirchhoff, p. C1. See also Noguchi, p. D1, and Theresa Poletti and Michele Quinn, "HP Engulfed in Extraordinary Boardroom Fight," *San Jose Mercury News*, September 6, 2006, p. C1.

175   See Peter Burrows, "HP Board Split Over Dunn," www.businessweek.com, September 11, 2006.

175   Hurd's remarks at Dunn's resignation and her response are found in Stewart, p. 13, and Dunn's Congressional testimony, p. 29. See also "Patricia Dunn Resigns from HP Board," HP News Release, September 22, 2006.

175   Hurd's treatment of Keyworth and Perkins is highlighted in Scot Ard, "Leak scandal costs HP's Dunn her chairman's job," www.CNETNews.com., September 22, 2006.

175–176   Grace Wong, "California investigating HP board fracas," www.CNN.Money.com, September 6, 2006. See also Matt Richtel and Miquel Helft, "Former H.P. Chairwoman Makes Court Appearance," www.nytimes.com, October 6, 2006.

176   The Court dismissal and attorney Brosnahan's comments are from Matt Richtel, "Charges Dismissed in Hewlett-Packard Spying Case," *New York Times*, March 15, 2003. See also "Patricia Dunn: I Am Innocent," CBS News 60 Minutes, October 8, 2006.

176   Dunn's dismissal statement may be found on www.ga6.org/pattiedunn.com, March 14, 2006.

176   Chairman Hurd's comments are extracted from Richtel, ibid. See also Ard, ibid. See also Adam Lashinsky, "Mark Hurd's Moment," *Fortune*, March 16, 2009, p. 98.

177   See Kaplan, p. 241.

177–178   Kirk Hanson's views are from Jessica Guynn and Ben Pimentel, "Scandal at Hewlett-Packard," *San Francisco Chronicle*, October 27, 2006, p. A2.

178   Eleanor Roosevelt's quote may be found in "Wisdom to Live By," *Investor's Business Daily*, April 11, 2008, p. A3.

179   Lance Armstrong is quoted in "Wisdom to Live By," *Investor's Business Daily*, December 28, 2005, p. A4.

CHAPTER 10. **Steve Case: Second Act**

183	F. Scott Fitzgerald's familiar quote is from his Hollywood novel, *The Last Tycoon*.
183	Case's quote is cited in "AOL founder calls for breakup of Time Warner," www.seattlepi.com, December 13, 2005.
183	His "willingness" quote is from Catherine Yang, "Another Case Entirely," *Business Week*, March 31, 2005, p. 62.
185	The Case quotes on strategic partnering and independence may be found in his June 12, 2004 interview at the Academy of Achievement in Chicago, p. 2.
185	See Gene Koprowski, "AOL CEO Steve Case," *Forbes*, October 7, 1996, p. 94.
186	Eric Schmidt's quote is from "The Online World of Steve Case," *Business Week*, April 15, 1996, pp. 3–4.
187	Will Rogers' quote is from "Wisdom to Live By," *Investor's Business Daily*, May 23, 2008, p. A3.
187	Case's quote on potential synergy is from the January 10, 2000 press release announcing AOL's acquisition of Time Warner.
187–188	For more of Case's views on brain-cancer research, see Suzanne McGee, "Personal Passions," *Barron's*, November 27, 2006, pp. 28 and 31; and Andrew Pollock, "Hints of Progress, and Longer Life, as Drug Makers Take on Brain Cancer," *New York Times*, May 23, 2008, p. A18.
188	The Case quote is from Howard Dicus, "Steve Case decides to resign from AOL Time Warner," *Pacific Business News*, January 13, 2003.
188	For his comments on "integration issues" and subsequent problems, see Lucy Kellaway, "Case study in textbook emotion," *Financial Times*, February 9, 2005, p. 8. See also his Academy of Achievement interview, p. 5.
188	Henry Haskins' quote may be found in "Wisdom to Live By," *Investor's Business Daily*, May 29, 2008, p. A3.
189	Case's quote on new market entry is from David Stires, "The (R)evolution of Steve Case," *Fortune*, November 14, 2005, p. 92.
189	The Gilburne quote is from Bob Van Voris, "Steve Case immerses himself in life after AOL," *Honolulu Star-Bulletin*, August 1, 2006, p. C1.
189–190	Case's remarks on consumerism are from Kellaway, p. 8. See also Thomas Heath, "Revolution Health Buys Stakes in Two Web Sites," *Washington Post*, December 5, 2007, p. D4.

191	The Williams reference is from his interview with Geoff Colvin in *Fortune*, May 12, 2008, p. 109.
191	Case's remarks on "time" are from Milt Freudenheim, "AOL Founder Hopes to Build New Giant Among a Bevy of Health Care Web Sites," *New York Times*, April 16, 2007, p. 4.
193	Case's views on the importance of synergy are found on www.revolution.com.
193	Case's newfound happiness is described in David A. Vise, "AOL co-founder having 'fun' in healthcare, resort venture," *Washington Post*, May 5, 2005.
193	Case's Hawai'i-based ventures are described in Van Voris, p. C3.
193–194	His views on linking technology and philanthropy are from "Give a Little, Help a Lot," *Parade*, January 20, 2008, p. 10. See also McGee, p. 31, and the Academy of Achievement interview, p. 6.
194	The Gibson quotes are from Stephanie Strom, "Foundation Lets Public Help Award Money," www.nytimes.com, June 26, 2007.
194	See Alan M. Webber, "Giving the poor the business," *USA Today*, May 21, 2008, p. A11.
194	Case's comments on extraordinary times may be found in his Academy of Achievement interview, p. 7. See also Ben Steverman, "Steve Case Made Sure to Put America Online," *Investor's Business Daily*, April 18, 2007, p. A3.

CHAPTER 11. **Strategies for a Bright Triumph**

197	See Richard Karlgaard, "Seven Lessons of Walt Disney," *Forbes*, December 25, 2006, p. 33.
197	For more on Churchill's many quotes, visit www.winstonchurchill.org. See also James C. Humes, *The Wit & Wisdom of Winston Churchill: A Treasury of More than 1,000 Quotations and Anecdotes* (New York: HarperCollins, 1994).
198	See Rabbi Harold S. Kushner, "How to Overcome Life's Disappointments," *Bottom Line*, February 1, 2008, pp. 9–10, and Sandi Dolbee, "Getting Over It," *The San Diego Union Tribune*, November 4, 2006, pp. E1 and E4.
198	Carly Fiorina is quoted in Del Jones, "It's lonely—and thin-skinned—at the top," *USA Today*, January 16, 2007, p. 2B.
199	For the Lowell quote, see "Creative Quotations from James Russell Lowell" at www.becomecreative.com.
199	The Thoreau quote is cited in "Quotes for Dreams," www.motivatingquotes.com/dreams.

199	For the Puller quotes, see Hoffman, *Chesty*, p. 397.
200	The Goldsmith quote may be found in Diane Brady, "Yes, Winning Is Still the Only Thing," *Business Week*, August 27/28, 2006, p. 55.
200	Daniel Webster's quote at the signing of the Declaration of Independence, Philadelphia, July 4, 1776.
201	See "Stephen Covey on Recharging Creativity," *USA Weekend*, November 17–19, 2000, p. 19.
202	See Erik Erikson, *Gandhi's Truth: On the Origins of Militant Non-Violence* (New York: W. W. Norton, 1969).
203	Theodore Roosevelt is quoted in Sandra Bienkowski, "From Weak to White House," *Success*, April/May 2008, p. 109.
203	Ethan Gologor is cited in Sonja Carberry, "How to Go the Distance," *Investor's Business Daily*, March 2, 2007, p. A3.
203	The Faulkner quote is from "Wisdom to Live By," *Investor's Business Daily*, June 19, 2008, p. A4.
203	The Drucker quote is from his "What Executives Should Remember," *Harvard Business Review*, February 2006, p. 146.
204	The Goethe quote is found in Robert B. Tucker, "Succeeding With Your Bright Ideas," *Creative Living*, Summer 1997, p. 32.

INDEX

PRODUCTION NOTES FOR

HEENAN / **BRIGHT TRIUMPHS FROM DARK HOURS**

Jacket and interior design by Julie Matsuo-Chun

Display type in Seria Sans; text in Warnock Pro Light

Printing and binding by The Maple-Vail Book Manufacturing Group